Toward a Liberalism

Toward a Liberalism · · ·

RICHARD E. FLATHMAN

Cornell University Press

Ithaca and London

First published 1989 by Cornell University Press.

International Standard Book Number (cloth) 0–8014–2243–4
International Standard Book Number (paper) 0–8014–9536–9
Library of Congress Catalog Card Number 88–47922
Printed in the United States of America
*Librarians: Library of Congress cataloging information
appears on the last page of the book.*

*The paper in this book is acid-free and meets the guidelines for
permanence and durability of the Committee on Production Guidelines
for Book Longevity of the Council on Library Resources.*

primun non nocere

Contents

Acknowledgments

The introduction and Chapters 1 and 6 of this volume are here published for the first time. The other chapters appeared earlier, and permission to reprint them was generously granted by the publishers: Chapter 2, "Liberalism and Authority," in *The Prospects of Liberalism*, edited by Timothy Fuller, Colorado College Studies, no. 20 (Colorado Springs, 1984), pp. 41–57; Chapter 3, "Citizenship and Authority: A Chastened View of Citizenship," *News for Teachers of Political Science*, no. 30 (Summer 1981) (Washington, D.C.: American Political Science Association, 1981), pp. 9–19; Chapter 4, "Liberalism and the Human Good of Freedom," in *Liberals on Liberalism*, edited by A. J. Damico (Totowa, N.J.: Rowman & Littlefield, 1986), pp. 67–94; Chapter 5, "Moderating Rights," in *Human Rights*, edited by Ellen Frankel Paul, Fred D. Miller, Jr., and Jeffrey Paul (Oxford: Basil Blackwell, 1984), pp. 149–71; Chapter 7, "Egalitarian Blood and Skeptical Turnips," *Ethics* 93 (January 1983): 357–66, © 1983 by The University of Chicago Press, all rights reserved. Chapter 3 is a somewhat shortened and otherwise revised version of the original; the other chapters have been changed only in minor ways.

Toward a Liberalism

Introduction

The essays presented here were not written to a program, certainly not to the program of developing a theory of liberalism or a liberal political theory. The terms *liberal* and *liberalism* are prominent in all of them, however, and a number of the themes that recur in the essays can be viewed as within or about liberal theory and practice. In bringing the essays together in this format, I hope to underline these themes and to this extent move "toward a liberalism."

I should say at the outset that the presence of these features and the fact that the same terms and themes appear with increasing frequency in books that I have written in roughly the same period as these essays[1] come initially as—if I may put it this way—something of a surprise to me. This is not because I have deceived myself about my disposition to some form of liberalism in practical politics. The surprise is due, rather, to the conjunction of the conception of political and moral philosophy in which I have been working over the past couple of decades and an understanding of liberalism which I have—perhaps less self-consciously—accepted.

The conception of philosophy, for which "analytic" is a usual if no longer especially helpful tag, has tended to produce differentiating, disaggregative studies rather than the more encompassing, synoptic formulations commonly associated with ideological thinking.

[1]Richard E. Flathman, *The Practice of Rights* (New York: Cambridge University Press, 1976); *The Practice of Political Authority* (Chicago: University of Chicago Press, 1980); and *The Philosophy and Politics of Freedom* (Chicago: University of Chicago Press, 1987).

Toward a Liberalism

At least for this reason, commitment to this conception of philosophizing would not seem to predict the use of ideological terms such as *liberal* and *liberalism* as thematic or organizing categories.

My understanding of liberalism has both historical and doctrinal components. As to the first, liberalism has never been a closely integrated or firmly fixed doctrine; its proponents have held to a considerable and frequently changing variety of views and its historians and critics have regularly disagreed concerning its main ideas and tendencies. As to the second, suspicion of systematic, programmatic, certainly dogmatic theorizing has been a persistent characteristic of liberal thought and practice. In the first essay I argue against the view that is most often invoked, at least by the philosophically inclined, to explain this characteristic, namely, that liberalism is wedded to philosophical empiricism and its attendant atomism and skepticism.[2] Notwithstanding this argument, however, many prominent liberals have been empiricists and numerous others have insisted on the empir*ical,* skeptical, individualist, and pluralist character of the liberal outlook. If I am correct in my understanding that these characteristics and the antisystematic tendency that frequently accompanies them are prominent in liberalism, we will expect to find its themes in the ideational elements of liberal practices and in the writings of liberal publicists, not in the treatises of philosophers.

Viewed in this perspective, the project represented by this collection has a certain anomalous quality. On further reflection, however, I have found my initial surprise and discomfort giving way to the view, or at least to recognition of the possibility, that the emergence of the language and the themes of liberalism in my work is in part a natural result of the very conjunction that at first made it seem surprising and doubtful to me. This is not, or not exactly, for the reasons that have been advanced for thinking that the conception of philosophy in question is inherently conservative and, given that liberalism is the dominant ideology in the culture in which the conception has found favor, has perforce gravitated toward a defense of liberalism.[3] Apart from the most general questions raised by explanations of this sort, there are a number of specific difficulties with this argument. On any reading of its history, the advent

[2]See, for example, Bertrand Russell, *Philosophy and Politics* (London: Cambridge University Press, 1947).

[3]See, for example, Herbert Marcuse, *One-Dimensional Man* (Boston: Beacon Press, 1964); Ernest Gellner, *Words and Things* (Boston: Beacon Press, 1959).

of liberalism substantially antedates the emergence of analytic philosophy; numerous liberal thinkers are decidedly not of an analytic orientation in their philosophizing and numerous analytic philosophers are opposed to liberalism; liberalism was initially, and in some settings remains, a radical not a conservative or an establishment view. And so forth.

Nevertheless, if the above characterizations of "analytic" philosophy and of liberalism are accurate, there may now be a greater consonance, perhaps even an affinity, between the two than between such philosophizing and any of the other currently influential ideologies. Analytic moral and political philosophers are committed to a close examination of the language actually employed in moral and political discourse, language that in our culture has been substantially influenced by liberalism. For this reason, and whatever moral and political convictions they may hold or conclusions they may reach, the work of philosophers of this orientation will concern, and to that extent may have a tendency to sustain, conceptions prominent in liberal theory and practice. More important here, on the variant of this understanding of philosophy that I find most congenial—that is, the Wittgensteinian—the philosopher's stance toward the language (and hence the practices) of moral and political discourse is at least akin to that which much liberalism urges us to maintain toward persons and sometimes even toward social groups and associations, namely, a respectful stance. (I explore this complex and importantly problematic comparison in the first essay.) Finally, insofar as liberalism is a cautious, skeptical, or antisystematic ideology, if any mode of philosophizing is congenial to it, the analytic is a promising candidate.

These last considerations help to relieve my concern that the present project is, at a very general level and hence pervasively, incongruous or even aberrant. They should also begin to prepare the reader for what might be called the immodest modesty of the several essays and of the collection as a whole. I continue this process by introducing in more substantive terms some of the main themes of the papers that follow.

The first of these themes, which manifests both the "modest" and the "immodest" elements in "immodest modesty," concerns the circumscribed possibilities of moral and political philosophy, especially as regards their role in political practice and more especially their role in political practice in liberal societies.

In its most general formulation, for which I draw heavily on

Wittgenstein, this theme involves claims about philosophy *sans phrase*. Although not passive, philosophy is primarily reactive in the sense that its materials and issues (and hence its possibility and its limits) are for the most part given to it, not created or constructed by it, given to it by thought and action that may come to be influenced by philosophizing but that are not themselves philosophical in character. In its application to moral and political philosophy, this general formulation is augmented by an understanding of what has traditionally been called practical as distinct from theoretical reasoning. It is further augmented in regard to liberal societies by the normative argument concerning "respect" (in something like the sense of "a decent respect for the opinions of mankind") already mentioned.

This theme is developed in the first essay and it is elaborated and applied, partly by way of criticizing the overweening ambitions of other moral and political philosophers, in the essays on freedom, citizenship, equality, and moderating rights. It represents "immodest modesty" of a kind familiar from various forms of skepticism: in insisting on a modest role for philosophy in moral and political practice, it perpetrates the immodesty of specifying the character and the limits of moral and political philosophy.

A consonant theme, or perhaps tendency, is represented in a form familiar from the history of liberalism by the essay on authority, in less familiar forms in the essay on citizenship, and in the several discussions of rights and of equality that occur in the volume. Liberals have been less suspicious of authority than they have been of power, and some among them have turned readily to authority not only to control power but to legitimate it and put it to effective use in pursuing their social and political objectives. The uneasiness about authority which is expressed in my essay is more characteristic of emphatically individualist liberal writers, particularly those who lean toward libertarianism, toward some version of laissez-faire doctrine, and of course it is also characteristic of those few (such as myself) who regard anarchism as a powerfully attractive ideal. It is less common to link citizenship to authority and power and to use that linkage, as I do in the third essay, as reason for what I call a chastened view concerning citizenship and especially concerning participationist and communitarian theories of citizenship and of democracy.

It is yet less common to draw parallels between authority and rights and to caution that rights—including rights to liberties that are (rightly) prized by most liberals and to forms of equality promoted by many liberals—need to be "moderated" lest they become weapons against values that many liberals have cherished. In one perspective, my arguments in these regards (especially my objections to so-called natural or otherwise absolute and inalienable rights and to libertarianism) are instances of the mildly skeptical, antisystematic, and antienthusiasm tendency of my entire discussion. In another, and especially in respect to rights, they reflect a desire to acknowledge and sustain deontological features of our morals and politics while accommodating them to the contextualist, pluralist, and consequentialist strains in the liberal tradition (strains that seem to me to provide welcome justification not only for civil disobedience to established authority but for what I call "civil encroachment" on established rights).

To elaborate somewhat, both rights and authority appear to be "content-independent" in the sense in which H. L. A. Hart used that characterization of rights:[4] rights and authority, especially in political life, are typically established through procedures such as promising, authorizing, subscribing, and consenting, procedures that are used to create, often into the indefinite future, entitlements not merely to this or that particular action at such and such times and places but to classes of actions taken or not at the discretion of all agents or agencies to whom or to which the right or the authority has been assigned. They are content-independent in that a great variety of entitlements, and corresponding duties, obligations, and so forth, can be created by use of these procedures and devices and that the entitlements and duties result from the correct or valid use of the procedure not from the merits of the actions or their consequences. Although valuable, arguably indispensable, features of our moral and political arrangements, these devices are nevertheless objectionable on theoretical grounds and are readily and frequently abused in even the best of the practices that include them. Political and moral philosophers, perhaps particularly philosophers of a liberal bent, have contributed importantly to clarifying these notions and to defending them against utilitarianism and various forms of collectivism, communitarianism, and traditionalism. My purpose is not to undo this work but to qualify what seem to me

[4]See H. L. A. Hart, "Are There Any Natural Rights?" *Philosophical Review* 64 (1955): 175–91.

unjustifiably strong conclusions that have been drawn from it. (I hope that the essay on abortion will testify to my belief in the value of the institution of individual rights. I see no reason to amend the main arguments or conclusions of that essay, but were I to rewrite it I would give greater emphasis to the provisions it makes—see especially pp. 200–204—for "moderating" the moral and legal right to abortion on demand. Doing so would diminish the tensions between the essay and the conception of the theory-practice relationship that informs the book.)

Much of my attempt to harmonize deontological and consequentialist (but not, I now think, utilitarian) considerations is carried out through discussions of what I call the liberal principle, or LP. I advanced this principle in *The Practice of Rights;* I argued for and from it in *The Philosophy and Politics of Freedom;* and it figures prominently in several of these essays. LP states that "it is a prima facie good for persons to form, to act on, and to satisfy and achieve desires and interests, objectives and purposes." My argument for the principle is naturalistic (hence immodest?) in the sense that it relies on claims about the usual characteristics of human beings and their circumstances, but it is also contextualist or culture-specific rather than transcendental or universalistic in that my claims about the characteristics and about what should be inferred from them are limited (!) to societies of Western modernity (hence modest?).

As is indicated by "principle," LP is intended to be (weakly) deontological; I argue that it should regulate thought and action in the very wide area of its applicability. This means that criticisms and condemnations of interests and desires, objectives and purposes, and their satisfaction, and attempted interferences with actions to serve and achieve them, require justifications sufficient to remove the onus that LP places on them. As indicated by "prima facie" and "good," however, LP is, in a logical sense, a weak principle; the good that it identifies gives way to adequately justified all-things-considered judgments about better and best, right and wrong. Such judgments, moreover, while always liable to challenges based on LP, can and do become codified in moral rules, in laws, and in social conventions. If the processes and procedures of codification satisfy further, locally various criteria, they sometimes yield conclusions— for example, that there should be certain rights and duties—which typically hold against whole classes of claims advanced on the basis of LP. Some conclusions of this kind (the conclusion that there is a duty not to commit murder or to inflict cruelty, for example) have become so widely and firmly accepted in our culture as generally to prevent or to deflect challenges to them and to place an exceptionally heavy burden of justification on those who nevertheless issue such challenges. In a society that accepts LP, however, all such conclusions are, in reason, subject to questioning proceeding from LP.

It is at least initially plausible to think of LP as stating a right to form and to act to satisfy desires and interests, objectives and purposes, and as stating a correlative duty not to interfere when others do so. The principle bears at least some resemblance to far-reaching notions such as the right to equal consideration, the right to consideration as an equal, and the like. It is yet closer kin, especially if we focus on conceptual form rather than the ideational substance poured into that form, to the "natural right" that Hart claimed is presupposed and qualified by the "special rights" that are created by procedures such as contracting and promising, to Hobbes's "Natural Right" to all the things I judge necessary to my well-being, and to Hohfeld's concept of "liberties" that correlate with "no-rights."[5]

We do better, however, to think of LP as a principle (as an element in our axiology or our set of authoritative values and beliefs) from which to reason for or against rights and duties and for or against construals and implementations of rights and duties. The essay on abortion and, in part, the essay on freedom argue from LP to the conclusion that there should be a right to abortion on demand and rights to certain liberties; and the essay on freedom and the one titled "Moderating Rights" invoke LP against various rigorist or unjustifiably strong deontological views of rights. This argumentation would be hampered, at least in the sense that the conceptualization in which it is presented would be much more complicated and might appear to be internally contradictory, if LP were treated as itself an asseveration of rights and duties.

My reasonings for and from LP are compressed expressions of the individualism, pluralism, and teleological thinking represented in various forms in these pages. The interests, desires, and so forth that

[5]See Hart, "Are There Any Natural Rights?"; Thomas Hobbes, *Leviathan* (Oxford: Basil Blackwell, 1955); Wesley Hohfeld, *Fundamental Legal Concepts* (New Haven: Yale University Press, 1919). On these points, see also my *Practice of Rights*.

LP protects, and the liberties and rights that are partly grounded in LP, are, first and foremost, formed and pursued, enjoyed and exercised, by individual persons. In treating individual persons and their good as the primary "unit" of thought and of evaluation, I align myself with the individualist strain in liberalism. One form of pluralism enters the discussions in my recognition that the interests and desires that individuals form are in important part the result of the location of those individuals in one of the many differing cultural traditions and societies and, more proximately, their associations and interactions with groups of individuals in their own cultures and societies. Neither the individuals nor the individualism presented here is "atomic" or "atomistic." Thus for important purposes the unit in and about which my theorizing occurs is not the individual but the culture or the society.

Individualism and pluralism of distinct but I think complementary kinds are represented here in a tendency toward a strong version of a view that is sometimes called voluntarism, sometimes antiperfectionism, sometimes other names. (In the sense in which I am using it, voluntarism was first a theological doctrine stressing the will and willfulness, and hence mysteriousness, of God and God's actions. God does as and because God wills, not as or because reason dictates. The following paragraphs, and further discussion in the next essay, indicate ways in which voluntarism in moral and political theory is a descendant of this theological view.)

In fact, individuals in modern Western societies, including in comparatively homogeneous and well-integrated societies and sectors of societies, form and pursue a considerable diversity of desires and interests, ends and purposes (conceptions of their good, as Rawls and others say). In varying degrees and on a variety of grounds, liberalism has approved and fostered this diversity and the understandings and arrangements that sustain and promote it. According to liberalism, individuals and groups not only do but should develop and pursue their conceptions of good "voluntarily," and where this is the case these conceptions have differed widely and can be expected to continue to do so.

It has not been a part of liberalism that this diversity and pluralism is, should, or could be without limit. By acculturation, socialization, and education, by example and argumentation, and through a varying but invariably substantial array of disciplinary and coercive devices, these societies evolve, adopt, and impose restrictions on the thought and action of their members. If as a generalization liberals have tended to be more suspicious of or cautious about these characteristics of modern Western societies, if they have tended to be selective concerning means of limiting diversity, they have denied neither the social and political importance of limitations nor the possibility of interpersonally convincing justifications for the particular limitations adopted and imposed. Liberalism is not radical antinomianism or individualist anarchism and, despite their voluntarism, few liberals have embraced doctrines as deeply subjectivist as emotivism or Sartrean existentialism. In these respects, the present essays are well within the liberal tradition.

But liberals have disagreed with one another concerning the appropriate scope or extent of restrictions on diversity and—more important here—concerning the best justifications for such limits. A word about these disagreements, a number of which are more fully aired in the essays that follow, will help further delineate "voluntarism" and the forms of individualism and pluralism that it involves.

In societies that in fact are diverse and pluralistic, endorsement of LP itself involves a weak form of voluntarism. But we might endorse LP for certain purposes and nevertheless think that we have or could in principle develop norms or principles that are—in fact, in truth, or in reason—unqualifiedly and indisputably superior to LP. If (1) those norms are thought applicable to a circumscribed range of thought and action they might be proposed as fixed qualifications of LP in that range or at least as shifting the burden of justification to those who propose to depart from them. In this case, LP would operate primarily if not exclusively outside of the ambit of the more highly ranked norms. Alternatively, (2) if we think that the valid or proper application of such norms is wide or even general, we might disavow LP altogether and seek to implement a thoroughgoing perfectionism or a strict deontology. While few would regard views of this sort as liberal in character, a liberal might entertain these possibilities but promote the superior norms or principles by example, argument, education, and the like, sustaining commitment to LP on the ground that it would be impossible or too costly to enforce the norms.

These possibilities are presented in concrete terms in a number of doctrines that are often regarded as liberal. Theorists of natural rights from John Locke on exemplify (1) in that they regard appeals to LP (or any comparable principle) as circumscribed by the natural rights and duties. By contrast, John Rawls's "Kantian constructivism" eschews the idea of natural rights and clearly adopts a voluntarist position concerning thought and action outside of the "basic structure" of society. Beyond the confines of that structure, Rawlsian liberalism presumes a wide and in any case an ineliminable diversity of conceptions of good. Within that structure, however, Rawls's view is akin to Locke's in proposing principles of justice that are to have "absolute weight" against all other considerations and hence against LP. As to (2), it is perhaps most clearly represented by religious thinkers who have no doubt about the superiority of their religious beliefs or the moral implications of those beliefs but who nevertheless promote toleration of a diversity of religious beliefs and practices in order to avoid the destructive conflicts that they believe invariably result from attempts to impose religious-cum-moral uniformity.

As it is understood here, voluntarism refuses these possibilities, but only in the sense that it rejects the idea that the rights, norms, principles, and the like have or could in principle be provided with incorrigible or indisputable foundations. On the one hand, rights, norms, and the like might in fact be undisputed in the society, and voluntarist liberals might have no actual, no "live," disposition to dispute them. On the other hand, voluntarism rejects the possibility that they are or could be put beyond cogent disputation. (Of course Rawls allows for dispute concerning his principles of justice, but he argues that consideration of them is fruitful only in the "original position and under the constraints of the "veil of ignorance." Once the principles are adopted, they can be reconsidered only by returning to that position and its constraints.)

A full development and defense of voluntarism would have to justify the particular "immodest modesties" that it involves. A leading instance is its claim that we can be certain that we cannot be certain about the justifiability of our moral and moral-cum-political conclusions. Yet worse, voluntarism makes this certain uncertainty into a kind of moral and political certitude, the certitude that we always are and will always be unjustified if we treat our moral and political conclusions as beyond cogent dispute. More proximately, development and defense of voluntarism would require showing how and why acceptance of it is consistent with commitment to regulative principles, even principles that are as "weak" as LP.

As I envisage it, such a development and defense would involve an elaboration, with particular reference to moral and political questions, of the Wittgensteinian understandings mentioned above. Moral and political certainties parallel to or at least analogous with the certainties Wittgenstein discusses in *On Certainty* and elsewhere are possible,[6] but claims to and indeed the quest for the further, superstrong certainties that he discredits involve deep misunderstandings. The first essay in this book considers elements of Wittgenstein's view and of the related views of Michael Oakeshott, as do passages in several of the other essays, but I do not address these issues in a concerted manner here.

As already suggested, however, voluntarist views are prominent in liberal thought and do support forms of individualism and pluralism beyond those already discussed. John Stuart Mill's "fallibilism," together with his closely conjoined case for a rich diversity of "experiments in living," particularly as interpreted by Isaiah Berlin, is a leading example, and Berlin's own moral and political thinking another.[7] As Berlin argues, Mill's individualism and pluralism are in sharp tension with the residues of classical utilitarianism in his thinking, and Berlin, Bernard Williams, Stuart Hampshire, and of course John Rawls are among numerous contemporary writers whose articulations of forms of voluntarism are by contrast with and in opposition to what they regard as the anti-individualist and homogenizing tendencies of utilitarianism.[8] I examine the differences among these views (to say nothing of similarities and differences between them and the Nietzschean and post-Nietzschean positions they resemble in respects pertinent here) only to the extent of offering objections (mainly in the fourth essay) to Rawls's in many ways minimal restrictions on individualism and pluralism. I hope, however, that my arguments against Rawls will also challenge views more rigid and far-reaching than his and do something to indicate the lines along which an insistently voluntarist liberalism might be developed.

The tendencies in liberal theory and practice which the foregoing

[6]See Ludwig Wittgenstein, *On Certainty* (Oxford: Basil Blackwell, 1969).

[7]See John Stuart Mill, *On Liberty* (New York: E. P. Dutton, 1951); and Isaiah Berlin, *Four Essays on Liberty,* esp. essay 4 (Oxford: Oxford University Press, 1969).

[8]See Bernard Williams, *Ethics and the Limits of Philosophy* (London: Fontana Paperbacks and William Collins, 1985); Stuart Hampshire, *Morality and Conflict* (Cambridge: Harvard University Press, 1983); John Rawls, *A Theory of Justice* (Cambridge: Harvard University Press, 1971).

themes affirm are of course susceptible to various kinds of distortion and corruption. Individualism can degenerate into privatism, egoism, and hero-worshiping romanticism, voluntarism into irrational subjectivism, pluralism into corporatism and ethnocentricity, chauvinism, and other forms of parochialism. "Chastening" our thinking about citizenship and "moderating" our practice of rights risk condoning antagonism to both, and entering cautions about egalitarianism may engender elitism and other vulgar and destructive forms of class and personal pretension. Even skepticism about and determined suspicion of paternalism, authority, and power— dispositions that in my judgment are at the vital if restless center of liberalism—may diminish inclinations to serve and hence the likelihood of service.

Success in moving "toward a liberalism" might itself do something to mitigate or at least to defer all too familiar declensions such as these. To the extent that the ideas and themes I have introduced can be integrated into an encompassing, a unifying, construction, they might support one another so as to create resistance to the tendencies discussed in the previous paragraph. An idea that coheres with others, that "hangs together" with other ideas to form a system or a set, is perhaps less vulnerable to misconstruction and misuse. For example, in company with a suspicious stance toward authority and rules, and with a generalized skepticism about unqualified assertions and claims, arguments for moderating rights and for chastening attitudes toward the political role of citizenship may present a different appearance than those arguments have when encountered one by one.

If the themes of these essays do cohere, collecting them in this format might advantage the several arguments in these ways. Expressing this hope, however, brings me back to the beginnings of this introduction and indeed to the title of this work. I aim at "a" liberalism out of conviction, not diffidence or self-abnegation. Like love, liberalism is a many-splendored thing; also like love, the "manyness" of liberalism is integral to "its" splendor. In less florid terms, there is neither an exhaustive nor a privileged inventory of the ideas and themes of liberalism, and there is no reason to think that there is an indisputably superior ordering of any of the numerous sets and subsets of ideas that are recognizably or even arguably of a liberal character.

All thinking strains (however weakly) toward order, toward integration, toward system, and all theorizing seeks to magnify these tendencies of thought. Insofar as it self-consciously subscribes to and promotes an "ism," liberal thinking and theorizing intensify these characteristics of their genres. But it is fundamental to liberalism that none among the orderings its thinking and theorizing achieve can be regarded as exclusive, entire, or immutable. If achieving coherence and system meant realizing a closed, strictly hierarchical, or fully harmonious construction, coherence and system would be antithetical to liberalism and liberals would have to find other ways of coping with their difficulties. These essays concern elements in thought and action that I have come to value, not a dogma or doctrine; they identify and follow tendencies, but they do not march toward a fixed or even a clearly delineated destination.

I

Theory and Practice, Skepticism and Liberalism

The first half of my title assumes that theory and practice are sufficiently distinct to permit consideration of relationships between them. This assumption is sharply controversial. Melding the two concepts, thinkers in the praxis tradition seem to exclude the possibility of a relationship between them. Other writers might replace my conjunction with a hyphen. There are no practices that are innocent of theory, and all theories presuppose some practice of which they are the, or among the, theories. Theories and practices form pairs not unities, but no instance of either of them can be identified or usefully discussed apart from the instance of the other with which it is paired. Numerous others who have reflected on this topic endorse one or another version of the assumption implicit in my title, and some among them further insist that, properly understood, theory and practice are not only categorically distinct but disjunctive in the sense that theory can play no role in practice.

We have to consider these disagreements. But we do not have to accept the view, which might be suggested by the persistence of the disagreements, that reflection about theory and practice can yield nothing better than a list, perhaps with additions, of stipulations. It is not, I think, tendentious to say that the parties to the controversies I have mentioned are advancing *theories* about theory and practice. Their theorizing occurs in concepts and makes use of ideas that have not been and almost certainly could not be fully appropriated by any of the past, present, or future contributors to it. There is reason for impatience with the topic of theory and practice, for doubt about the richness of its yield, but there is no reason to think that theorizing about it has been or must be merely and hence fruitlessly sectarian.

Similar concerns arise about, and an analogous stance is appropriate concerning, the other elements in my topic—that is, liberalism and the roles of theory and of skepticism in liberal practice. There is a tendency to think that it is with "liberal" and "liberalism" as Hobbes said it was with "good" and "evil"—that is, that these words "are ever used with relation to the person that useth them: there being nothing simply and absolutely so; nor any common rule ... to be taken from the nature of the objects themselves."[1] This tendency of thought commits an exaggeration. Leaving aside the historian's question of just when liberalism emerged, the term is now widely and often vigorously used of ideas and people who hold them, of institutions and policies, of governments and nations. Features prominent in liberalism do give us reason to doubt that we can significantly reduce the diversity of recognizably liberal idioms; certainly there is reason to doubt that we can fully resolve the disputes among self-designated liberals and between them and opponents of liberalism. But this circumstance, commonplace in moral and political philosophy, is hardly reason for dismissing the disputes as spurious or for rejecting the possibility of contributive thinking about them.

There is an easy transition from the foregoing remarks to some preliminary comments concerning skepticism. In its "Academic" and "Pyrrhonian" variants,[2] respectively, classical general skepticism denied or doubted the possibility of knowledge when "knowledge" was taken to require true, warranted, or at least reasonable beliefs and when the beliefs pertinent to knowledge claims were (or are now usually) taken to consist of integrated sets of general propositions. Let us say, at least provisionally, that such an integrated set of truth-evaluable general propositions is a necessary feature of a theory. On this construal of theory, if we embrace general skepticism we will thereby have answered a main question concerning theory and practice. We will either (1) have to deny that theory can or should play any affirmative role in practice or (2) we

[1]Thomas Hobbes, *Leviathan* (Oxford: Basil Blackwell, 1955), chap. 6.
[2]See Richard H. Popkin, *The History of Scepticism from Erasmus to Spinoza* (Berkeley: University of California Press, 1983); Miles Burnyeat, "The Sceptic in His Place and Time," in *Philosophy in History*, ed. Richard Rorty, J. B. Schneewind, and Quentin Skinner (London: Cambridge University Press, 1984).

will have to say that theory can and should guide practice despite the fact that theories cannot be true (dogmatic skepticism) or that thus far no theories are known to be true (undogmatic skepticism). On the widely received position that true or at least well-warranted answers to questions that practice confronts are the distinctive contribution of theory to practice, the stronger of these two conclusions will follow. Either way, the classical forms of general or doctrinal skepticism seem to require us to reject the idea that theory is necessary to practice, and dogmatic general skepticism requires us to reject the possibility that theory can contribute to the quality of practice.

According to Miles Burnyeat, the Pyrrhonian skeptics of classical antiquity drew very definite practical conclusions from their epistemological doubts and denials. Unable to resolve the issues of moral and political life, they sought "tranquillity" by withdrawing as far as possible from it.[3] If we regard skepticism as a theory about the possibility of true or contributive theory, their theory of theory and practice had material implications for both theory and practice. As Burnyeat puts it, there was no "insulation" between their theory of theory and practice and their practical judgments.[4]

Burnyeat's account suggests several contrasts with more recent thinking on these topics. As he remarks, a number of modern and contemporary thinkers have reached dogmatically skeptical conclusions about moral and political theory but have put a thick layer of insulation between these conclusions and their thinking about moral and political practice. The "first-order" judgments of moral and political practice are not diminished by the unavailability of true "second-order" theories of the kind traditionally sought by moral and political philosophers. What is increasingly called "commonsense morality" gets along nicely without the assistance of such theories. By denying that practice has any need for such theory, these theories of theory and practice insulate practice from the effects of their own skepticism about theory.

An alternative to (variant of?) the position just sketched is pro-

---

[3]Burnyeat, "The Sceptic in His Place and Time," esp. pp. 238–47.

[4]Ibid., pp. 225ff. There may be a suggestion in Burnyeat's account that the Pyrrhonians adopted skepticism *because* the suspension of judgment it required implied withdrawal from practical affairs. Their desire for tranquility was primary, their skepticism a justification and protection of it. See esp. Burnyeat, "Can the Skeptic Live His Skepticism?" in *The Skeptical Tradition* (Berkeley: University of California Press, 1983).

vided by "antifoundationalism." Instead of saying with the classical skeptics that we cannot establish the truth of theories, or that we do not know whether we can do so, antifoundationalists contend that these epistemological questions are misbegotten and that we should address ourselves to other issues.

In Burnyeat's terms, antifoundationalism might be characterized as putting a double layer of insulation between skepticism and practice. If we adopt this position, we insulate practice not only from (truth-seeking) theory but from that species of theory about theory and practice that is epistemology. Antifoundationalism is a theory about theory and practice which makes not only theory of or about practice but theory about theory and practice (or, more exactly, all theories about theory and practice other than its own) irrelevant to theory and practice.

Wittgenstein's position, which some regard as a version of this view, will concern us below. For now, however, the more striking point is the lack of success of antifoundationalists in their campaign to banish epistemological concerns from moral and political philosophy. Writers of this persuasion may have moved epistemology to the wings of the general philosophical stage, but the concerns traditional to it remain prominent in the domains of morals and politics—perhaps particularly so in the work of self- or widely other-designated liberal thinkers. Leaving aside the early history of liberalism, writers such as Isaiah Berlin, Bruce Ackerman, and a bevy of neo-Kantian thinkers led by John Rawls have rejected utilitarianism and what Rawls call perfectionism and insisted on the ineliminable plurality of conceptions of the good and the good life. The voluntarism, subjectivism, or agent-relativity of these views has provoked vigorous rejoinders from other neo-Kantians (for example, Alan Gewirth) and from neo-Aristotelians (Alasdair MacIntyre), neo-Hegelians (Charles Taylor), and communitarians (Roberto Unger), who claim that moral and political theory can and should provide interpersonally and even interculturally valid specifications of the good. And because some of the liberals who have abandoned the search for a true or a best theory of the good have nevertheless tried to circumscribe pursuit of the conceptions of good that people in fact form with general theories of the right, of justice, and of rights, their efforts have prompted skeptical reactions from a diverse array of writers who deny the possibility, the usability, or the desirability of such theories. Very little of this argumentation extends its reach to general skepticism or the "dog-matisms" that have opposed it, and to this extent these thinkers may show the influence of antifoundationalism. But within the domains of concern here, including within and about liberalism, we continue to find a range of views extending from insistent skepticism about the possibilities of true or otherwise contributive theorizing to soar-ing aspirations for this mode of reflection. If antifoundationalists claim that the epistemological flavor of this work reveals it to be archaic or even reactionary, they must be pressed to defend the certitude with which they advance their own theories of theory and their own theories of theory and practice.

I

A familiar construal of liberalism, at least of its anglophone variants, gathers the four terms of this essay under the philosophical rubric of empiricism. Most versions of this view posit a hierarchy descending from the general to the particular with epistemology (and sometimes metaphysics) or "first philosophy" governing moral and political theory, which in turn governs moral and political practice. Empiricism correctly determines how we know and what we can and cannot know. Accepting and thinking within these determinations, liberalism as moral and political theory determines how we can know about morals and politics, what we can and can-not, do and do not now know about them. Liberals as moral and political agents act within the determinations of liberalism and at-tempt to implement their findings and conclusions in moral and political practice.

A slightly modified but forceful articulation of these connections was presented by Bertrand Russell in 1947. After identifying Locke as the founder ("so far as the modern world is concerned") of both empiricism and liberalism, Russell asked:

> What has theoretical philosophy to say that is relevant to the validity or otherwise of the Liberal outlook? The essence of the Liberal out-look lies not in *what* opinions are held, but in *how* they are held; instead of being held dogmatically, they are held tentatively, and with a consciousness that new evidence may at any moment lead to their abandonment. This is the way in which opinions are held in science, as opposed to the way in which they are held in theology. . . . Science is

empirical, tentative and undogmatic; all immutable dogma is unscientific. The scientific outlook, accordingly, is the intellectual counterpart of what is, in the practical sphere, the outlook of Liberalism.[5]

As with Locke, Hume, Mill, and numerous others, Russell then identifies empirical science with empiricist philosophy: "The empiricist's theory of knowledge—to which, with some reservations, I adhere—is halfway between dogma and scepticism. . . . Scientific theories are accepted as useful hypotheses to suggest further research, and as having some element of truth in virtue of which they are able to colligate existing observations; but no sensible person regards them as immutably perfect."[6] His conclusion is that "in our day as in the time of Locke, empiricist Liberalism . . . is the only philosophy that can be adopted by a man who, on the one hand, demands some scientific evidence for his beliefs, and, on the other hand, desires human happiness more than the prevalence of this or that party or creed."[7]

It may strike some students of liberalism that, as with related accounts from the same period (accounts by "cold war liberals" as they are now, usually with derision, commonly called), Russell modifies understandings that were predominant in the thinking of earlier and some later liberals. As with Russell (and ignoring the transition from "psychological" to "logical" empiricism), many nineteenth- and early twentieth-century liberals regarded empiricism as the philosophical position that best accounted for and regulated natural science; in at least partial contrast with Russell, however, for them the startling successes of science provided the basis for a robust optimism about moral and political matters. Beginning with the sensationalist-associationist psychologists and early utilitarians, at least in part in John Stuart Mill, and continuing among some of the founders of the Liberal party in Great Britain (for example, Graham Wallas), the ambition of many liberal thinkers has been to bring empiricist-based scientific thinking and investigation to bear on social life, expecting thereby to achieve improvements in that realm at least approximating those Newtonian science had made possible in the understanding and control of nature. If

[5]Bertrand Russell, *Philosophy and Politics* (London: Cambridge University Press, 1947), p. 22.
[6]Ibid., p. 24.
[7]Ibid., p. 27.

present-day liberals are less likely to celebrate science, aspirations of this sort remain alive among them.

This difference between Russell and his predecessors and successors represents a phenomenon—namely, proponents of a single general philosophical position drawing divergent practical inferences from it—which is important to the concerns of this essay. The point for immediate attention, however, is the *agreement* between Russell and most of his empiricist liberal predecessors concerning the proper relationship between theory and practice.

Empiricism gives an account of our access to reality, and a further account of science as the means of achieving knowledge and truth. Russell puts more stress on the limitations on scientific knowledge than do most of his predecessors (albeit he denies that he does so out of the "sceptical intention" of Hume, who of course anticipated him in this emphasis), but he has only minor reservations concerning the main elements of the empiricist epistemology and metaphysic and no doubt that science, as construed by empiricism, gives us the best knowledge we can have.

Theory, then, is construed as at once plural and hierarchical: that part of theory which comprises epistemology and metaphysics ("theoretical philosophy" in Russell's terms) is the basis of science, and that part of it which is scientific is the basis of the most reliable of all further knowing. Upending the metaphor, epistemology and metaphysics dominate science in that they identify the subject matters and criteria of science and scientific knowledge, and science dominates all other forms of knowing in that conclusions arrived at scientifically and "colligated" in scientific theories are superior to all conclusions lacking these characteristics. Scientific theories are subject to revision in light of new evidence and reasoning, and nonscientific beliefs are subject to revision and rejection in the light of changes in scientific theory. Theory in the sense of theoretical philosophy dominates scientific theory and practice, and scientific theory dominates all nonscientific theory and practice. Insofar as we arrive at scientific theories concerning social and political life, those theories properly dominate social and political practice. Insofar as liberalism incorporates the methods and findings of science, it properly dominates social and political practice.

Thus the more emphatically fallibilist character of Russell's view does not alter the fundamentals of the picture that this conception gives us of intratheory and theory-practice relationships. The mildly diffident tenor of Russell's empiricist-based liberalism is not due to any regard that is owed to practice as against theory. Because his cautions about scientific theory apply even more strongly to beliefs reached nonscientifically, he gives us no general reason or principled ground on which to hesitate about supplanting the latter with genuine instances of the former. Scientific theory is superior not because it helps us to understand practice as it is but because it discovers and orders an independent reality to which practice ought to conform. Theory is relevant to practice not because it is consonant with but an improvement on the understandings and beliefs of practitioners, but because it provides a basis on which to reject and replace the latter. Until such time as scientific theory has supplanted prescientific beliefs and understandings, the contributions of theory will be based on the discrepancies and disjunctions between theory and practice. In political language, empiricist scientists and those who have mastered their theories should rule. They should rule with a due awareness of the limitations of their theories, but equally with awareness of the yet more severe limitations of nonscientific beliefs.

Despite or perhaps because of its long-standing association with liberalism, it is worth asking whether this is a view that *liberals* should endorse.

II

We can begin to answer this question, and also give skepticism a more prominent place in the discussion, by recalling that this conception of theory and practice is anything but unique to empiricism or empiricist liberalism. It would be more accurate (albeit an exaggeration) to say that it is the conception that has dominated Western philosophy, certainly moral and political philosophy, from Plato to Jürgen Habermas. Despite the many differences among them, Platonists, Rationalists, Marxists, Critical Theorists, and numerous others have also posited several levels of theory and have had no doubt that theory should dominate practice.[8]

[8]Cf. Anthony Giddens's generalization, advanced in the context of a discussion of the relations between philosophy and social sciences, about social science: "Given their naturalistic presumptions, the proponents of the orthodox consensus assumed that the practical connotations of social science have a 'technological' form. The social sciences correct false beliefs that agents have about social activity or institutions. As we get to know the social world better, just as in the case of the natural world, we are in a position to change it." Anthony Giddens, *Social Theory and Modern Sociology* (Stanford: Stanford University Press, 1987), pp. 70–71.

Despite this commonality, empiricist liberals have regarded the views just mentioned as the deadly enemies of liberalism. This hostility is of course due in part to their conviction that theories not resulting from empirical inquiry as empiricism construes and directs it will almost assuredly—happenstance aside—be false. For this and other reasons they have viewed such theories and the theorizing that produces them as dangerous. Echoing Karl Popper, Russell insists that Platonism, Hegelian idealism, and Marxism are like religions not only in lacking any basis in evidence and reason but in that they engender fanaticism. Unburdened by the need to demonstrate the fit between their conclusions and observed fact, their proponents have afflicted us with grandiose moral and political visions and with futile but destructive attempts to enact those visions in moral and political practice.

Many philosophers, empiricists and otherwise, have thought that empiricism entails or at least engenders philosophical skepticism. Some of those favorable to it have argued that it is this among its features (whether emphasized or even clearly recognized by this or that liberal theorist) that immunizes empiricist liberalism against the virulent diseases of thought and conduct that Popper and Russell attack. The unique advantages of empiricist-based liberalism result from the combination of the scientifically warranted certitude it yields on some questions and its philosophically grounded doubt on all others. Although emphasized much more strongly by some liberals than by others (perhaps most strongly by the "cold war liberals"), this combination has been present in empiricism not only from Locke on but from its beginnings in the thought of Sextus Empiricus.

For reasons already mentioned, however, this feature of empiricist liberalism, rather than allaying the apprehensions generated, for liberals, by the conception of theory-practice relationships in question, puts empiricist liberalism in conflict with itself. On the one hand, if empiricism entails a robust skepticism it will not support so much as Russell's mildly chastened conception of theory-practice relationships (to say nothing of the more enthusiastic liberalisms that we might now associate with phrases like "the best and the brightest"). The possibility of "scientific theory," and hence also the expectation that such theory could properly rule practice, would be narrowly circumscribed if not eliminated. Hume's more potent skepticism would not be a matter of this or that theorist's personal "intentions"; it would be a logically necessary consequence of empiricist epistemology. On the other hand, the logical implications of empiricism would not prevent empiricist liberals from "insulating" their practical thinking and acting from their skepticism, maintaining their conception of theory and practice, and going right ahead with their moral and political projects.

III

Later I consider the role of skepticism in conceptions of theory and practice that are sharply divergent from all of those mentioned thus far, conceptions that might provide an alternative orientation to liberalism. Before taking this more affirmative turn, however, we should recognize affinities between my remarks about empiricist liberalism and the views of leading antiliberal writers. Sharp criticism of empiricism is pervasive in modern philosophy.[9] Influential writers have accepted the connection between empiricism and liberalism and have argued that the defects of the former vitiate the latter. Whatever we may think about Hegel's relation to liberalism, his is a major refutation of empiricism: neo-Hegelians have accepted that refutation and drawn the inference about liberalism that I just stated. (Charles Taylor and perhaps Roberto Unger are contemporary examples.) Marx and many Marxists take parallel positions, and analogous patterns of argumentation can be found in Nietzsche, in Heidegger, and in neo-Aristotelian views such as those advanced by Alasdair MacIntyre. The several elements that constitute empiricist liberalism—the atomic entities that constitute all matter; the logically unrelated sensations and percepts through which we experience those entities; the passive, structureless minds in which our sensations and perceptions associate; above all, the isolated, self-subsistent "individuals" standing in no more than radically contingent but usually adversarial relations with one another which we as persons are said to be—are all dismissed as, in F. H. Bradley's frequently quoted phrase, "delusions of theory."

For these critics, then, as a philosophical matter empiricism and

9The essays in ibid. provide one of a number of recent surveys of these developments, Giddens's account being valuable in the present context because of his concern with the relationships among "first" or "theoretical" philosophy, social theory, and social and political practice.

23

liberalism can only be scorned and dismissed. Of course they recognize that liberals have induced many to think and act as if their philosophical hallucinations are true. Turning Russell's rhetorical move back against liberal theorists, they pay the latter the same "compliment" that Russell accorded proponents of religions and of political theologies, namely, allowing that they have successfully propagated their false and destructive creeds. But sharing as they do the fundaments of Russell's conception of theory as properly ruling practice, these critics nevertheless think what he thought about Christianity, Marxism, and fascism—namely, that their refutations of empiricism *ought to* discredit liberalism.

As a historical matter, this form of antiliberal argumentation overlooks liberal theorists—such as Kant and various neo-Kantians, Green and his residually idealist successors—who are among the most determined and effective critics of empiricism. In some cases, moreover, neo-Kantian and other at least vestigially idealist liberalisms, although sponsoring conceptions of theory-practice relations that are substantially analogous to those I have been discussing up to now, have entered important modifications in those conceptions. In company with numerous antiliberal praxis theorists, they have sustained the idea that theory can and should improve practice in various significant ways but rejected the empiricist view that theorists properly go about improving practice by displacing practitioner understandings. Theory might modify practice, might over time contribute to a transformation of practice, but it cannot do so *à la* empiricism.

To this extent, these alternative forms of liberalism open up the question that is most important for present purposes. Insofar as we reject (as both doctrinal skeptics and antifoundationalists do), or qualify (as some alleged skeptics and some alleged antifoundationalists have done and as I attempt to do below), the conception of theory and practice I have been discussing, we may be able to: (a) recognize that empiricism has often been associated with liberalism; (b) reject empiricism; but (c) embrace liberalism. The liberalism that we embrace, however, will have to involve a quite different conception of theory and practice.

I discuss some recent formulations of liberalism that are arguably idealist in philosophical orientation later in this essay. But if I am correct that these views partly endorse the understanding of theory as dominating practice, considering them will not provide a genuine alternative to the conceptions of that relationship which I have thus far discussed. For this reason, and because empiricism and idealism are widely thought to exhaust the array of philosophically informed and motivated versions of liberalism, I first look outside of liberalism for different ways to assemble the elements of this essay. In making this sojourn abroad, however, we will have to take seriously the possibility that "first philosophy" of any sort has little more than prophylactic or perhaps antidotal value for either moral and political theory or moral and political practice.

IV

Let us consider views, those of Michael Oakeshott and the later Wittgenstein, which reject not only empiricism but all arguments to the effect that theory can or should direct, guide, or in any way contribute to practice.[10]

According to Oakeshott's theory of theory and practice, theory is categorially distinct from and hence categorically irrelevant to practice. Attempts by "theoreticians," "rationalists," and other "impudent mountebanks"[11] to deny this and to impose their abstractions on practice are double failures: they abandon theorizing in the only distinct and defensible sense of the term and they distort and damage the practices into which they intrude.

The basis for this position is laid in *Experience and Its Modes*.[12] In Part II of this unduly neglected work, Oakeshott rejects as self-contradictory the several elements of empiricism mentioned above. The key distinctions on which it depends, between subject and object, among sensation, perception, and intuition on the one hand and between them and thought or judgment on the other, are

---

[10]Wendell John Coats, Jr., has argued persuasively that Oakeshott's thought provides a distinctively coherent formulation of a liberal view. With few and minor exceptions, I agree with his analysis of Oakeshott's thought and further agree that the elements Coats emphasizes are central to a form of liberalism. As Coats recognizes, however, Oakeshott himself would hardly condone this classification—or appropriation—of his thinking. See "Michael Oakeshott as Liberal Theorist," *Canadian Journal of Political Science* 18 (December 1985):773–87.

[11]Michael Oakeshott, *On Human Conduct* (Oxford: Clarendon Press, 1975), p. 30.

[12]Michael Oakeshott, *Experience and Its Modes* (Cambridge: University of Cambridge Press, 1933).

"abstractions" from the "world of ideas" which is experience as a "concrete whole," abstractions that depend for their intelligibility on the whole of which they are a part and from which they have been abstracted. In denying this, in claiming that "things" or "individuals" are self-subsistent and that sensations and perceptions stand apart from one another and hence from thinking, empiricism denies presuppositions of what it attempts to affirm.

In privileging these abstractions, empiricism also abandons philosophy and philosophizing. "It is our business in philosophy to avoid abstractions." Uniquely, philosophical experience is "experience without presupposition, reservation, arrest or modification." As distinct from all other thinking, philosophy seeks experience that is "critical throughout," that pursues the coherence of the world of ideas until it provides "the evidence of its own completeness" in the sense that all of the suppositions of and all of the connections among the ideas that constitute that world (*the* world) have been identified and purged of incoherence.[13]

The notion of a fully coherent, fully concrete world of ideas, and of philosophical knowledge as complete knowledge of that world, although the only notion that is entirely free from abstractness, "is necessarily fleeting and elusive."[14] But it is also indispensable in the sense of logically necessary to all thinking, and its unremitting pursuit is the defining characteristic of philosophy. Coherence is the *criterion* of intelligibility and hence of truth, of reality, of all that is "satisfactory" in experience. It is implicit in the partial coherence of all that is intelligible; it presents itself more distinctly as the philosopher notices unappreciated suppositions and attempts to rectify disjunctions and inconsistencies.

For Oakeshott, then, philosophy does not probe beneath, behind, or outside of pre-, non-, or extraphilosophical thought. There is one world, the world of ideas. In this respect, and notwithstanding the uniqueness of its objectives, philosophical thinking is continuous with, inseparable from, all other thinking. Rather than correcting nonphilosophical thinking by reference to philosophical discoveries brought back like gifts from some other realm, it explicates the world of ideas.

In his later *On Human Conduct* and related essays, Oakeshott narrows his focus from philosophizing concerning experience as a

[13]Ibid., pp. 9, 2.
[14]Ibid., p. 3.

whole to what he calls "theorizing" conduct *inter-homines*. Confined as it is to seeking the coherence of the "mode of experience" he earlier called the "practical," this activity allows of being "arrested" and "abstract" in ways that philosophizing as analyzed in *Experience and Its Modes* has to suffer but cannot endorse. In respect, however, to their implications for empiricist liberalism and other doctrines that promote the dominance of theory over practice, philosophizing and theorizing are as one.

Both theorists and practitioners of human conduct seek coherence in thought and action. They both "begin" (in a logical not a temporal sense) by "recognizing" various "goings-on" as having certain distinguishing characteristics, "identify" them as consisting of compositions of characteristics gathered under "ideal characters," and seek to extend further the intelligibility of their experience by "mapping" the relationships among the latter. To the extent that they succeed, they attain to a "platform of conditional understanding" that is a "considerable advance" on the coherence among the mere recognitions with which they "began."[15] Theorists then press on to an activity in which, for reasons we will consider below, practitioners cannot engage—that is, identifying and "interrogating" the "postulates" of platforms of understanding. But here too theorists are dependent on practitioners because the postulates they interrogate and theorize are postulates of the ideas and understandings of practitioners. In this and other ways, this understanding of theorizing discredits the conceptions of theory and practice discussed above. The ideas common to those conceptions—namely, leaving practice wholly or partly behind, discovering a truth or a reality independent of it, and bringing that truth back as a substitute for or corrective to practice—are "delusions of theory." There is no truth or reality apart from practice for theorists to theorize.

As we have seen, Oakeshott rejects much more than the doctrine that philosophy and theory can and should supplant and dominate practice. Despite the views I have summarized, he holds that philosophy and theory are categorially distinct from and categorially irrelevant to practice. His reasons for this conclusion, surprising and puzzling given his insistence on the continuities between theory and practice, will be assessed below. But first let us consider another formulation with a strongly analogous combination of features.

[15]Oakeshott, *On Human Conduct*, p. 6. It should be emphasized that Oakeshott's account is not to be construed as a chronicle, as identifying temporally calibrated sequences through which these steps pass.

Wittgenstein rejects Oakeshott's idea that the unique purpose of philosophy is to discern and examine something that can be of no interest to nonphilosophers, that is, the world of ideas as a concrete whole or the postulates of their own thinking and acting. "Philosophy simply puts everything before us, and neither explains nor deduces anything.—Since everything lies open to view, there is nothing to explain. For what is hidden, for example, is of no interest to us." "If one tried to advance *theses* in philosophy, it would never be possible to question them, because everyone would agree to them." "And we may not advance any kind of theory. There must not be anything hypothetical in our considerations. We must do away with all *explanation,* and description alone must take its place. . . . The problems are solved, not by giving new information, but by arranging what we have always known." "Philosophy may in no way interfere with the actual use of language; it can in the end only describe it. For it cannot give it any foundation either. It leaves everything as it is."[16]

We might treat the foregoing passages as a radical extension, an extension to "everything," of Oakeshott's views about theory and practice. Oakeshott argues that philosophy and theory may not interfere with practice, that they leave practice as it is. But he also posits further, categorially distinct, kinds of reflection that are exclusively the province of philosophy and theory. Rejecting (albeit not *refuting*) the idealist notion of a single, entirely coherent world of ideas that lies behind Oakeshott's conception, Wittgenstein denies that philosophy has any distinct subject matter. Philosophy is continuous with all other thinking in respects yet deeper than those Oakeshott insists on.

It is tempting to go further and say that for Wittgenstein "everything" is what Oakeshott calls practice, that none of us is other than a more or less adept practitioner of various practices or activities, and hence that there is *no* distinct role for philosophy to play, no special purpose for "it" to pursue.

Although not simply mistaken, this further inference fails to take account of features of Wittgenstein's thinking which are especially pertinent here. Despite the passages I quoted above, Wittgenstein made investigations he called "philosophical" and his writings in-

---

[16]Ludwig Wittgenstein, *Philosophical Investigations* (New York: Macmillan, 1953), I, 126, 128, 109, 124.

clude various remarks about the distinctive characteristics and objectives of philosophical work. We cannot substitute these passages
for attention to the detail of his investigations, but several of his
more programmatic statements will repay immediate notice.

"The philosopher's treatment of a question is like the treatment
of an illness." "There is not *a* philosophical method, though there
are indeed methods, like different therapies." What illnesses does
the Wittgensteinian philosopher treat; what are the maladies to
which philosophers administer their various therapies? "Naming,"
he says, sometimes "appears as a *queer* connexion of a word with
an object.—And you really get such a queer connexion when the
philosopher tries to bring out *the* relation between name and thing
by staring at an object in from of him and repeating a name or even
the word 'this' innumerable times. For philosophical problems arise
when language *goes on holiday*."[17] Captivated by a picture or ideal
of what must be the case, the philosopher fails to attend closely to
language actually at work in thought and action. Removing concepts from the contexts or circumstances that are integral to their
meanings, in which they are "in order," philosophers perplex themselves with paradoxes of their own creation. The therapies Wittgenstein provides vary from case to case, but they all involve dissolving
the picture or disqualifying the ideal by bringing the concepts in
which they are expressed back to the settings in which they are
unproblematic.

V

We might say that Oakeshott and Wittgenstein treat practice as
"theory-like" and practicing as a form of theorizing. Among the
main elements of practice are concepts, ideas, beliefs, and the like.
As with the components of any formation that deserves the name of
a theory, these elements make up ensembles each of which has a
more or less definite and discernible pattern or order. These patterns
are produced, maintained, and altered by the practitioners who
think and act within and about them. As with good theorists, adept
practitioners understand the patterns of the various ensembles
(ideal characters, language games) in which they think and act and

[17]Ibid., I, 255, 133, 38. Cf. ibid., 52, 131, 194, 295, 393, 520, 588–90.

perhaps something of the larger patterns (forms of life, traditions and practices) formed by constellations of ensembles. Although necessarily accepting much of what they have come to understand, their thought and action may enhance, diminish, or otherwise change the existing patterning by altering or rearranging some of its elements. Like unaccomplished theorists, less adept practitioners may fall into and create confusion.

Characterizing their views in this way underlines some of Oakeshott's and Wittgenstein's objections to the conceptions of theory and practice promoted by empiricism and a variety of other doctrines. To say that practice is theorylike and that "practicing" is like theorizing is to affirm that they have properties such as intelligibility, internal consistency, and coherence; that is, that all practices and practicing have at least some of the properties that theorists with overweening ambitions say practices acquire only *after* they have been remade by Scientific, Rationalist, or other philosophizing (remade to meet criteria not internal to them prior to the successful intervention of the theorist).

The same characterization, however, seems to open up a possibility that Oakeshott insistently denies and that Wittgenstein occasionally seems to deny and more frequently disparages—namely, that theory might make distinctive contributions to practice. If philosophy or theory are inseparable from and continuous with practice in the ways I have been discussing, why can't theory contribute to practice *as* it pursues its distinctive activities and purposes, in the course of conducting those pursuits? Do not the same considerations that discredit empiricism and related views suggest that success in enhancing the coherence of the world of ideas and ministering to confusions in thought would contribute something of at least modest value to practice? Might we not go further and say that the views sketched in Section III of this chapter articulate a praxis conception of theory and practice and hence make theory not only valuable but integral to practice? If there is an objection to the idea that theory can contribute to practice, it might be the one to which I adverted at the outset, namely, that there is no clear distinction between them and hence no basis for saying that "the one" can or cannot assist "the other." It is now time to assess Oakeshott's and Wittgenstein's reasons for rejecting these inferences.

Beyond passages already quoted, such as "philosophy leaves everything as it is" (and leaving aside his pessimism about the likelihood that his thinking would be so much as understood), Wittgenstein frequently takes a derisive attitude toward the philosophical therapies he performs. Like a medical doctor curing diseases that other doctors have inflicted on themselves by bad medical practice, his recognition that his patients are genuinely in distress is not enough to suppress a certain disdain for them and for their illnesses. In these passages philosophizing presents a dismal appearance. "What we are destroying is nothing but houses of cards and we are clearing up the ground of language on which they stand." "The results of philosophy are the uncovering of one or another piece of plain nonsense." "My aim is: to teach you to pass from a piece of disguised nonsense to something that is patent nonsense." "A whole cloud of philosophy consensed into a drop of grammar."[18]

Better, it might seem, if philosophy had never made an appearance.

By contrast with Wittgenstein's occasional and enigmatic remarks on this subject, Oakeshott argues explicitly and at length that philosophy and theory are categorically irrelevant to practice. Because his arguments will help us to identify the combination of limitations on and possibilities for contributions of theory to practice, they are worth considering in some detail. I concentrate on his discussion of theorizing in *On Human Conduct,* taking up with the "platforms of conditional understanding" to which I earlier brought my discussion of his theory of theory and practice.

For practitioners, the identifications assembled to form these platforms are "diagnoses" and "verdicts." As these terms imply, they are invitations to action. "The identities disclosed in 'this is a case of the measles,' 'that is a bank robbery,' . . . are understood [by practitioners] to prescribe utterances such as 'isolate the patient,' 'sound the alarm,' . . . or performances that correspond to these utterances." "An utterance which provokes laughter is an utterance diagnosed as a 'joke.'"[19] These identifications can be meaningful only to the extent that they are part of a more or less coherent set of understandings; but for practitioners their meaning is, in J. L. Austin's sense, exclusively perlocutionary; understanding them *is* knowing how to perform in response to the diagnoses and verdicts they issue.

[18]Ibid., I, 118, 119, 464; II, p. 222.
[19]Oakeshott, *On Human Conduct,* pp. 7–8.

By contrast, the theorist (as with the philosopher of *Experience and Its Modes*) must decline the invitation to action and accept another that the practitioner cannot entertain, namely, to question further the ideal characters and the platforms of understanding they compose. In order to act on verdicts, the practitioner must accept them and hence also the set of identifications that compose the platforms of understanding from which they issue. The practitioner is, and as practitioner must remain, "in the prison of his current understanding."[20]

It is from this prison that the theorist "seeks release," release that can be obtained only by understanding the identities "in terms of their postulates." As Odysseus did with the songs of other Sirens, theorists must close their ears to the invitations to action accepted by practitioners and set out instead on an "unconditional adventure in which every achievement of understanding is an invitation to investigate itself and where the reports a theorist makes to himself are interim triumphs of temerity over scruple." For the theorist, platforms of understanding are not instruments to be used in action but objects of further interrogation. "The irony of all theorizing is its propensity to generate, not an understanding, but a not-yet-understood."[21]

Thus far, theory is held apart in order to protect *it* from the distractions of practical activity. Theorizing, however, is not itself unconditional, and just as philosophy in the fullest sense cannot hope to achieve complete coherence, theorizing has no prospect of arriving at a "terminus in an unconditional theorem." As with the actions of practitioners, theorizing is and must always be from a platform of understanding parts of which the theorist cannot *now* be interrogating. As Wittgenstein says, to think about *this,* the theorist must accept much else. What distinguishes the theorist from the practitioner, rather, is the determination of the former to be "perpetually *en voyage,*" to regard success in delineating the postulates of previous understandings as reason for neither action nor rest but for questioning the conditions of that success.[22] This labor is not Sisyphean in the sense of having endlessly to do again exactly what was already done; nor is it interminable for the reason that empiricists sometimes suggest—namely, that we can never be

[20]Ibid., p. 9.
[21]Ibid., pp. 8, 11.
[22]Ibid., p. 11.

certain we have correctly identified all of the "facts" that need to be "colligated" by the scientific theorist. Theorizing can be stopped but never finished because every stopping place involves suppositions that require interrogation.

The illusion that the theorist has achieved an unconditioned theorem is one source of the mistaken and "impudent" view that theory can and should govern practice. Convincing themselves that they have achieved "an unconditional understanding of the world in terms of its postulates," Platonists, Rationalists, Marxists, and even some empiricists (for example, Bentham) dismiss the conditional understandings of practitioners as "worthless nescience" and promote their own self-admired constructions as "a complete *substitute* for," as "a definitive understanding and language to supersede and *to take the place of* all other understandings and languages." In addition to being a self-congratulatory philosophical fantasy, this species of presumption badly underestimates those whose thought and action it dismisses. Practitioners "are not at all inadequately equipped for understanding and dealing with the world in which they live." There are "expert map-makers and adept diagnosticians" among them and their unconcern for the conditional character of their identifications does not diminish their prowess as practitioners.[23] Rather, the theorist's theorems about postulates are irrelevant to conduct and cannot possibly substitute for or improve on the diagnoses and verdicts of practitioners.

Holding as it does for all theorems not merely for supposedly unconditional ones, the last claim is the most general and the most important for our purposes. Platonists, Marxists, and self-described scientific empiricists are distinctive in their readiness to discard practitioner understandings, but they are not the only theorists who desert their calling and become "theoreticians"—imposters who claim that their abstractions entitle them to govern practice. "This deplorable character has no respectable occupation. In virtue of being a theorist he purports to be concerned with the postulates of conduct, but he mistakes these postulates for principles from which 'correct' performances may be deduced or somehow elicited. He understands it to be his business to umpire conduct, certifying performances . . . [as] 'correct' [or] . . . 'incorrect' inferences from the theorems of an alleged understanding of conduct in terms of its conditions. But since such theorems are incapable of specifying

[23]Ibid., pp. 26, 29, 29–30.

performance, the engagement of the 'theoretician' is a spurious engagement in conduct itself, an undertaking to direct the activities of map-makers, diagnosticians and agents by systematic deception. He is a fraudulent tutor; and the certificates he issues are counterfeit, acceptable only by those who share his belief in the truth of his theorems and share also his delusions about their character."[24] In their futile attempts to close the gap between the postulates that theorists discern and interrogate and the verdicts and diagnoses of practitioners, theoreticians commit "the most fatal of all errors," *ignoratio elenchi;* they fall victim to "the most insidious and crippling of all forms of error—irrelevance."[25]

These last passages align Oakeshott with views about "practical reasoning" and "judgment" which go back at least to Aristotle, are closely akin to Wittgenstein's discussions of rule following and (more generally) "knowing how to go on," and embody what is most important in both Oakeshott's and Wittgenstein's views concerning the limits of philosophy and theory *as they understand them.* I return to these views by way of concluding this essay. But first we must see why the arguments just considered do not support the restrictive conclusions that seem to be implied by some of Wittgenstein's remarks and that Oakeshott insistently draws.

As with the inference that philosophy is indistinguishable from thinking *sans phrase,* the conclusion that it would have been better if we had avoided it altogether exaggerates an element that was genuinely a part of Wittgenstein's thinking. We should note a sense in which even his most disdainful responses to the work of other philosophers serve to modify his assertion that his own philosophizing "leaves everything as it is." In curing their diseases of thought, Wittgenstein returns them and perhaps us to the *status quo ante philosophicum,* restores the health and good order that their misguided thinking had corrupted. And if one thinks, as Oakeshott sometimes seems to think about theoreticians, that philosophers can transmit their viruses to nonphilosophers, such immunization of thought, the practice of such preventive philosophical medicine, would deserve higher regard than he appears to accord it.

This modification takes on substantially greater significance when we see that there are wider grounds for thinking that the illnesses

[24]Ibid., pp. 26–27.
[25]Oakeshott, *Experience and Its Modes,* p. 5.

to which philosophers fall victim are not purely "iratrogenic" in the sense of resulting exclusively from bad *philosophical* practice. Whereas Oakeshott typically writes as if the only (if any) practical contribution of philosophy and theory is to cleanse practice of the pollutants discharged by theoreticians, Wittgenstein thinks that philosophers are especially prone to diseases to which we are all susceptible. "Philosophy [as Wittgenstein himself practices it] is a battle against the bewitchment of our intelligence by means of language." "The problems arising through a misinterpretation of our forms of language have the character of *depth*. They are deep disquietudes; their roots are as deep in us as the forms of our language and their significance is as great as the importance of our language." Language (*langue*) is in order as it is in the sense that there is no ideal language and no extralinguistic reality by comparison with which the languages we have can be judged, corrected, or improved. But speech (*parole*) and thought are often not in order. "We do not *command* a clear view of our use of our words." "The aspects of things that are most important for us are hidden because of their simplicity and familiarity. (One is unable to notice something—because it is always before one's eyes.) . . . We fail to be struck by what, once seen, is most striking and powerful."[26]

Those who engage in what "used to be called 'philosophy' " are distinctively but not uniquely susceptible to these difficulties. The "forms of language" are deep in us all, and the "hiddenness" of the familiar makes it difficult for any of us to see those forms clearly. It is not only in doing philosophy that we become "entangled in our own rules" and fall into the kinds of contradictions that lead us to say things such as "I didn't mean it like that." "The civil status of a contradiction, or its status in civil life: there is the philosophical problem."[27]

An implication of these views, writ large in Wittgenstein's philosophical practice, is that philosophical therapy cannot be brisk. As their counterparts in psychoanalytic therapy are wont to claim as their achievement, philosophical therapists must appreciate the depth, the complexity, and the power of the disquietudes to which they minister. "Philosophy unties knots in our thinking; hence its result must be simple, but philosophizing has to be as complicated

---

[26]Wittgenstein, *Philosophical Investigations*, I, 109, 111, 122, 129.
[27]Ibid., 125.

as the knots it unties." "In philosophizing we may not terminate a disease of thought. It must run its natural course, and *slow* cure is all important."[28]

Contrary to interpreters who dismiss Wittgenstein as some sort of Panglossian or apologist, these are not the remarks of a thinker complacent about the subject matters of his reflections or disposed to diminish the importance of his thinking. To untie the knots in our thinking, to cure the diseases of thought from which we suffer, to achieve a clearer view of our practices and activities, these accomplishments, even if modest by comparison with the ambitions of traditional philosophers, would be far from negligible.[29]

Returning to the more difficult matter of Oakeshott's arguments, I have no disposition to deny the significance of his paired distinctions between the postulates and, for example, the principles of a practice and between thinking in and thinking about postulates. These distinctions are less clear-cut than he supposes, but they do mark important differences such as between doing historiography and doing history, between the philosophy of science and science, and between the primarily metatheoretical enterprise of this essay and the more usual (or at least the more widely proclaimed) purposes of both political theorists and political practitioners.

Developing this perspective a bit further will help us to appreciate both the somewhat anomalous character of the programmatic Oakeshottian and Wittgensteinian views about philosophy-practice and theory-practice relations and the admittedly circumscribed but nevertheless larger possibilities for theory that are implicit in the views I have been discussing.

Assuming that we have gotten in hand serviceable distinctions

[28]Ludwig Wittgenstein, *Zettel* (Oxford: Basil Blackwell, 1967), 452, 382.

[29]It is of course true that Wittgenstein was deeply pessimistic about the prospects of success in these endeavors. But deep pessimism does not overtake us in respect to the trivial or the merely foolish. See especially the Preface to *Philosophical Investigations*. It might be added that there is at least an analogy between Wittgenstein's conception of philosophy as therapy and conceptions of genealogists such as Nietzsche and Foucault. Wittgenstein's work does not have an explicit historical component and it is concerned primarily with the ideational and conceptual rather than the institutional dimensions of practice. The first point is important, marking as it does Wittgenstein's rejection of all forms of historicism. The second is less so, the distinction itself being difficult to draw clearly on Wittgenstein's views. But I introduce the comparison to further discredit the view that Wittgenstein's work is somehow complacent or Panglossian. That he thinks the diseases he treats are in principle curable does not alter his view that they are deep and serious afflictions.

between the elements of practice about which practitioners think and act and the postulates of those elements (neither an innocent nor an unproblematic assumption), it may be true that one and the same person cannot simultaneously think within and think about those postulates. And it is certainly false that self-conscious thought about postulates is necessary to thinking and acting within them—albeit it is doubtful, as Oakeshott says, that anyone could think about a set of postulates that they had never thought within. Oakeshott himself denies the possibility of a life given exclusively to philosophy or to theory.[30] Persons who are practitioners may never think about the postulates of their practices, but persons who are theorists are sometimes practitioners and therefore must sometimes think within the postulates of practices. Moreover, the world of ideas that is experience is a whole; however differentiated and complex it may be internally, philosopher-theorists must work on the assumption that every element of it connects to and can be made to cohere with every other.

The perspective just described is the one from which Oakeshott the philosopher-theorist identifies and distinguishes modes of experience such as history, science, and practice,[31] "orders of inquiry" such as the procedural and the processual, the "idioms of inquiry" that form the basis of the several conventional academic disciplines,[32] and the platforms of conditional understanding discussed above. It is also at least implicitly the perspective from which Oakeshott makes his distinctions between morality as a vernacular and an authoritative specification of ends; between a civil society and an enterprise association; between authority and power; between law (*lex*) and other types of rules; and between politics and (roughly) administration.[33] The perspective does not invalidate or diminish the importance of these distinctions: the world of ideas is a whole, but it is a whole consisting of parts that must be distinguished and related. Rather, the perspective enables the distinctions, gives the philosopher-theorist a standpoint from which to draw them. If the distinctions are drawn in a manner that enhances coherence, then so far from committing category mistakes *à la* the theoretician, the philosopher-theorist not only exposes the misun-

[30]Oakeshott, *Experience and Its Modes*, p. 3.
[31]Ibid., chaps. 3–4.
[32]Oakeshott, *On Human Conduct*, pp. 13–17.
[33]Ibid., esp. pp. 61ff.; essay II; pp. 127–38, 161–84.

derstandings of theoreticians (and to that degree protects practice and practitioners against them) but enhances the satisfactoriness of experience.

Oakeshott's claim that philosophy and theory are categorically irrelevant to practice, and—though less clearly so—Wittgenstein's argument that philosophy can be no more than therapeutic, are most convincing when construed as directed against positions that are incoherent because they deny conditions necessary to their own intelligible formulation. In denying what I have called the theorylike character of practice, in arguing that practice will acquire this characteristic only after it has been remade by theory, proponents of these positions in effect claim that there can be and is thought and action (experience) which are intelligible or meaningful despite the absence of order, pattern, or integration among their elements. They claim that they understand practice, understand it well enough to identify its defects and to determine how those defects should be remedied. They may even allow that in some degree practitioners of unreformed practices understand themselves and one another. But they characterize practice and practitioners in ways that on Oakeshottian and Wittgensteinian views make understanding impossible.

The anomaly is that, despite these views about practice, in their most programmatic statements about philosophy, theory, and practice, Wittgenstein and especially Oakeshott insist on distinctions that deny to philosophy and theory the very possibilities for contributing to practice that their views about practice open up.

Philosophers, theorists, and practitioners are and must be alike in that they pursue and to some considerable extent achieve coherence and intelligibility, seek to and to some considerable extent succeed in eliminating inconsistency, disjunction, and the like from their thinking. But (bracketing the Oakeshottian idea of *complete* coherence) coherence, intelligibility, meaningfulness, and the like are matters of greater and lesser, not all or none, and it is undeniable that much thought and action succeeds by various criteria despite the presence in them of inconsistency, confusion, and misunderstanding that are unnoticed, unresolved, and even deliberately introduced and maintained.

Realizing this, we can draw valuable but less than categorial distinctions among philosophy, theory, and practice. Oakeshottian philosophers differ from theorists (Wittgenstein does not make this distinction), who differ from practitioners, not in some notional sense of kind but in the centrality they respectively accord to criteria such as coherence and integration and more particularly the single-mindedness with which they pursue these rather than partly complementary but sometimes competing objectives. Remembering that all philosophers and theorists are also sometimes practitioners, we might say that there is something of a division in the labor of achieving and sustaining what Oakeshott calls satisfactoriness in experience. Philosophers and theorists are specialists in detecting confusions and other maladies in the "theory" implicit in practice; practitioners specialize in acting on the invitations that theory extends. To the extent that philosophers and theorists identify and help to "cure" diseases of thought, they may contribute something that is—by standards practitioners also at least implicitly accept—of value to practice. Although Oakeshott officially denies and Wittgenstein frequently diminishes the idea of such contributions of theory to practice, their respective theories of theory and practice provide reasons for entertaining that idea.

VI

Are these possibilities worth pursuing? Are they and the views from which they emerge more consonant with or appropriate to liberalism than those discussed earlier in this essay? Does skepticism play any role in the combination of possibilities for and limitations on moral and political theory which are suggested by Oakeshott and Wittgenstein?

The last of these questions is the easiest and answering it will be of some help in addressing the first two. Both Oakeshott and Wittgenstein can be described as skeptical in the nondoctrinal, perhaps dispositional sense of tending to look with suspicion on claims and arguments, especially those advanced by philosophers. (It is probably also accurate to say that they are both, perhaps congenitally, pessimists.) But neither of them accepts the view that warranted belief is impossible or cannot be known to be possible. Oakeshott has no doubt that he has refuted empiricism, rationalism, and indeed doctrinal skepticism itself, has demonstrated that they are incoherent and hence false. Again, while he has no hope of achieving the fully coherent world of ideas that philosophy seeks, he is entirely confident that this is the proper objective of philosophy. This means that philosophers and theorists can never rest content, must always seek to enlarge the coherence of the world of ideas. But it does not impugn their partial achievements. Most important here, it does not impugn the claims of practitioners. By the criteria appropriate to their activities, those claims can be and often are adequately warranted. Wittgenstein does not refute empiricism, idealism, or skepticism, but rather dissolves them by showing that they fail to give intelligible formulations to key concepts such as "truth" and "knowledge," "certainty" and "doubt." By the criteria established in the language-games and forms of life in which they are made, claims to knowledge, certainty, validity, and the like, claims to have "gone on" or to be going on correctly in various activities, are sometimes justified, sometimes not. Claims to and demands for some further, some philosophically superstrong justification or disjustification, are misguided, are chief sources of "diseased" thinking.

Moving toward liberalism, let us look at these aspects of Oakeshott's and Wittgenstein's thinking in the perspective of the concern of Russell and other liberals to erect barriers to theory-driven utopianism, arrogance, and fanaticism. Earlier I argued that empiricist liberalism is at odds with itself in the following respect: its skepticism and fallibilism, which it claims expose dogmatism and block unwarranted intrusions into practice, conflict with its equally deeply grounded ambition to replace erroneous practice with scientific truth. Because this conflict is internal to the theory, its resolution is left to the "intentions" of this or that soi-disant liberal, to the determination liberals bring to "insulating" their scientific faith from their skepticism or vice versa.

Empiricist liberalism (and perhaps other doctrines that promote or at least entertain the possibility of the dominance of theory over practice) seeks to get beneath, above, outside of language, convention, practice. By contrast, for Wittgenstein there is no beneath, no outside. "Our *acting* is at the bottom of our language games."[34] "There is no outside; outside you cannot breathe."[35] For Oakeshott there is one world, the world of ideas. Wittgensteinian and Oakeshottian *theory* excludes as misconceived or incoherent this empiricist and all similar projects. Philosophers and theoreticians who

[34]Ludwig Wittgenstein, *On Certainty* (Oxford: Basil Blackwell, 1969), 204.
[35]Wittgenstein, *Philosophical Investigations*, I, 103.

nevertheless adopt and pursue that project may or may not be arrogant and dogmatic, may or may not have effects on practice; it is certain that they make vitiating mistakes in their theorizing.

Oakeshott's and Wittgenstein's views of what theory cannot do for practice, then, rest on affirmations not denials, on what they believe to be warranted conclusions, not on skepticism about the possibility of such conclusions. The same is true of the more constructive possibilities for theory which, despite their official disclaimers, are opened up by their theories of theory and practice.

There is a world of ideas that is and is known to be (partly) coherent, a form of life that is "in order." Thinking within that world or form of life and by its criteria of coherence and incoherence, order and disorder, theorists attempt to identify confusions and inconsistencies and thereby to enlarge (at least in the sense of restoring) order and coherence. In doing so they are of course liable to make mistakes. The more important point is that the wherewithal for identifying mistakes as such and for correcting them is provided (to all participants not only or distinctively to philosophers and theorists) by the world of ideas or the form of life. This conception of philosophy and theory is confined in ways that will make it unwelcome to some liberals, but it is affirmative not skeptical.

In disqualifying on philosophical grounds the soaring, self-promoting aspirations of some moral and political philosophers, Oakeshott and Wittgenstein buttress recurrent if unsteady tendencies in liberalism. Let us now consider affinities between some other persistent (but also unsteady) liberal propensities and the more constructive possibilities that are licensed by the positions of these two nonliberal thinkers. In making these comparisons I restrict my remarks to one of a number of possibilities, namely, the notion of "respect," first as in "a decent respect for the opinions of mankind" and second in the sense in which many liberal theories (perhaps especially nonempiricist theories) strongly promote "respect for persons" and arrangements that sustain and enhance "self-respect."

For Jefferson and his fellow signers, respect for the opinions of humankind was a moral and political imperative. Of course the imperative did not require them to agree with or accede to the opinions of others. The signers of the Declaration discharged this among their duties by taking seriously the opinions of humankind—by trying to understand opinions other than their own, by explaining their own views to others, and by attempting to justify their actions in ways responsive to objections and disagreements. Self-respect and respect for persons are more complex and perhaps more elusive notions, but no one would say that they require accepting the beliefs and values of all those to whom respect is owed or whose self-respect one is trying to sustain and enhance. Serious, perhaps sympathetic, consideration is due, but conflicts among the beliefs and values of persons make agreement with all of them impossible, and in many circumstances the duty itself is thought to require attempts to correct the mistaken or ill-considered views of those to whom respect is owed.

Neither these imperatives nor the concepts in which they are expressed make any appearances in Wittgenstein's thought, and they appear in Oakeshott's, if at all, in a diction quite different than those usual in liberalism. But if "a decent respect" and respect for persons consist in the elements I just sketched, it is clear that a commitment to something akin to them is *entailed* by those of Wittgenstein's and Oakeshott's views which I have emphasized in this essay.

Recall Oakeshott's rebuke to theoreticians for dismissing the thinking of practitioners as "worthless nescience" and Wittgenstein's view that those who do "what used to be called philosophy" fall into confusion because they refuse to give close attention to "the language of every day." To dismiss, to refuse to take seriously, the thinking and acting of practitioners is to dismiss elements of experience and reality themselves. Whatever effects doing so may have on practice and practitioners, it guarantees the failure of philosophy and theory.

Here again Oakeshott and Wittgenstein, qua practitioners, are not therefore committed (or, as it happens, particularly disposed) to agree with the beliefs, opinions, and practical judgments of other practitioners—no more so than Jefferson and his colleagues committed themselves to agree with the opinions of all of humankind about American independence, Kant with Roman Catholics, Green with the pro-alcohol lobby, or Rawls with those who reject religious toleration. Qua philosopher or theorist, however, Wittgenstein, Oakeshott, and anyone who accepts their philosophical positions must "take seriously," must seek to grasp the coherence and incoherence, the order and disorder, of the thinking and acting in which beliefs and opinions are embodied and expressed.

For reasons having to do with "practical reasoning" and with which I will conclude, "respecting" thought and action, thinkers and actors, in this sense will not itself guarantee Kantian respect for persons, the self-respect of persons as Rawls and others have construed that notion, or any other moral or political achievement. But if, contrary to Oakeshott's and Wittgenstein's official view, general philosophical positions are nevertheless pertinent to practice, the position I have attributed to them is promising in this regard—more promising than the positions of liberals whose theories feature respect and self-respect as moral and political imperatives and desiderata.

In much liberal thought, the notion "person" bears little resemblance to either the Oakeshottian concept of "practitioner" or to Wittgenstein's characterizations of participants in language games and forms of life. As Oakeshott would put it, the "persons" of liberal theory are, by intention, abstract not concrete; they are described in ways deliberately chosen to eliminate the effects of traditions, conventions, and rules, shared languages, beliefs, and values. In Wittgensteinian parlance, these "persons" are not understood as parts of "wholes" such as language games and forms of life. Treated as "atomic entities," as denizens of "states of nature" or parties to "original positions" veiled in ignorance, they are abstracted from the "mechanisms" in which they can be "somethings" rather than "anythings" or "nothings."[36] These differences stand out in yet bolder relief when we look at the attempts of leading liberal theorists to give content to the ideas of respect, regard, and consideration. Respecting persons and contributing to their self-respect are made to consist in protecting their "natural rights," fostering their "self-realization," or contributing to their "full autonomy." Rather than looking within the traditions and conventions of actual societies to see what their members regard as showing respect and disrespect (looking, for example, at the conventions of polite conduct, the forms of address, of demeanor, of gift and return of gift, and the like), liberal theorists set such considerations aside in favor of criteria that, they argue, deserve acceptance and implementation whether or not they accord with already accepted norms and expectations. The objective of devotees of these notions is to resolve conflicts among and otherwise to improve on the think-

---

[36]Ibid., I, 6.

ing and acting of practitioners. Thus natural rights must be protected even if their putative bearers find the idea of such rights incomprehensible or the measures proposed to protect them strongly objectionable. Again, views about self-realization, autonomy, and like notions that conflict with the theory-generated criteria that properly govern them, however widely accepted those views might be, are to be given no weight in moral and political deliberation.

To the extent that these (admittedly casual and underdefended) characterizations of theories of respect and self-respect are accurate concerning identifiable liberal thinkers,[37] they support my earlier suggestion that non- and antiempiricist liberals are prone to conceptions of theory and practice at odds with the theory of theory and practice I have attributed to Oakeshott and Wittgenstein.

Of course a detailed defense of this suggestion would not discredit the moral and political substance of these theories—no more so than refutations and dissolutions of empiricism discredit the specifically moral and political proposals of self-styled empiricist liberals such as Mill and Russell. If, *per impossible* on Oakeshott's and Wittgenstein's theory of theory and practice, a "theory" were formed or a "proposal" advanced which was genuinely independent of practice, which owed *nothing* to practitioner understandings, "it" would discredit itself in the deep sense that it would be unintelligible (including to its proponent).

This comment may explain why Oakeshott insists and Wittgenstein sometimes suggests that philosophy and theory in their senses are irrelevant to practice. Because all theories in other senses, and all proposals, must satisfy the Oakeshottian criteria of intelligibility and the Wittgensteinian criteria of meaningfulness, those criteria cannot discriminate among theories or proposals. And because those criteria are all that philosophy and theory in their senses provide, philosophy and theory are irrelevant to practice.

Even if strictly correct as regards philosophy and theory in the most insistently circumscribed construals I have considered, this position underestimates their prophylactic value to practice. To the extent that Oakeshott's and Wittgenstein's theories of theory and practice are accepted, practice is protected against the *claims,* com-

---

[37]I will not attempt to document the characterizations here. Thinkers to whom I think they apply are Ronald Dworkin on the notion of respect generally, T. H. Green on self-realization, Kant on autonomy, Alan Gewirth on natural rights, John Rawls on self-respect and "full autonomy."

monplace in our civilization and culture, of "theoreticians" and proponents of "what used to be called philosophy" to the authority to dictate to all other practitioners. (Those persuaded by my discussion of liberalism and authority in Chapter 2 might agree that at least in this regard the views of Oakeshott and Wittgenstein are congenial to liberalism.)

We have seen reason to say more than this. If practice itself is "theorylike," we need distinctions within theory and philosophy as well as between them and practice, and we cannot get along with one distinction between theory and practice. One possibility is to say that philosophy is concerned with the criteria of intelligibility or meaningfulness as such and therefore has no more (but no less) than prophylactic value for practice (a stipulation for which there is warrant in Oakeshott's own distinction between philosophy and theorizing). Theory, then, will be the attempt to discern and enhance the intelligibility (coherence) or meaningfulness of this or that practice or language game, these or those performances of particular practitioners or participants. Insofar as theorists succeed in such attempts, they may contribute something of value to practice and to practitioners. This distinction, drawn as it is in terms of differences in purposes or objectives, all of which are pursued within the world of ideas or within forms of life, cannot be categorial in Oakeshott's sense; but it is no less valuable for that.

With this distinction in hand we can discern an understanding of great importance in Oakeshott's and Wittgenstein's otherwise exaggerated assertions that theory is irrelevant to practice. Theory in the sense just distinguished is integral to practice and hence to practical reasoning or judgment. As delineated and elaborated in Oakeshott's and Wittgenstein's theories of theory and practice, however, theory itself can never bring practitioners all the way to the practical conclusions necessary to action. This is not because theory and theorizing must be superseded by "will," "decision," or some kind of "leap" that is to be understood (if at all) in terms of impulses, inclinations, or some other characteristics that owe nothing to the traditions and practices, language games and forms of life in which they occur. As with all "exhibitions of intelligence,"[38] judgment, decision, and action are possible only in traditions and practices, language games and forms of life. Rather, it is because theory and theorizing are always general, always concerned with classes or

[38]Oakeshott, *On Human Conduct*, p. 13.

45

categories and the relations among them, whereas judgment and action are concerned with particulars. Without what I am calling theory and theorizing, particulars would be "bare" and hence "any-things" or "nothings," not "somethings." But for this very reason theory and theorizing will not themselves single out this or that particular from the class or category in which it is intelligible and hence will not carry through to action. In order to act, the theorist must become a practitioner; or as the tradition to which this dimension of Oakeshott's and Wittgenstein's thinking contributes says it, theoretical reasoning must stop and practical reasoning must begin.

We might say that the discussion of practical reasoning began when Plato argued that philosophers must become kings. Having no doubt that philosophers could arrive at the truth about morals and politics, Plato nevertheless concluded (reluctantly and regretfully) that they could make their truths effective in practice only if they became that species of practitioner known as a king. But Plato's reason for this conclusion seems to have been that only philosophers can be relied on to do in practice what the truths of theory require. Philosophers must become practitioners because of defects or deficiencies in the understanding, the rectitude, and so on of nonphilosophers, not because of any difficulty intrinsic to putting theory into practice.

By contrast, from Aristotle to Oakeshott and Wittgenstein a number of thinkers, including some who have been confident that they could discover, develop, or construct warranted general truths or principles, have argued that such truths and principles necessarily underdetermine moral and political decisions and must be supplemented by kinds of thinking and acting that may be influenced by theory but that are not themselves theoretical. Aristotle's *phronesis*, the scholastic doctrine of casuistry, the Kantian concept of judgment, Oakeshott's notion of pursuing the intimations of a tradition, Wittgenstein's treatment of rules, rule following, and "knowing how to go on" (perhaps the most radical of these doctrines)—all exemplify this position. According to it, claims that a general principle or set of such principles enjoin or prohibit a particular judgment or action can always be successfully rebutted; genuine commitment to a theory or theoretically derived principle is always consistent with a variety of actions; it is never possible to disqualify, exclusively by appeal to theoretical considerations, all but one decision or course of action. The difficulty is not that there may be slips between theoretical cup and practical lip, but that getting from cup to lip requires particularization and the abilities and skills to effect it which the theoretical cup cannot contain.[39]

Those parts of Oakeshott's and Wittgenstein's theory of theory and practice which I styled "philosophy" teach anew the lesson of this limitation on itself and on theory and theorizing. In doing so they do all that they can to expose and protect practice and practitioners from the pretensions and presumptions of theoreticians masquerading as theorists. As with the arguments of the earlier theorists of practical reasoning whom I mentioned, however, and despite their programmatic statements to the contrary, the Oakeshottian and Wittgensteinian theories of theory and practice give us reason not to deny or to dismiss but rather to value and to augment the contributions that good theory can make to practice.

With the possible exception of Kant, none of the theorists of practical reasoning I have mentioned in the last pages is a liberal, and it would be absurd to suggest that their theories of theory and practice entail, imply, or recommend any of the self-styled liberal moral and political theories. But if liberalism acknowledges and welcomes the variety and changeable character of moral and political practices, if it recognizes and delights in the restless diversity of moral and political practitioners, these conclusions concerning the limitations and possibilities of theory and theorizing are neither surprising nor disturbing, neither to be resisted nor regretted. More than this the theorist of theory and practice cannot and should not try to say.

[39]Valuable recent discussions of practical reasoning include Ronald Beiner, *Political Judgment* (Chicago: University of Chicago Press, 1983); and Charles Larmore, *Patterns of Moral Complexity* (Cambridge: Cambridge University Press, 1987).

2

Liberalism and Authority

Discourse about liberalism and authority suffers distracting embarrassments. If the discourse aspires to contemporaneity it may well be accused of necromancy or even necrophilia; liberalism and authority are dead. Nor can it easily take refuge in historicality; one set of eminent authorities avers that liberalism has existed nowhere outside the pages of hopelessly unhistorical "histories" of political thought, another that authority has enjoyed but a fleeting presence in one or two times and places.[1] Should one be so heedless as to persevere with the discourse, the choices would appear to be unattractive: unmasking one's supposed subject matter or perpetuating mythologies.

The bold categoricality of these contentions arouses suspicion of lurking essentialisms. If "liberalism" is dead and "authority" is gone—*sans phrase* as it were—the least we must say is that each of "them" must have lived and been among us in forms pretty definite and well understood. Medical examiners need bodies to pronounce over. Even the proposition that liberalism is a figment would seem to betray certitude about what "it" has been thought to be and confidence that the supposititious entity will elude our most assiduous researches. The Exorcisor needs to know what the ghost was thought to be like and where it was said to lurk.

[1] The death of liberalism has been announced so often that documenting even the more prominent such assertions would be tedious. The demise of authority is also a recurrently popular theme, but by far the most interesting and important statements are by Michael Oakeshott in *On Human Conduct* (Oxford: Clarendon Press, 1975) and Hannah Arendt, especially in "What Is Authority?" in her *Between Past and Future* (New York: Viking Press, 1961).

Uncomfortable with such convenient but almost certainly over-simplifying assumptions, I hope for nothing so dramatic as confirmation or refutation of the sweeping empirical contentions I have mentioned. As suggested, however, the very presuppositions of those contentions encourage the thought that there are subject matters—if only at the level of ideas—available for examination and reflection. Equally important, the uncommon fervor with which the contentions are commonly advanced engenders the suspicion that examining these subject matters may tell us something about our political estate. I will use the terms *liberal* and *authority* without further apology, but I will not make a concerted effort to define *liberalism* or to document the past or present reality of authority. I will be examining a number of ideas that are familiar and, I think, commonly associated with these terms. Insofar as I have a theme it is also familiar, namely, that the deep tension between liberalism and authority, the deep ambivalence of liberals concerning authority, could hardly be otherwise. I hope also to suggest that this is no bad thing; that our political estate is the better for it.

I

Getting this examination under way will require some initial simplifications of my own, especially concerning the tenets of liberalism. Conveniently, Bruce Ackerman's recent book in, but ultimately against, liberal thinking helps us to arrive at a serviceable abbreviation.[2] (1) Human beings are purposive, goal-seeking creatures whose actions and patterns of action cannot be understood apart from their conceptions of good. (2) Conceptions of good and goals of action are irreducibly plural. There are no criteria of good that exclude the possibility of cogent disputation, and application of the available criteria frequently leads to conflicting judgments and conclusions. (3) There is a scarcity of at least some of the goods that human beings seek and of the resources necessary to effective pursuit of those goods. (4) Hence there is certain to be disagreement and competition and very likely to be conflict among human beings. (5) Disagreement, competition, and conflict neither can nor should be eliminated, but conflict must be contained within nondestructive

[2]Bruce Ackerman, *Social Justice and the Liberal State* (New Haven: Yale University Press, 1980).

limits. (6) The primary objective of politics is to promote an ordering of human interaction which allows each person the greatest possible freedom to pursue goals compatible with effective constraints on destructive conflict.

These propositions, of course, are neither exclusive to liberalism nor somehow exhaustive of all of the ideas that have ever been claimed for or ascribed to it. Self-designated non- or antiliberals might accept some of them, and some self-denominated liberals would want to alter the formulation of one or more. Certainly numerous contemporary liberals would insist on adding to the list, most particularly by including propositions about equality. But even if the list does not give us the historical gist or the philosophical essence of liberalism, it provides an interrelated set of ideas that engender a distinctive understanding and assessment of authority.

In respect to authority, our initial need is less for a list of tenets than for a set of distinctions. Following with one largish addition, the important account of Richard B. Friedman, we may distinguish among *in* authority, an *authority,* and *the authoritative.*[3] Presidents and police officers are *in* positions of authority. They hold offices that are invested, and that invest their occupants with, authority to promulgate rules and issue commands concerning classes of action, rules, and commands that are binding on all those subject to the jurisdiction of the office. Charles Goren holds no such office and hence possesses no such *in* authority. Rather, by virtue of his exceptional knowledge of and skill at playing the game of bridge, he is *an* authority on that game for numerous persons who play it. To my knowledge, Edmund Hoyle never held any office and is in any case long since deceased. Yet play "according to Hoyle" is *authoritative* for players of poker and numerous other games.

In Friedman's view, the distinction between *in* and *an* authority is categorical. Their presuppositions or conditions, the character of relations conducted in terms of them, are not only entirely different but antithetical. *In* authority presupposes disagreement and equality among the parties to the authority relationships; *an* authority assumes consensus (or at least the realistic possibility of achieving it) and inequality. As Thomas Hobbes has taught us to think, *in* authority arises because persons more or less equal in the respects

[3]Richard B. Friedman, "On the Concept of Authority in Political Philosophy," in *Concepts in Social and Political Philosophy,* ed. Richard E. Flathman (New York: Macmillan, 1973).

salient in their interactions fall into intractable disagreement over issues that cannot be sidestepped or postponed. To prevent destructive conflict, those persons create an office of authority and agree in advance to abide by all *intra vires* decisions of the occupant of that office. In the colorful language that is commonly employed in this connection, for purposes of action in regard to matters that have been regulated by the authority, they "surrender their judgment" to it. By contrast, *an* authority develops because one person (Able) achieves superiority of wisdom, knowledge, or skill over another (Baker) in respect to matters of interest or importance to both. As with *in* authority, Baker defers to Able. But this deference is based not on the assumption that agreement cannot be reached as to the proper resolution of substantive issues or questions, but on the belief that Able's judgment and actions are likely to be correct, wise, skillful. This belief is grounded in and justified by the quality of Able's previous performances as judged by criteria accepted by Baker. Accordingly, it will be proper for Baker to give up the belief and withdraw the deference if Able's performances deteriorate. Thus *an* authority relations are integrally concerned with the substantive merits of Able's performances. They presume not that there is intractable disagreement between the parties but rather that the parties will agree once Able has discerned and enunciated the truth, displayed the correct technique, and the like. Whatever terminology we choose to employ, *in* and *an* authority are radically different concepts and (if instantiated in practice) phenomena. The tendency to assimilate them has been productive of dangerous confusion. (Later we will see that in Michael Oakeshott's view a closely related confusion has engendered the mistaken belief that the modern state is possessed of the desirable property of *in* authority and, indeed, is responsible for the distinctive evils of modern life.[4])

No one acquainted with Friedman's acute analysis will deny that there are important differences between *in* and *an* authority. Our discussion of those differences, however, has already displayed at least one important commonality between them. There are others as well and they are material to understanding liberal attitudes toward political authority.

In both *in* and *an* authority Able's performances constitute considerations that are not only relevant to but ordinarily decisive

[4]Oakeshott, *On Human Conduct.*

concerning performances on Baker's part. We might say that Able's performances constitute reasons for *this* as opposed to *that* performance by Baker. (Later, however, we will have to give further attention to the notion "a reason for.") Whether this commonality explains or justifies our use of one and the same term, some such deference is rudimentary to both concepts and both relationships.

I want to try to understand this common feature by examining the relationships between *in* and *an* authority and what I called the authoritative. Expressions such as "that's according to Hoyle" and "that's not kosher" are used well beyond the confines of card play and dietary practice. As with notions such as "the done thing," "that's not on," and even (though with a harder, not necessarily a sharper, edge) "Christian," "un-American," and their ilk, these notions invoke beliefs and values that the speaker regards as strongly settled and widely shared among the members of her culture, community, or group. Conduct that accords with those beliefs and values is approved "as a matter of course," while actions that deviate from or conflict with them are therefore suspect and in need of explicit and detailed justification. Social scientists refer to such beliefs and values as forming the culture, the mores or folkways, the national character, and so forth of the societies they study. The philosopher Wittgenstein seems to have them in mind in such of his statements as the following: "It is what human beings *say* that is true and false, and they agree on the *language* they use. That is not agreement in opinions but in forms of life." "If language is to be a means of communication there must be agreement not only in definitions but also (queer as this may sound) in judgements."[5]

Attending to such "agreements" helps us to understand features of *an* authority relationships that are otherwise puzzling and perhaps objectionable. If Able's standing as *an* authority depends on the truth, wisdom and skill of her performances, it appears that Baker must be able to judge those performances. But if Baker is in fact competent to make such judgments, it would seem that Baker has no need for Able's authority; it would seem that there is no work for Able's authority to do. On the other hand, if Baker is

[5]Ludwig Wittgenstein, *Philosophical Investigations*, I, 241, 242 (New York: Macmillan, 1953). I have discussed the notion of the authoritative and other aspects of the present topic at greater length in my *The Practice of Political Authority: Authority and the Authoritative* (Chicago: University of Chicago Press, 1980).

incapable of judging Able's performances but nevertheless defers to Able, Baker is deferring not to Able's authority but to Able herself.

These considerations have led Michael Oakeshott to conclude that *an* authority is a bogus, but also an extremely dangerous, notion. Where use of the notion is more than a way of giving cheap compliments to Able, it shows that Baker has become an "individual manqué" who has willingly submitted to a despotism.[6] No one who has worried about the burgeoning role of "experts" in our society will entirely dismiss Oakeshott's view. Understood as a critique of much of what passes for *an* authority relationships his conclusions are disturbing in their perspicacity. Moreover, he helps us to see why *an* authority relationships, especially if viewed from the perspective of liberalism, are inherently unstable. Nevertheless "*an* authority" is more than a frequently encountered misnomer. Nor are genuine *an* authority relations necessarily more dangerous or objectionable than authority relations of other kinds.

Consider the *an* authority of medical doctors—say, Michael de-Bakey's standing as an authority on heart disease and treatment. Few of deBakey's patients are competent to assess the technical details of his diagnoses, prescriptions, surgical performances. But it does not follow that they *must* choose between caring for themselves and submitting to his personal despotism (of course, they may in fact do either). Other members of the medical and related professions are competent to and have in fact judged his technical performances. His standing as *an* authority is, in part, a result of the fact that such judgments have been made and have generally been favorable. Using Wittgenstein's language, we might say that there is agreement on the opinion that deBakey is exceptionally knowledgeable about and skillful in the treatment of heart problems. As important as it is, however, this is not the main point in the present context. Such agreement in "opinion" is possible only because there is also agreement at levels at once deeper and more general. Among medical practitioners, life scientists, biomedical engineers, and the like, there is substantial agreement on a body of general knowledge about human and other organisms, about various questions of procedure and technique not specific to the heart and its treatment, and so forth. At least some of this knowledge is shared widely in the

---

[6]Oakeshott, *On Human Conduct,* esp. chap. 2.

society. Yet more generally, there is substantial agreement on such questions as the objectives of medicine and on what counts as health and illness, successful and unsuccessful treatment. As parties to an agreement, as sharers in these authoritative beliefs and values, patients have the criteria necessary to a variety of judgments, judgments that, when made and collected, support or fail to support deBakey's standing as *an* authority. The judgments also support (or not) the belief that it is appropriate to accord his decisions and actions distinctively respectful consideration. When we understand that *an* authority is grounded in the authoritative, we see how puzzles concerning it can be resolved and major objections to it parried.

In the light of the tenets of liberalism set out above, the inherent instability of *an* authority relationships results from the very features that make such relationships possible. As the term itself implies, the beliefs and values that make up the authoritative are in part normative in character. Agreement concerning them must therefore be more as opposed to less firm, more as opposed to less widespread; it can never be entirely firm and it is unlikely that it will ever long remain entirely encompassing. Wittgenstein and numerous others have given us powerful reasons for thinking that it is impossible to question all of the elements of the authoritative at once. To put the same point another way, if we could imagine a number of people who lived in spatial proximity but who agreed on nothing, we would have imagined a group of people for whom *an* authority (among other things!) would be impossible. But because (on the liberal view) each and every belief and value is logically subject to dispute, because no element of the authoritative can be logically immune to cogent questioning, the basis of *an* authority relationships must on principle be uncertain. More important, perhaps, from the liberal point of view the relation ought in fact to be kept in something of an uncertain condition. As John Stuart Mill emphasized so forcefully, a society that has ceased to question its most basic values and beliefs has no basis for them, has regressed into a kind of nonage, and is vulnerable to one or another form of despotism.[7]

Liberals treasure knowledge and wisdom; such progress as human societies have made from barbarism to civilization is largely

[7]John Stuart Mill, *On Liberty* (New York: E. P. Dutton, 1951), esp. chap. 2.

calibrated by the development of these.[8] Moreover, few liberals
(certainly not Mill) believe that such progress is possible without
divisions of labor and specializations of function that are all but
certain to produce *an* authorities and *an* authority relations. Yet the
tenets of liberalism positively require suspicion and distrust not
only in respect to *an* authorities but of the very suppositions of *an*
authority relationships.

The school of thought running from Hobbes to Oakeshott celebrates *in* authority precisely because it breaks the connection between authority and the authoritative and hence is not encumbered
by these complications and liabilities. Subscription to an office of *in*
authority, so far from assuming or depending on shared beliefs and
values, presupposes the absence of any such consensus. Subscribers
defer or "surrender judgment" to the decisions of *in* authorities not
because they agree with them and not because they are confident
that they would agree with those decisions if they possessed the
special competence or expertise of those who made them. *In* authority has (is said by these writers to have) nothing whatever to do with
Able's knowledge, expertise, or skill, with the content or merits of
Able's decisions, and nothing to do with beliefs, values, or opinions
held by Baker or the members of Baker's society.

Or rather—the difference is of the utmost consequence—*in* authority has to do with these phenomena in the single respect that the
members of the community share the belief that they will be unable
to reach agreement on numerous and important of the issues that
arise in the course of their interactions with one another. It is this
postulate that justifies their common willingness to conform, without regard to content, to the decisions of those invested with authority.

As with Oakeshott's views about *an* authority, this account and
assessment of *in* authority has much to be said for it. Moreover, we

[8]Some of the complexities and paradoxes in the subject of authority, and perhaps
much of the appeal of Oakeshott's and related attacks on it, stem from the well-
established tendency to characterize the development of civilization as a movement
away from "authority" and relations dominated by "authority." On this conceptualization uncivilized societies (often called "traditional") are organized and dominated by a set of values and beliefs for which there is no basis in evidence or reason
but which are treated as "authoritative" in the sense of being immune to question.
The history and anthropology that inform uses of this conceptualization are deeply
suspect. But insofar as they are correct, no liberal should treat them as histories or
anthropologies of authority and authority relations.

see below that basic contentions of the Hobbes-Oakeshott theory have great prominence in liberal thinking about authority. I suggest that much of this thinking about authority consists in an attempt to accept those contentions without fully embracing the suppositions on which Oakeshott thinks they depend. Liberals have recognized that favorable judgments of the content of the rules and commands cannot be the only good reason for obeying them, a recognition that informs and is elaborated by their enthusiasm for such notions as the rule of law, government of laws not of men, constitutionalism, and procedural as opposed to substantive due process. Yet liberals have balked at the notion of surrender of judgment and the intimately related view that *in* authority relations should or even could be entirely independent of substantive beliefs and values and judgments derived from them.

On the question of "could," liberals are undoubtedly correct. As important as it is, the distinction between *an* and *in* authority cannot be drawn in the manner Oakeshott (and Friedman) suggests. The relationship between *in* authority and the authoritative is not the same as between *an* authority and the authoritative, but there must be such a relationship.

There are several lines of argument that support this conclusion. In my judgment, the most powerful of these is grounded in Wittgenstein's analysis of language and meaning, particularly his analysis of key notions such as rules, following a rule, and "knowing how to go on." These notions are not only salient in but constitutive of *in* authority on the understanding thereof that we are considering. If Wittgenstein's analysis of them is correct, Oakeshott's understanding of *in* authority is not just mistaken, it is incoherent in crucial respects.

Fortunately, Oakeshott himself has provided us with a closely analogous but shorter route to the same conclusion. Subscription to *in* authority is human conduct. All human conduct is informed by, is incomprehensible apart from, beliefs and values, objectives and purposes, accepted by the agent or actor. Nor are these features difficult to discern in the discussion of authority itself in this tradition. Hobbes was as keen to promote surrender of judgment as any writer previous to Oakeshott. But as the proverbial "every schoolboy" knows, Hobbes urged such surrender *on the ground that, in order that,* we might escape from or avoid that intolerable condition he called the state of war. Oakeshott is much more circumspect, much more parsimonious, in his formulation of the same point. But his *cives* or citizens subscribe to the *in* authority of the state in order to "abate" somewhat the "contingency" that is at once the condition and, if entirely unabated, the deadly enemy of their liberty.[9] A person who cared not for her liberty, or one who did not believe that surrender of judgment to authority is necessary or at least contributive to preserving it, could not maintain subscription to authority. In a society lacking consensus on at least these values and beliefs authority would be what it presently appears to be in places like Lebanon, Haiti, and El Salvador (and what Oakeshott thinks it has been in much of human history), that is, an impossibility. Moreover, "abating contingency" is a portmanteau objective that requires a good deal of elaboration and specification if it is to yield guidance in formulating, applying, and most important for present purposes, in obeying or disobeying the rules and commands issued by *in* authorities. These processes of elaboration and interpretation will of necessity be informed by any number of further, more specific beliefs and values. Where there is no tolerably wide consensus on some number of such further beliefs and values these processes cannot be sustained.

II

In company with such students of authority as Tocqueville and Weber, then, I contend that *in* authority shares with *an* authority dependence on the authoritative. Not every decision and action in a practice of *in* authority must or even could express or congrue with authoritative beliefs and values. But if there are no such beliefs and values, or if practitioners do not find a general and continuing congruence between them and the workings of authority, authority is an impossibility.

Because of this parallel between the two types of authority, the liberal's wariness of *an* authority must extend to *in* authority as well. In the nineteenth century this suspicion was expressed most forcefully in the concern over the tyranny of the majority and the despotism of society over the individual. In our time it presents itself

[9]Oakeshott's views about human conduct are presented most systematically in the first essay of *On Human Conduct*. The discussion of *cives* and their subscription is primarily in the second essay. The notion of abating contingency is at p. 74.

in the antipathy to communitarian thinking, whether emanating from the New Left, Jonesville, the Moral Majority, or even academic political theorists committed to strongly participationist theories of democracy. Celebrating as they tend to do some body of substantive moral and political truths and goods, all of these modes of thought threaten to still critical thinking over the fundaments of social life. The liberal nightmare, instantiated in the waking state by totalitarianism, is the circumstance in which an entire union, embracing action as well as thought, is effected between an encompassing body of uncritically held beliefs and values and the activities of the most powerful bearer of authority, the state.

But liberals have been and remain endlessly ambivalent concerning the authority of the state. As with their closely analogous attitude toward the *an* authority of experts, this ambivalence is rooted in the tenets discussed at the outset and can be expected to continue as long as those several tenets are accepted. The first two of those tenets require skepticism about if not rejection of *in* authority. But there is a standing temptation, at least partly grounded in one or more of the other four tenets, to use *in* authority to contain conflict and in this and other ways to maximize liberty. If liberalism has a history, that history is replete with attempts, never more than partially successful, to reconcile, or at least to achieve a practicable coordination between, these two impulses. In the space that remains I comment on these attempts in the light of the foregoing discussions.

I said in passing that Able's authority provides Baker with a reason for deferring to Able's decisions and judgments. It might well be thought, however, that this claim about, this characterization of, authority relations is precisely what liberalism cannot allow. The notion "a reason for" is difficult to explicate. Most of its uses, however, involve a distinction between the arbitrary and the nonarbitrary. The former often implies subjectively held or merely personal opinion, while the latter suggests evidence and argumentation deserving of interpersonal standing. *A* is a reason for *B* if *A* is correct, true, justified, and the like by virtue of the evidence and argumentation that support it. *A* is not a reason for *B* if it lacks these characteristics. Now, if Able's authority is grounded in the authoritative, and if the authoritative consists in disputable beliefs and values, indeed if it is a condition of Baker's liberty that Baker realizes this and in fact disputes those beliefs and values, then it follows that Able's authority cannot provide Baker with a reason for accepting and/or acting on Able's decisions and judgments.

Oakeshott's treatment of *in* authority can be interpreted as an attempt to solve this problem. It would be oversimplifying and otherwise seriously misleading to categorize Oakeshott as a liberal. But his skepticism about the possibility of true or justified belief concerning the substantive questions of moral and political life ("practical" questions in the language of his *Experience and Its Modes*), while grounded in philosophical convictions different from the skepticism of most liberals, is at least as deep as theirs. And their antipathy to the use of authority to impose such beliefs on those who do not accept them pales by comparison with his. Thus he entirely rejects the notion of *an* authority, seeks to found *in* authority exclusively on procedural considerations, and proposes to restrict its activities to questions about which issues of true and false, correct and incorrect, are not allowed to arise.

As already suggested, the generic impulses that move Oakeshott in this regard are also at work in liberal attempts to solve the problem we are considering. The rule of law, constitutionalism, the notion of an office, the rules of procedure characteristic of legislatures, courts, and rational-legal bureaucracies—all of these are intended less to resolve moral and political questions than to put constraints on which questions will be taken up and on the manner in which those that are addressed are debated. Viewed in the light of our discussion of liberalism, they can be interpreted as attempts to give the notion "reason for" a standing as compatible as possible with basic liberal tenets. If we regard "reasons" as propositions that are undoubtedly true, perhaps even that could not be false, then no such reasons are available. But some propositions have better standing than others; some considerations are less subject to dispute than others. If we can ground authority in, constrain its activities by, those propositions and considerations that deservedly enjoy such standing, we will as a practical matter have provided ourselves with reasons for accepting and deferring to authority.

In a number of political societies this project seems to have met with sufficient success to have sustained authority and authority relations over considerable periods and despite a great deal of disagreement at the level of Wittgenstein's "opinion." So far as I can judge, not many Englishmen or Americans think of provisions of the British and the United States constitutions as necessary truths. A preponderance of these two populations nevertheless appears to believe that those provisions are defensible and do accord a deserved legitimacy to the arrangements, institutions, and practices of British and American government. Indeed, the fact that these constitutions are not repositories of immutable truths, and hence that their provisions are subject to discussion, interpretation, and deliberate change, is viewed in many quarters as among their merits.

On this understanding, however, the notion "a reason for" and everything that depends on it has no better than a comparative and a contingent standing. Given other beliefs that for the moment we are choosing not to question, we can say that *A* is a better reason for *X* than is *B*, perhaps that *A* is the best reason for *X* which is now known to us. And we can sometimes say that the reasons for *X* are better than the reasons for *Y*. But the comparative, contingent, and hence hypothetical character of these judgments leaves them in an unstable, a vulnerable, condition. This circumstance may or may not disquiet citizens, but it is unsettling to many philosophers— including, oddly enough, many philosophers who are also liberals.

Perhaps as a consequence, the ambivalence of liberal philosophers toward authority is rehearsed, in more insistently philosophical terms, as ambivalence concerning tenets basic to their own position. Attempts are made to amend or qualify the idea that conceptions of the good and related axiological conceptions are irreducibly plural. Arguments are sometimes advanced that there are at least some things that must be good; arguments are more frequently advanced that there are some that are not and cannot be.

If liberalism begins in the seventeenth century and if John Locke is a liberal, this ambivalence makes its appearance at the very beginning of the liberal tradition. An empiricist and a nominalist, a voluntarist, contractarian, and believer in negative liberty, Locke nevertheless argued that moral and political good and right are constrained by certain natural rights. Because political authority must be grounded in good and right, authority is also so constrained. The efficacy of these natural rights is of course contingent on their having achieved authoritative standing in this society or that. But their philosophical standing, their standing in reason and as reasons for action, is necessary not contingent. To deny them is to make a discernible, a correctable, error of reasoning: any individual who fails to respect them is thereby convicted of immortality. Any political system that does not conform to them is a tyranny.

The inconsistencies within Locke's thought have delighted his enemies, confounded his friends, and bedeviled his commentators for three centuries. On the face of things, his natural rights are simply dogmatic, representing either residues (in Pareto's sense) of previous natural law and natural right thinking or ad hoc devices adopted to solve or to conceal glaring difficulties in his moral and political thought (an appearance that, for me, natural rights doctrines continue to present—most notably in the work of Robert Nozick).[10] Later writers, however, at least some of whom are insistent in their claim to be liberals, have continued and refined Locke's effort to stabilize or solidify morals and politics by putting philosophical constraints on conceptions of good. The most sophisticated of these attempts, particularly fascinating when compared to the arguments of Oakeshott, take their inspiration from Immanuel Kant (whether legitimately so I will not here venture to say). They reach what appears to be their apogee in the work of Rawls and have attained to a kind of reductio ad absurdum in the recent argument of Bruce Ackerman.

Oakeshott accepts the premises that human action is purposive and that the conceptions of good that inform its purposiveness are irreducibly plural. From these premises he infers that we may not use political or any other kind of authority to limit the diversity, substantively speaking, of thought and action. Individuals pursue their purposes as they see them. If some individuals happen to share a purpose, they may form an association to pursue it in concert. Such associations are founded entirely on the consensus that informs them and properly cease to exist the instant that consensus disappears. Any attempt to maintain such an association by use of authority will explode it in conflict or transform it into a tyranny. As the encompassing political entity, the state cannot hope for consensus on substantive issues. It must rigorously exclude such issues from its concerns and restrict itself to maintaining "civility" in the pursuit of individual and group objectives. Its sole task is to see to it that its members pursue their multifarious purposes within the confines of "adverbial rules" adopted exclusively to minimize (they can never eliminate) conflict of an uncivil variety. Purposiveness and the diversity it engenders are treasured, not banished or even reduced. But they are excluded from politics; they are excluded from interactions involving authority.

Liberals such as Rawls and Ackerman share many of Oakeshott's

---

[10]Robert Nozick, *Anarchy, State, and Utopia* (New York: Basic Books, 1974).

premises but do not want to accept (all of) the politically restrictive inferences he draws from those premises. As suggested above, they want better to secure the foundations of authority. In part for that reason they are committed to objectives over and above civility. Yet they recognize that there is sharp disagreement concerning those objectives and they are convinced that the objectives will not be achieved if their pursuit is left to individuals and groups lacking public authority. Hence they seek to justify, consistent with the premise that there are no incorrigible axiological truths, the use of authority to attain and maintain goals beyond civility. They need somehow to derive exceptionally powerful normative conclusions from exceptionally weak premises.

Their inventiveness in this enterprise is often a wonder to behold. But they cannot conceal the fact that they are in the impossible position known proverbially as trying to get, or rather claiming to have gotten, blood out of a turnip. A veritable barrage of criticism has shot down the crucial Rawlsian claims. Acceptance of maximin and the difference principle is not rationally compelled for those equipped with the concept of justice, a capacity for instrumental reasoning, and such information as is available on the nether side of the veil of ignorance. It can be said with entire confidence that the same fate awaits Ackerman's astonishing contention that a distribution rule requiring no less than strict arithmetic equality in the division of most resources follows deductively from no more than a skeptical metaethics. If I am correct that these conclusions are not compelled by reason, imposing them by authority would have a decidedly illiberal appearance.

III

Having insinuated my largely favorable judgment of the liberal position into these remarks, it would be fitting for me to say something in defense of that judgment. Happily, competing civilities ordain brevity. I restrict myself to three connected remarks.

Liberals argue that liberty engenders diversity. In a number of its classic formulations this argument relies on empiricist and emotivist assumptions that are something of an embarrassment. I have to recognize that my own attachment to the liberal outlook may be explained by a native distaste not only for the dogmatic but for the evangelical and even the enthusiastic. There are, however, better philosophical foundations for such a position than those provided by Ayer's *Language, Truth and Logic* and its ilk. I can't do much more than drop a name, but I suggest that these better foundations may be found in Wittgenstein, particularly in his discussions of what certainty, agreement, and related notions are not and cannot be, are and can become. These discussions might be called skeptical, but they are only skeptical of mythological, hypostasized notions of certitude which, being unattainable, generate a general and a destructive skepticism with which Wittgenstein has nothing to do. Are certainty, well-founded agreement, justified belief, distinctions between better and worse arguments, possible among free human beings? Properly understood, they are not only possible but humdrum in their homely ordinariness. But they are not given, they are achieved and reachieved, earned and earned anew, through discourse within practices and conventions. They cannot be posited or asserted.[11]

On this understanding, we can say that a good deal of agreement, well-founded judgment, and certainty have been achieved in respect to many features of our politics. This is my second point. I can amplify it just a bit by saying that it explains why Oakeshott's argument about *in* authority works as far as it does and why in this and some other societies the rule of law, constitutionalism, certain basic rights, are quite firmly established. From a stance outside of the tradition that he presumes, Oakeshott's adverbial rules and procedural principles, what for him and for most of us are the canons of civility in politics, would represent highly doubtful conclusions concerning deeply substantive issues. Our agreement in these judgments constitutes the language of our politics. It is a language arrived at and continuously modified through no less than a history of discourse, a history in which we have thought about, as we became able to think in, that language.

It is not inconceivable that this agreement, this language, might be achieved in respect to matters about which there is now no more than a mix of agreement and disagreement in opinion. For example, it might be achieved in respect to those questions of social justice about which Rawls has written with much eloquence. But such certainty as we have achieved or may achieve is not necessary in any

[11]Wittgenstein's discussions of these points are most accessible in his *On Certainty* (Oxford: Basil Blackwell, 1969).

of the usual philosophical senses; it is not a deduction from the categorical imperative or a deliverance of God, Nature, or any notional Archimidean Reason.

Thus my third point. Liberals are correct that authority is dangerous. If we understand the grounding of authority in the authoritative and the ways in which it therefore requires rather than excludes the exercise of judgment, we understand how authority relations are possible for us. Nevertheless, by comparison with our other practices, authority abbreviates and truncates the processes of reflection and judgment through which agreement develops among free human beings. It asserts and commands the certainties distinctive to it. The view that we cannot do without such abridgments and that we ought not to do comfortably with them is not the least of liberalism's contribution to our political estate.

3

Citizenship and Authority:
A Chastened View of Citizenship

My purpose in this essay is to present and defend what I think of as a chastened view of citizenship. "Chastened" means subdued or tempered as compared with some alternative understanding that is more enthusiastic, celebratory, or evangelical in tone and character. Because this essay is addressed primarily to professional political scientists, and because the most influential recent discussions of citizenship in the political science literature could hardly be called celebratory, characterization of my view as chastened needs immediate explanation. Chastened as opposed to what?

We can make a (rough) beginning by adverting to the familiar distinction between empirical and normative theories. Much recent writing about citizenship—for example, the works of Schumpeter, Downs, Lipset, Berelson and his associates, Dahl, Sartori[1]—adopts something like the following stance: the "classical" ideal of citizenship, deriving from such daunting personages as Pericles, Aristotle, and Rousseau, elevates citizenship to the highest moral and political standing. Citizens are free, equal, and engaged with one another in pursuing matters of high and distinctively human import. Citizen-

---

[1]See Joseph Schumpeter, *Capitalism, Socialism, and Democracy*, 4th ed. (New York: Harper & Row, 1954); Anthony Downs, *An Economic Theory of Democracy* (New York: Harper & Row, 1957); Seymour Martin Lipset, *Political Man* (Garden City, N.Y.: Doubleday, 1960); Bernard Berelson et al., *Voting* (Chicago: University of Chicago Press, 1954); Robert Dahl, *A Preface to Democratic Theory* (Chicago: University of Chicago Press, 1963), *Pluralist Democracy in the United States* (Chicago: University of Chicago Press, 1967), *After the Revolution* (New Haven: Yale University Press, 1970), and *Polyarchy* (New Haven: Yale University Press, 1971); Giovanni Sartori, *Democratic Theory* (New York: Praeger, 1965).

ship is the distinctive human activity and the distinctively important feature of a political society. Whatever the merits of this ideal from a normative perspective (most of the recent writers just mentioned, one surmises, do not rate them very highly), the ideal is unachievable in and hence irrelevant to political life and practice in the modern nation-state. The continuous, intense, morally uplifting interactions that the ideal presumes can obtain, if at all, only in and among subgroups within the large, complex, and impersonal societies of the modern world. Attempts to achieve and sustain such interactions at the level of the political society are distracting and destabilizing. Accordingly, political scientists must resolutely set the classical ideal aside and investigate the realities of and realistic possibilities for citizenship in the political societies of our day. The empirically grounded descriptions and prescriptions that result, uninspiring though they may be, will have the greater merits of accuracy and realism.

These "empirical" accounts and theories of democracy and citizenship are not chastened in the sense I intend here. Rather than temper or refine the classical theories against which they are (in part) reactions, they abandon the normative objectives and commitments characteristic of the latter. They are less a chastened species of an explicitly normative genus than a covertly moralistic species of an allegedly empirical or scientific genus.

The prevalence of these notionally scientific theories of citizenship has (along with numerous other factors) spurred a revival of insistently normative theorizing that takes its bearings from the classical theories of Aristotle and Rousseau. Writers such as Arendt, Barber, Pateman, Thompson, and Walzer[2] have insisted that the fundamentally normative questions raised by the classical theories cannot be disposed of by showing that the practice of those contemporary societies conventionally labeled democratic do not comport

[2]See Hannah Arendt, *The Human Condition* (Garden City, N.Y.: Doubleday, 1959), *Between Past and Future* (New York: Viking, 1961), and *On Revolution* (New York: Viking, 1963); Benjamin R. Barber, *The Death of Communal Liberty* (Princeton: Princeton University Press, 1974), *Superman and Common Men* (New York: Penguin, 1971), and *Strong Democracy* (Berkeley: University of California Press, 1984); Carole Pateman, *Participation and Democratic Theory* (Cambridge: Cambridge University Press, 1970), and *The Problem of Political Obligation* (Berkeley: University of California Press, 1979); Dennis F. Thompson, *The Democratic Citizen* (Cambridge: Cambridge University Press, 1970), and *Political Participation* (Washington, D.C.: American Political Science Association, 1977); Michael Walzer, *Obligations* (Cambridge: Harvard University Press, 1970) and *Radical Principles* (New York: Basic Books, 1980).

with any of the versions of the classical ideal. If practice does not satisfy ideal, we must conclude not that ideal should be scrapped but that practice is unsatisfactory and should be changed. Several of the recent revivalists of the classical ideal, moreover, insist that the ideal is much more compatible with, could be much more fully realized in and by, contemporary societies than "scientific" critics of that ideal contend.[3]

It is by comparison with the classical ideal and its recent revivals and restatements that the view presented here is chastened. Insofar as the "normative-empirical" distinction can be sustained, I agree that the normative issues raised by the classical view cannot be settled by adducing some set of alleged facts about modern societies. If (1) there were such a thing as a set of ideal-neutral factual observations, or such a thing as an "empirical theory" that was independent of ideals, if (2) those facts or that empirical theory were discrepant from the classical ideal, but (3) the ideal were nevertheless normatively superior, then our task would be to attempt to alter the facts. It would fall to us to act politically and morally to try to bring the facts and hence the empirical theory into conformity with the ideal. Or at least it would fall to us to lament the discrepancy between the two. As my sometime colleague Ralph Lerner used to say, we may be swept down the stream, but we are not therefore obliged to shout hosannas to the gods of the river.

Of course clauses (1) and (2) in the previous paragraph are patently counterfactual. Leaving aside general questions in the philosophies of meaning, theory construction, and scientific method, no reader of studies and theories of democracy such as Berelson's Lipset's, or Sartori's can fail to see that those works are imbued by moral and political values and preferences sharply at variance with those that inform the thought of Aristotle and Rousseau. More fundamentally, no student of the moral and political practices over which these theories claim to generalize can fail to see that the participants in those practices accept and act upon a set of beliefs and values which, while residually influenced by the classical ideal of citizenship, include understandings and orientations difficult to accommodate to the classical ideal.[4] The notion that we could study

[3]See esp. Thompson, *Democratic Citizen;* Pateman, *Participation and Democratic Theory;* Barber, *Strong Democracy.*

[4]See Gabriel Almond and Sidney Verba, *The Civic Culture* (Princeton: Princeton University Press, 1963); J. David Greenstone and Paul E. Peterson, *Race and Authority in Urban Politics* (Chicago: University of Chicago Press, 1973).

and theorize about democracy and citizenship without addressing the normative issues raised by the classical ideal is no better than a more or less willful misunderstanding.

The present view, then, is intended to be chastened in the sense that it seeks to temper the moral and political ideal of citizenship that comes down to us from the deepest thinkers on the subject. It addresses the question of whether the third of the above subjunctive clauses is counterfactual; whether the beliefs and values that constitute that ideal deserve our reflected allegiance. It is intended, moreover, to be chastened, not antagonistic. The initial, the immediate, moral appeal of the Aristotelian and, on some readings, Rousseauean variants of the classical ideal seems to me undeniable. There is even reason to doubt whether a self-respecting human being could justifiably accommodate to a politically organized society that is not committed to and that does not substantially realize the values and objectives of this ideal of citizenship. To put this point another way, it is not surprising that many of those who have rejected the Aristotelian view have been led to a strongly antipolitical stance. Even the most scrupulously chastened—as opposed, again, to antagonistic—view of the ideal of high citizenship tends toward a political withdrawalism, the fully developed expression of which is now philosophical anarchism.[5] One way to state the question that will concern me is to ask whether this tendency can be arrested; whether a stable, ratiocinatively defensible position can be established between a politics of high citizenship and a non- or antipolitical stance. I suggest possibilities along this line. But we should note that to put the matter this way is to assume that anarchism or other extreme versions of withdrawalism are not choiceworthy and hence that the classical ideal of citizenship must be tempered, not rejected or abandoned. I am not able to defend this assumption systematically in this essay, but I try to say something concerning it.

As indicated by the title of this essay, I address these questions by attending to the relationship between citizenship and authority. A step toward doing so can be taken by recalling a well-established position—namely, Plato's—which is distinct from both the high

[5]Of course withdrawalism was not anarchistic in its most notable premodern expressions. Political withdrawalists such as the Stoics, Augustine, Pascal, Montaigne, and Hobbes found it possible to be in but no more than marginally of (as opposed to against) their political societies, a position revived by recent libertarian thinkers and, to my mind more interestingly, by Michael Oakeshott.

citizenship argument of Aristotle and withdrawalist views such as those of the Stoics, Pascal, and nineteenth- and twentieth-century anarchists. No one would accuse Plato of amoral scientism in his thinking about politics. For Plato, active, vigorous political arrangements and processes are indispensable to the well-being of all but the most superior members of the human race. Yet for all save those superior few (who take on an active political role as a painful duty), human beings should be subjects not citizens. Their well-being will be achieved by submitting to the moral-cum-political authority of the philosopher-kings. A political society that accords anything like citizenship to any very large segment of its populace is unjust in itself and will of certainty produce severe instability and moral degeneration. The choice is not between a politics of high citizenship and withdrawal from political society; it is between a political order that fosters moral excellence through the proper distribution and exercise of authority and a moral and political disorder in which the many are encouraged to meddle in matters beyond their ken.

In its insistently anticitizenship Platonic version, this understanding is no more a serious contender for the intellectual allegiance of the twentieth-century political mind than is philosophical anarchism. Few among us would accept Plato's identification of justice with a society employing a division of labor in which significant moral and political decision making is the all but exclusive prerogative of a narrow elite. As attenuated as citizenship has become in even those societies of our time with some justification for their self-designations as democratic, not many of their members would exchange the values of citizenship for the stability, order, economic efficiency, or other desiderata said to be the yield of all but entire subordination to—what Plato was prepared to call—political authority.

The Platonic view is nevertheless important for my present purposes. This is so generically because it presents insistently normative arguments against citizenship; it is important specifically because the arguments it presents invoke authority and subordination to authority as essential elements in a proper moral and political order. It is made to appear that the moral values and objectives of political society are to be achieved not by interaction among citizens but by the subordination of subjects to those who are deservedly in possession of public authority. We are to think about political society and

69

its moral characteristics and objectives not in an undifferentiated manner as if all members or participants contribute to those objectives in the same ways, but in terms of highly organized specializations of function and insistently hierarchical patterns of superiority, subordination, and deference.

From Aristotle on, much of the argumentation for high citizenship has been in reaction to the Platonic understanding. Sharing the objectives of moral excellence in human life, and sharing the conviction that an organized political society is at least a necessary condition of such excellence, proponents of such citizenship have tried to show that the excellence can be achieved—perhaps can only be achieved—in a politics of citizenship as distinct from and opposed to a politics of authority on the Platonic model. By defining citizens as persons who are equal in the sense that they share in offices and who rule and are ruled in turn,[6] and by celebrating political societies characterized by citizenship in this sense, Aristotle at least appears to have banished (what Plato had taught him to regard as) authority to the private realm. He believed that Plato was correct that the naturally, the necessarily, superior should rule over the naturally inferior. Masters should rule over slaves, parents should rule over children, husbands over wives. But politics occurs in the realm of freedom not of necessity; at its best, political life takes place among persons who have no claim to Platonic authority over one another. When Rousseau said that in a proper political society "every person while uniting himself with all . . . obeys only himself and remains as free as before,"[7] he restated, in radically democratized form, this same understanding, this same opposition between a politics of citizenship and a politics of authority.

Whatever we may think of its epistemological foundations, Plato's position depends on an untenable, indeed an incoherent, conception of authority. The notion he seeks to articulate is of authority in the sense of someone who is *an* authority concerning a subject matter—for example, Corwin as *an* authority on the United States Constitution or Samuel Beer as *an* authority on British politics. Plato is correct that this notion presupposes a sharply drawn inequality between those who are authorities and those who are not. Corwin is *an* authority concerning constitutional law because

---

[6]Aristotle, *Politics*, 1275b, 1279a.
[7]Jean Jacques Rousseau, *The Social Contract* (New York: E. P. Dutton, 1950), I, vi.

he knows more about that subject matter than most others who are interested in it. But because the latter must be able to recognize the superiority of Corwin's knowledge, at least some among them must know a good deal about it. Authority, even of the kind Plato sought to delineate, involves a relationship not just with the subject matter on which one is *an* authority but between the person (a) who is *an* authority and those others persons (b) for whom (a) has that standing. Keen to establish the unqualified superiority of philosopher-kings, Plato made it impossible for them to attain or sustain authority as opposed to power or domination.[8]

The foregoing criticism of Plato's understanding of authority is important to my attempt to find stable conceptual and normative ground between the ideal of high citizenship and political withdrawalism. My more immediate concern is with an incoherence into which, by the wrongheaded brilliance of his formulations, Plato induced the partisans of high citizenship who reacted against him. If Plato had been correct that authority and citizenship are incompatible, then a politics of citizenship would have to exclude authority. But this is an impossibility. Citizenship, I argue, presupposes authority. Those "offices" in which the Aristotelian citizen shares are established by rules (for example, the rules of a constitution) which are themselves invested with authority and which invest the offices and their officeholders with that same property. That "ruling and being ruled in turn" which defines the Aristotelian citizen would be incomprehensible apart from laws and commands that, once adopted, are binding on rulers and ruled alike because invested with authority accepted by both. However the array of offices may have been decided on, through whatever process it may have been invested with authority, a citizen dissatisfied with it must accommodate to that array unless and until it has been changed by established procedures—by procedures themselves invested with authority. In the same way, a citizen discontent with a law or command must obey it until those whose turn it is to rule—which of course may include the dissenter—have seen fit to repeal or alter it. In both cases the "must" in question is an obligation of citizenship, one that is supported by sanctions that may include the loss of the status of citizen itself. In the absence of such authority, the notion of citizen-

[8]I have elaborated the understanding of authority that informs this criticism of Plato (and much of the discussion in this essay) in *The Practice of Political Authority* (Chicago: University of Chicago Press, 1980).

ship has the echoing political emptiness of the phrase "citizen of the world."

As these remarks indicate, it would be overstating the case to assert that proponents of high citizenship propose, implicitly or explicitly, to eliminate public authority altogether. However we resolve the controversy about the presence or absence of the concept of authority in Aristotle, he is not only aware but insistent that citizens *rule* one another.[9] Nor can there be any doubt that the decisions of the Sovereign of Rousseau's *Social Contract* bind all citizens until those decisions have been changed; or, for that matter, that the decisions of what he calls government bind the citizenry until such time as the latter have acted as Sovereign to override those decisions. Something akin to authority is and must be at work in at least these respects.

An adequate treatment of these matters will require some refinements concerning the concept of authority. Leaving these refinements to later sections, it remains the case that my discussion thus far commits no worse than an exaggeration. The politics of high citizenship is intended to be sharply contrasted with a politics of authority. Interactions among citizens are distinctive just in that they are interactions among equals; they are among persons who have no binding authority over one another in respect to the subject matters of their interactions as citizens. And it is this interaction itself that is distinctively valuable. Familiar sociological language may help us here. There is a kind of recognition that citizenship is a status or office defined by rules that are invested with authority. But the more powerful tendency is to think of it as a role rather than as a status. There are proprieties and improprieties in the performance of the role; indeed it is through the identification of those proprieties, through delineation of the notion of citizenship, that theorists of high citizenship give expression to some of their deepest values. These proprieties, however, are to be defined less by legal rules invested with authority than by customs and conventions that develop in the course of the interactions and by moral principles derived from thinking about the objectives and purposes distinctive

[9]I am thinking of Hannah Arendt's argument that there is no genuine, differentiated concept of political authority in either Plato or Aristotle, that the concept was an invention of the Romans. See her "What Is Authority?" in *Between Past and Future.* See also Elizabeth Anscombe, "Modern Moral Philosophy," in *Ethics,* ed. Judith J. Thomson and Gerald Dworkin (New York: Harper & Row, 1968).

to the role itself. Salient among those objectives and purposes is the aim of fostering interaction as little inhibited as possible by authority. The thought seems to be that success in pursuing this objective will reduce authority (over and among citizens) to the minimal possible proportions.

No one suspicious of or wary about authority will be insensitive to the appeal of this understanding. Even if one is skeptical (as I have been and remain) concerning the project of seeking a moral transformation of human beings through a politics of high citizenship, one can appreciate the ways in which active citizenship can improve the quality of the decisions reached and can limit the excesses to which political authority—and its all but invariable handmaiden, political power—has shown itself to be prone. But if I am correct that citizenship is itself inseparable from authority, if a commitment to citizenship is itself a commitment to some species of political authority as a feature of one's political arrangements, then the very considerations that lead one to value citizenship are also reasons for tempering one's enthusiasm for it. If authority is objectionable, and if citizenship does not come without authority, then citizenship cannot be an unalloyed good.

Such at least is the thought I explore in these pages. I propose to reexamine the ideal of high citizenship in light of the relationship between that ideal and a political phenomenon, authority, about which proponents of the ideal have themselves been ambivalent if not skeptical. This program requires closer attention to authority than is usual in the literature concerning citizenship;[10] it requires an attempt to articulate and to assess the complex relationships among the suppositions, elements, and implications of both authority and citizenship.

Types of Authority

There are two main types of authority and two basic kinds of argumentation supporting a place for authority in a political association.[11] The first type has been called by a variety of names,

[10]An exception is Dahl's *After the Revolution*.

[11]I elaborate the following distinctions in *The Practice of Political Authority*. See also Richard B. Friedman, "On the Concept of Authority in Political Philosophy," in *Concepts in Social and Political Philosophy*, ed. Richard E. Flathman (New York: Macmillan, 1973).

including "substantive" and "personal" authority. It is perhaps most clearly exemplified by a person who is *an* authority on a subject matter such as a body of knowledge or an activity. Arguments for authority of this kind in politics are presented in Plato's thought, in Thomism and some other moral and political doctrines substantially influenced by religious dogma, in Marxism, and by sociological theories of a strongly functionalist bent. I have elsewhere called political theories that are primarily about and that argue for authority of this kind "substantive-purpose" (S-P) theories. The second main type is often called "positional" or "formal" authority. Authority of this kind is most familiar to us as vested in an office and thereby accruing to the holders of that office. Persons who hold such an office are therefore *in* authority; that is, they are invested with authority to make certain decisions whether they are *an* authority on the subject matters that the decisions concern. Max Weber's discussion of "rational-legal" as opposed to "charismatic" and "traditional" authority is one of the most influential treatments of formal authority.[12] Forceful arguments for it are to be found in Thomas Hobbes, in the tradition of the rule of law as opposed to men (especially in the theory of the so-called *Rechtsstaat*), and most recently and powerfully in the writings of Michael Oakeshott.[13] I refer to theories of this type as formal-procedural (F-P) theories.

Substantive Authority

Arguments for personal or substantive authority typically have a large factual dimension. They involve propositions of the form "It is the case that . . ." and frequently "By nature . . ." or "In the nature of things . . ." It is the case that Charles Goren knows more about the game of bridge than most other people. In the nature of things there are classes of human beings who are fitted for reflection and for rule, others for military service, for household or menial work, and for being ruled. These propositions, which in principle are supportable by evidence about what is indeed the case, establish (claim to establish) differences or inequalities that are the basis of the distinction between those who possess authority and those who do not. These inequalities are a distinctive feature, perhaps the distinctive feature, of authority of this type. The truth of some such

[12]See the selections from Weber in ibid.
[13]See esp. Oakeshott's *On Human Conduct* (Oxford: Clarendon Press, 1975).

propositions is therefore a necessary condition of authority of this kind being justified, and the belief that some proposition of this kind is true is a necessary condition of any person actually achieving the standing of *an* authority concerning any particular subject matter or activity.

The existence or believed existence of such a factual inequality, however, is not a sufficient condition for either the existence or the justified existence of personal authority. I might concede that there are philosophers who know more about morals and politics than I do and yet insist that personal authority has no proper place in political life. Perhaps making and learning from mistakes is regarded as integral to the pleasure of the game of bridge. Perhaps I think that a politics in which decisions are made by authority destroys or derogates from the dignity or autonomy of those who accept that arrangement. As already indicated, to be *an* authority is to stand in a distinctive relationship not just with a subject matter or activity but with other persons who are interested or involved in it. The latter must recognize, accept, accede to, that relationship. And a justification for authority of this type must take account of the significance of that relationship for those who are party to it. It is interesting to note that even Plato accepts a version of this understanding. He seems to think that the superior wisdom and goodness of philosophers is itself sufficient to justify, though not of course to establish or sustain, the political subordination of nonphilosophers. In the peculiar ontological-cum-deontological manner in which he uses the term *justice,* such subordination is just in itself and needs no further justification. (Of course he also believes that the subordination is to the advantage of the nonphilosophers.) But the task of ruling is worse than merely uncongenial or distasteful to the philosophers; it is unnatural in that it forces them to return to the cave of appearance and opinion. Thus there is an ontological wrong involved in requiring philosophers to be kings, a wrong that cannot be justified by the sheer superiority of the philosophers. Accordingly, both Plato and his opponents must supplement their claim that there is in fact inequality with further arguments for basing authority on it.[14]

A great many such arguments have been offered. Of those with

[14]It is primarily because Plato describes subjects as incapable of understanding and acting on such further argumentation that authority—as distinct from power or domination—is an impossibility in his theory.

which I am familar, all are instrumental in character. Some end will be attained, some good will be achieved, some value served, by including relationships in terms of personal authority among the arrangements and practices of the society or group. That good or value—among political writers justice, stability, order, efficiency, and community have been among the favorites—is of sufficient importance to justify what would otherwise be objectionable aspects of authority relations. In short, a tradeoff is proposed. The philosopher-kings give up some of the elevation and nobility of a life in communion with the good in order to contribute to the justice and well-being of all of the members of their society (or perhaps they give up some of the nobility that they wish for in exchange for a measure of protection against the demos); free, autonomous persons give up some of their freedom and autonomy in order to obtain material well-being, substantive justice, security, or stability.

Owing to this combination of characteristics, the argument for substantive authority can be attacked by objecting to either its factual or its instrumental premise. The classical exponents of the ideal of high citizenship, who have without exception opposed any very large role for personal authority among citizens, have done so primarily by attacking the factual premise. As we have seen, Aristotle accepts Plato's view that some human beings are by nature fit to rule, some only fit to be ruled. But he diminishes the qualities or characteristics necessary in order to be fit for rule, thereby enlarging, as against Plato, the number of those who fall into that category. By the same move, he largely rejects Plato's view that personal or substantive authority has a proper place in political life. Political life occurs among citizens; all citizens are equal in the sense of being eligible for or fit to rule; therefore no citizen is entitled to personal authority over any other citizen. In a society featuring the politics of high citizenship, personal authority is largely if not entirely banished to the private realms in which the requisite inequality obtains. Rousseau's theory of citizenship involves an analogous move. He does not, however, so much lower the requirements for participation in rule as change their content from the primarily cognitive capacities and attainments insisted on by Plato to moral or dispositional characteristics. And he contends not that all in fact possess those characteristics but that participation in a properly ordered political society will itself develop the characteristics in all (adult males) who engage in it. (Substantive authority does retain what might be called a protopolitical role in the vital activities of that Platonic figure who haunts the *Social Contract,* the Legislator who establishes—and sustains?—Rousseau's ideal political society.)

These moves by theorists of high citizenship, however, produced difficulties of a high order of theoretical complexity and practical significance. These difficulties may have contributed importantly to the emergence of formal or positional authority in politics, and in any case realization of them did much to foster the development of F-P theories of authority. But neither the practice nor the theory of formal authority resolved the difficulties, and they continue to beset both thought and action concerning citizenship and authority. I will first identify the difficulties as they present themselves in Aristotle's uncertain movements toward a formal-procedural theory of authority and then look at some of the more salient moments in the later history of attempts to deal with them.

In rejecting, as regards politics, the premise of a natural inequality that justifies the rule of some citizens over others, Aristotle's theory of high citizenship abandons what seems then to have been the only accepted foundation for political authority.[15] But this leaves Aristotle in a difficult position. On his understanding of politics, including the politics of high citizenship, political life does involve ruling and being ruled. But as already suggested here, it is difficult if not impossible to invoke these notions without also invoking, however implicitly, some mode or kind of authority. Holding that tyranny is rule exclusively in the interest of the ruler, Aristotle does not make the modern equation between rule without authority and tyranny.[16] Yet ruling and being ruled have to be distinguished from other forms of superiority and subordination, dominance and submission. Drawing this distinction requires a theory of the nature and basis of authority. In other words, Aristotle has left himself with political authority for which he lacks a satisfactory basis or justification.

Formal Authority

Insofar as he recognizes and tries to resolve this difficulty, Aristotle does so by forseeing, albeit dimly, the possibility of a formal concept of authority and by foreshadowing later F-P arguments for

[15]Cf. the discussions cited in n. 9, above.
[16]See *Politics,* 1279a *et seq.*

its instrumental value. As in all F-P theories, his argument begins with the premise that equality (in relevant respects) obtains among those party to the authority relationship. Citizens are equal to one another in the sense that each of them possesses those qualities and characteristics requisite to participation in the ruling of the polis. In terms I have already used, citizens are equal in that each of them participates in the offices of the polis and thereby "rules and is ruled in turn." These famous formulae anticipate the later understanding that persons otherwise equal to one another could nevertheless be *in* authority over one another by virtue of having acceded to an office invested with formal authority. Acceding to such an office did not assume, and consistent with the premise of natural equality, could not be allowed to have created, personal superiority of the kinds that yield standing as *an* authority. Rather, justifications for the authority had to respect the foundational assumption of the equality of citizens.

A certain discomfort with this situation on Aristotle's part may already be intimated by the formula that citizens rule and are ruled in turn. True, Aristotle suggests that this arrangement itself contributes to the *telos* of political life. Learning to be ruled is said to be part of learning to rule.[17] But even if we allow him this somewhat unspecified notion, it remains unclear why the process of learning to be ruled cannot be completed at a relatively early age, thereby allowing all mature citizens to rule themselves continuously rather than intermittently.[18] If politics is conceived of as an activity through which development toward the fully and distinctively human end is achieved, any limitations on full participation qualify the ideal in unacceptable ways. Insofar as reliance on offices of authority creates divisions of labor or specializations of function, those excluded, however temporarily, from some tasks must thereby be deprived of some of the distinctive benefits of political life. Thus when Aristotle says that citizens rule and are ruled in turn, it looks as if he is trying to give the most favorable appearance to an arrangement that he knows to be discrepant from the ideal he is advancing.

It was of course Rousseau who sought to remedy this defect in the

---

[17]Ibid., 1277b.

[18]To put this difficulty somewhat differently and in a manner that anticipates discussion below of a further problem, if a citizen hasn't already learned to be ruled, how can that citizen safely be permitted to participate in ruling?

ideal of high citizenship. His emphatic rejection of representation[19] is, among other things, a rejection of the notion of a distinct office or set of offices invested with the authority to act on behalf of—that is, to rule over—those not occupying that office or those offices. All citizens must participate equally and continuously in all of the actions of the Sovereign. But there is a further difficulty in reconciling offices invested with formal authority with the ideal of high citizenship. I have noted Aristotle's acceptance of Plato's view that politics have the high moral purpose of making it possible for citizens to achieve a morally excellent life.[20] Of course Aristotle thinks of morals and politics as practical not theoretical sciences, indicating thereby his rejection of Plato's view that incorrigible or undeniable truths can be attained concerning the good life.[21] He nevertheless holds firmly to the conviction that morals and politics allow better as opposed to worse understandings, superior as opposed to inferior judgments and conduct. And while he dismisses the view that there are infallible philosopher-kings, he believes with equal firmness that there are some who are morally and politically wiser, who consistently (dispositionally) choose and act in a morally and politically superior manner.[22] Because the class "morally and politically wiser" does not coincide with the class "citizens,"[23] the arrangement by which all citizens rule and are ruled in turn seems to guarantee periods in which the morally and politically less wise will rule over those who are wiser than they.

Awareness of this difficulty may inform Aristotle's discussions of the good man versus the good citizen and the practical versus the contemplative life,[24] discussions that with hindsight might even be read as anticipating the reflections of political withdrawalists such as Montaigne and Pascal. The truly superior person, the person capable of the fully contemplative life, will *not* participate in politics. At the end of this essay I suggest a quite different interpretation of these among Aristotle's discussions, one that may help in arriving at a defensible conception of citizenship and political participation. However this may be, there is undeniably a tension (one we will

---

[19]Rousseau, *Social Contract*, II, i.
[20]Aristotle, *Politics*, 1278b, 1282b.
[21]Aristotle, *Nicomachean Ethics*, 1140a–43a.
[22]Ibid., 1104b–43a.
[23]Or rather, the two coincide only under an ideal constitution: *Politics*, III, iv.
[24]Ibid., VII, iii; I, ii; *Nichomachean Ethics*, IX, ix; I, vii.

encounter again) between the procedural aspects of Aristotle's theory of high citizenship and its substantive or moral purposes. This tension compounds and deepens the more general difficulty of reconciling authority and high citizenship. In addition to limiting participation itself, it appears that including offices of formal authority within the arrangements of a polis will allow the morally less wise to rule over the morally wiser. Insofar as it is the objective of high citizenship to achieve the morally good life among the members of a society, it is not easy to see how this arrangement can be justified.

I consider Aristotle's responses to these objections below. But first I want to note a kind of justification that, while almost certainly not intended by Aristotle, might be read into his discussion. The formula "rule and ruled in turn" suggests at least that offices of authority circulate among citizens over time, perhaps even that all citizens occupy one or more among the array of offices at any given moment in time. We have to qualify somewhat the ideal of fully and continuously equal participation in political life, but we attempt to do so fairly or equitably. The sense of the fairness of the arrangement, moreover, might be augmented somewhat by the following consideration: perhaps Able disapproves of Baker's decisions during the latter's tenure in office. But because Able can look forward to her own turn as holder of that office, it is unreasonable for her to object to the arrangement. Perhaps Able can reverse Baker's decisions or undo the effects of Baker's actions. Even if such steps are impracticable, Able can take comfort, perhaps even satisfaction, in the thought that Baker will like Able's rule no better than Able liked Baker's. The outcome of this arrangement may not otherwise be very edifying, but the reciprocity it involves makes it fair and to that degree justified.

These last thoughts are not in the idiom characteristic of Aristotle the theorist of high citizenship. (Of course high citizenship is not Aristotle's sole moral or political concern and its vocabulary is not his exclusive moral and political diction—a caveat that must be entered with respect to this entire discussion.) Read in the perspective of later discussions of citizenship and authority, they do evoke familiar images and set by now conventional reflections in motion. Acceptance of offices of formal authority does qualify and require compromises concerning the attributes and objectives distinctive of citizenship. But because the same qualifications are required of all citizens, because the qualifications are distributed fairly or justly and maintained reciprocally among the entire citizenry, it is reasonable for each citizen to agree to them.

Authority as Authorization

To understand the notion of reasonable agreement to a just arrangement of offices of authority we must consider a subtype of authority relations not obviously classifiable as either substantive or formal. This subtype is represented by the concept "authorization." In the simplest case, I authorize you to act on my behalf, to be my agent, to represent me. This arrangement may involve elements of personal or substantive authority. I may authorize you to represent me in part because I believe that you are *an* authority concerning the matters with which you will deal in acting on my behalf. Once again, however, we need more than the premise of inequality. My belief that you deserve standing as *an* authority is neither a necessary nor a sufficient condition of the relationship in question. I may give authorization to a person who lacks standing as *an* authority and I may withhold it from a person who deserves that standing. At the same time, the arrangment involves some of the elements of formal authority. You do not occupy an office in the sense of a position in a hierarchy that may remain constant through changes in officeholders, and thus far your "jurisdiction" is limited to me. But my authorization itself permits you, within the scope of the authority I have accorded you, to bind me to what may be a considerable array of performances. If I dislike the content of your actions, I may withdraw my authorization. But my assessment of the merits of those of your actions that are within the authority I have accorded you is, at least often, irrelevant to my obligation to perform as you have committed me to do.

In the simple case I am discussing, your authority and the authority relation between us are less a feature of a collectivity than a personal, even a private relationship. This feature of the arrangement, especially the fact that your authority results directly from, is limited by, and terminates with the withdrawal of my authorization, may do much to make it attractive to me. Clearly I have more control over the arrangement than is available to me in the more collective, institutionalized arrangements characteristic of political authority. If political authority could be founded on such authorizations, the qualifications effected against the ideal of equal citizenship would be justified not merely by the fact that they apply equitably but by the further fact that they would arise from and depend on each party's decision or choice.

Before developing the significance of these considerations for the concerns of this essay, it will be well to put them in perspective by noting that authorizations commonly acquire important social, public, and even legal characteristics that constrain the conduct of those who are party to them. In some cases they become practices in the sense exemplified by law and medicine. If I engage a lawyer to represent me, our relationship takes its character not merely from my authorization but from the customs and conventions, and indeed the legal rules, that surround and to some extent govern the conduct of lawyers and their relationships with clients. Although my lawyer as such does not hold an office with a specified authority and jurisdiction, she does occupy a social status and does play a socially and in part legally defined role. The norms and rules that define and govern her status and role place restrictions and requirements on her relationships with me and her actions on my behalf. Thus despite the fact that my lawyer's authority depends on my authorization, I cannot hope to have entire control over her authority in relation to me.

The attractions of authority relations based on authorizations have nevertheless been considerable. Because each such relationship requires an authorization from the person or persons over whom the authority will be held and exercised, the arrangement appears to accord a measure of respect to the basic equality that is fundamental to the ideal of high citizenship. Regardless of the distribution of authority that has been made in a society, all members remain equal in the fundamental sense that each is under authority by her own decision or choice. And even if authorizations are made in part in recognition of inequality in respect to a particular subject matter or activity, equality in respect to actions concerning that subject matter can in principle be reasserted at any time. Moreover, in all other respects the presupposition of equality remains unqualified.

In light of these considerations we cannot be surprised at the recurrence of efforts to build other more specifically political modes of authority on the foundation of individual authorizations. At least from Hobbes, the classic versions of consent and contractarian theories of authority have followed this path. The chief and remarkably constant suppositions of the theory are closely similar to those I "read into" Aristotle's discussion of ruling and being ruled in turn. Citizens (or in Hobbes's case subjects) are equal one to the other in that no one of them is sufficiently superior in morally and politically relevant respects to be entitled to personal authority over any others. "By nature" or "in the nature of things" the only authority that is politically germane is the authority that each person has over her own decisions and actions. Political authority can be justified only if it takes its origins from authorizations through which equal individuals transfer some of their authority over themselves to some other agent or agency. If such authorizations are given, and if they yield a distribution of authority and correlative obligations that is fair, then political authority can be justified.

Reconciling Authority and Citizenship

The consensus on these points, of course, coexists with very sharp disagreement on vital questions about the relationship between citizenship and authority. Debate concerning these questions, which has been waged from Hobbes to the present, can be viewed as a continuing attempt to resolve tensions already evident in Aristotle's theory of citizenship. Very roughly, the debate is between Hobbes and his (in respects to be discussed) followers on the one hand and Rousseau and later Rousseaueans on the other. The former give explicit and insistent development to Aristotle's foreshadowing of the notion of formal authority and embrace the inference that any very high citizenship is incompatible with authority and everything that depends on it. The imperative generated by the fact of natural moral equality is more or less fully satisfied by consent to the creation of offices of authority. From the moment of that consent on, ruling is and ought to be done primarily by those invested with that authority. The latter, proponents of high citizenship, may allow that authority can be created, perhaps that it can only be created, in this way. Individual consent or authorization provides a solution to the problem of how offices invested with binding authority—above all the office of citizen—can be justified. These theorists, however, insist on high citizenship and they struggle to reconcile their commitment to that ideal with their own acceptance of formal authority grounded in a collection of authorizations.

Toward a Liberalism

Aristotle and Hobbes

I proceed by examining Hobbes's classic version of the first of these modes of argumentation. I argued above that Aristotle gets into difficulties by trying to maintain authority as a feature of political life despite rejecting Plato's contention that political authority is founded on natural inequality. I now suggest that Hobbes tries to justify a more decisive role for political authority (more decisive than the role Aristotle assigns it) by deepening and extending the egalitarianism of Aristotle's theory of citizenship. It must be recognized, however, that the problem of justifying authority presents itself in importantly different terms in the two theories. They agree that there is no natural basis for personal authority in political life. But Aristotle thinks the equality that excludes personal authority opens up the possibility of cooperative, mutually beneficial political interactions among citizens. Thus for him the question would seem to be why political authority is necessary at all; why should the values of unrestricted, fully equal participation be qualified in any way in the political realm? Insofar as he answers this question, he does so by arguing that rule through offices of authority and the laws they promulgate maximizes the influence of that human characteristic—namely, the capacity for rational self-rule—the possession of which distinguishes citizens from slaves, from women, and from barbarians. Law is "reason without passion" and rule by its means is thus rule by reason itself rather than rule by "men" in the sense of rule by creatures with a variety of characteristics in addition to reason. Authority qualifies but does not replace citizenship. Or as we might better put it, authority contributes to a politics of high citizenship by helping to insure that those human beings with the capacities necessary to citizenship act largely or primarily out of those capacities and not out of the characteristics that they share with noncitizens.

A variety of modulations on this theme achieved prominence in the later theory of the rule of law and of constitutionalism. But no such argument is available to Hobbes. He believes that the very equalities that forbid personal authority make human interactions conflictive and deeply destructive. The most notorious feature of Hobbes's theory of equality is his insistence that every person is vulnerable to being killed by any other.[25] Equality in this raw

[25]Thomas Hobbes, *Leviathan* (Oxford: Basil Blackwell, 1955), chap. 13.

respect excludes the possibility that any of us will be able, by our own efforts, to assure our security. Natural equality excludes dominance on the basis of violence, power, and deception or manipulation as well as dominance on the basis of authority.

But it had scarcely been left to Hobbes to discover that human beings are rudely vulnerable to one another. The more interesting question that Hobbes addresses is why, in the absence of authority or some form of effective domination, personal security must be the constant, the overweening, human concern. Granting that others are physically capable of taking my life, why should they be disposed to do so? The explanation, Hobbes says, lies in the fact that human beings are equal in three further respects. First, although human interests and desires, purposes and objectives, vary in content from person to person, all human beings are interested and purposeful.[26] Second, human beings share an environment in which the supply of resources necessary to satisfy their desires and achieve their objectives is inadequate to the demand for them.[27] Third, and for present purposes most important, every person's well-being or satisfaction, as she defines or conceives them, are as good or deserving or legitimate as any other person's.[28] There neither is nor can be any convincing reason why one person should sacrifice or subordinate her interests or objectives to those of anyone else. Equality in the first two respects guarantees that human beings will come into conflict; equality in the third respect excludes the possibility that the conflict can be contained or even moderated by the parties to it. Taken together, the three equalities exclude the possibilities that inform Aristotle's theory—namely, that equal citizens, acting in a setting of shared authority and law, can readily interact in a cooperative and mutually beneficial manner.

Ever in quest of parsimony and consistency, and finding uncommon delight in the intellectually arresting, Hobbes's solution to the problem is formed largely out of the very elements that constitute the problem itself. Individual interests and purposes remain of equal legitimacy, but with the crucial qualification that each and every one of them is subordinate to the one overriding interest—namely, avoiding the "contranatural dissolution" that prematurely terminates the pursuit of all interests and purposes. Persons who are

[26]Ibid., chap. 6.
[27]Ibid., chap. 13.
[28]Ibid., chap. 6.

equal in the respects indicated, and hence equal in the further, supervenient respect that they know only the authority each exercises over herself, agree one with the other to create an office of authority to which they are severally and equally subject. The occupant of that office differs from others in no respect save that she is invested with the authority of the office. In particular, the interests and desires, the beliefs and values, the judgments and decisions, of the occupant of the office (qua natural person) possess no distinctive epistemic, moral, or prudential virtues or qualities. Subjects do not conform to the Sovereign's laws and commands because they approve of the content or the likely consequences of doing so. If, as Aristotle seems to assume, they could agree on (even in the sense of jointly recognizing once put before them) the merits of the laws and commands, laws and commands would be largely if not entirely superfluous. Subjects conform, rather, because the matters regulated by the laws and commands have proven to be the sources of intractable disagreement and mutually destructive conflict. In short, subjects obey the Sovereign for the same reasons that they created the office of Sovereign and made themselves its subjects—namely, to escape the horrendous consequences of their natural equality.

It would be no worse than a slight exaggeration to say that Hobbes's political theory seeks to "resolve" the difficulty of reconciling citizenship and political authority by eliminating citizenship and making relations in terms of authority the exclusive *political* relationship. Human beings as such may relate to one another in a wide variety of ways, but political persons, persons qua subjects, must relate to one another as subscribers to an office invested with authority. If they severally achieve the self-discipline necessary to maintain this thin but essential relationship, they may therefore find greater profit in their non- or extrapolitical relations; some among them may even hope to attain the felicity that consists in assurance of the more or less continuing satisfaction of their personal interests and desires and that is the highest estate God has permitted earthly humankind.[29] If they fail in the requisite discipline, if they succumb to the temptation to pursue what Aristotle called the good life in and through politics and the political relationships of citizenship, they will succeed only in recreating—perhaps in a yet more dangerous form—their original predicament.

[29]Ibid.

With these reflections—which some find dispiriting—in mind, I return to my earlier suggestion that arguments for authority have both a factual and an instrumental premise. The factual premise is that human beings are by nature equal in the several respects already discussed. This premise excludes personal authority. But it also opens the possibility of formal authority grounded in authorizations and yielding a distribution of obligations that is fair to all subjects. The premise that, despite the differences among their interests and purposes, all persons require security sufficient to allow them to pursue their interests, is an instrumental argument for accepting authority. If the condition specified by the factual premise is satisfied, the second premise implies that it is rational for each person to subscribe to authority in order to obtain the security.

This argument alters the specific form but does not resolve the generic character of the difficulties in Aristotle's theory. To restate them in the light of the intervening discussion, those difficulties consist in a tension between the factual premise of equality and the instrumental premise that some undeniable good or advantage is provided by authority. Using authority to pursue the good is problematic because doing so qualifies and encroaches on equality and the goods represented by it and served by respecting it fully. In abandoning the particular goods that Aristotle sees in equal citizenship, Hobbes renounces the attempt to reconcile authority and citizenship. But Hobbes's argument fails to resolve the closely analogous problem posed by his own recognition of equality. Is authority compatible with equality among (not citizens but) persons? Granted that all subjects have authorized the creation of the Sovereign, and granted also that they are equally subordinate to that office, there is an enormous inequality between the occupant of that office and each subject. And that inequality is at least as threatening to the values Hobbes treasures as authority is to Aristotle's values. Thus there is serious question whether Hobbes has made any progress toward justifying authority in a society of equals.

Hobbes's response to these objections depends heavily on two related ideas. The first is that the good sought by instituting authority has been reduced to minimal and incontrovertible proportions. The second is that the authority is formal or positional, not personal or substantive. The first point invites further comparison with Aristotle. The latter looks to politics—and hence in part to the authority that is an integral element of politics—for the highest (or perhaps the next to highest) and most complex aspects of the good for humankind. By contrast, Hobbes insists that each person must define and pursue her own good in her own way and he looked to politics and its authority to do nothing more than maintain a condition necessary to (but far from sufficient for) such private activity. By thus restricting the objectives of politics and its authority, by reducing those objectives to a common denominator on which all persons could be expected to agree, he hopes to make authority acceptable to all. As to the second point, Hobbes is of course aware that the office of authority will be occupied by a person or persons with the usual complement of passions and desires. He makes no attempt to deny that the occupant(s) of the office will use its authority in self-interested ways, and he firmly opposes all proposals to prevent such abuses by limiting or restraining the exercise of the authority of the office. (Hobbes prefers monarchy on the sobering ground that it reduces to the minimum the number of officeholders, thereby allowing satisfaction of the officeholder's personal interests at the lowest possible cost to the subjects.)[30] But he insists on a sharp distinction between the *authority* of the decisions of the office and the *merits* of those decisions. Subjects are to obey laws and commands not because they approve of or agree with their contents, but simply and exclusively because they are invested with authority. They are to obey authority because it is only when authority is obeyed that security can be maintained.

Hobbes's argument concerning the second point is of undeniable cogency and significance. To put the point in conceptual terms, if our sole reason for conforming our actions with laws and commands is our agreement with their content, we are acting on agreement or advice, not on obligation to authority. "Authority" and "law" are doing no work in our thought and action. Aristotle's argument that law is reason without passion, suggesting as it seems to do that citizens should obey laws because reason is embodied in them, confuses this point. Similarly, Rousseau's argument that in a politics of high citizenship "justice and utility may in no case be divided,"[31] and indeed the assumption of the entire tradition of which he is a chief exemplar—that a politics of high citizenship will yield better law and policy than any other mode of politics—might be thought to involve the same confusion. In language that Hobbes

[30]Ibid., chap. 19.
[31]Rousseau, *Social Contract,* I, 1.

88

himself might have used, to take this stance would be to recreate the very difficulty that prompted the attempt to create authority. Authority cannot be the same as, cannot be equated with or reduced to, agreement concerning the substantive merits of policies or laws. Individuals and groups who disagree about the desired content of policies and laws cannot sustain political arrangements and relationships on the basis of agreement concerning that content. In a characteristically trenchant formulation, Hobbes says that "this device therefore of them that will make civil laws first, and then a civil body afterwards (as if policy made a body politic and not a body politic made policy) is of no effect."[32]

Despite the seeming clarity of his understanding on this point, Hobbes does not in fact break the connection between the authority of laws and their content and purpose. His subjects create and obey authority in order to achieve what Michael Oakeshott calls an "imagined and wished-for" outcome or state of affairs—namely, peace and security. Agreement on the overwhelming importance of this objective is what explains and justifies the agreement to create and maintain authority. Accordingly, obedience to authority that does not in fact yield this outcome is irrational. Of course Hobbes *urges* subjects largely to forego judgment on this question. Except in those cases in which laws or commands themselves directly and unequivocally threaten the life of a subject, the subject is urged to let the Sovereign decide what will and will not conduce to security. But the logic of Hobbes's own argument prevents this from being more than advice, more than prudential counsel. Owing to the instrumental, end-oriented character of Hobbes's argument for authority and obedience to it, it is logically impossible for the authority of any law or command to be a sufficient reason for obeying it. Agreement on the proposition that peace and security are of paramount importance, and agreement on the further proposition that *these* laws and commands will yield peace and security here and now, is precisely what "makes" the Hobbesean body politic.

These considerations might tempt us to say that, appearances to the contrary notwithstanding, neither Hobbes nor Aristotle has a theory of authority. If it is a condition of such a theory that it make authority a sufficient, an invariably decisive, reason for action, then neither of these theories qualifies. This requirement is too stringent;

[32]Thomas Hobbes, *Elements of Law* (Cambridge: Cambridge University Press, 1928), p. 152.

if we insist on it, authority among human agents becomes both a theoretical and a practical impossibility. Just below I develop this argument by examining Michael Oakeshott's more vigorous attempt to satisfy the requirement in question. Assuming in advance that I can make good on the contention I just advanced, a better way to describe my conclusions to this juncture is to say that neither Hobbes nor Aristotle succeed in eliminating the tensions that we first encountered in discussing Aristotle's theory. In both cases persons aware of their natural equality and concerned about sustaining the good represented by it must recognize that subscription to authority deeply qualifies the equality and puts the good it represents in serious and continuing jeopardy. They may nevertheless decide that, all things considered, the qualification and the jeopardy are preferable to the available alternatives. Hence they may make the authorization, engage in the subscription, requisite to the creation of authority. But extraordinary good fortune apart, some laws and commands will threaten the very values that induced them to subscribe to authority. Thus whether on the perhaps depressing Hobbesean assumptions about politics and political interactions, or on the more elevated and gratifying Aristotelian assumptions, authority may be tolerated and sustained but it can hardly be celebrated. Once the assumption that there is some inequality that (in company with an agreed objective) justifies authority was abandoned, it became impossible to arrive at an unproblematic theory of authority.

As I indicated at the beginning of this chapter, my own response to this circumstance is to recognize, or rather to insist, that political authority *is* a deeply problematic feature of our arrangements. Arguments for it are inescapably less than conclusive or dispositive, are irremediably vulnerable to objections that are not only cogent but powerful. To accept authority and authority relations as a feature of human arrangements is to make a dangerous compromise; it is to act contrary to beliefs and to risk values of the first importance. And because it is certain that there is no such thing as citizenship without authority, highly doubtful that there is any such thing as a political society without authority, it follows that accepting citizenship and political society takes on these same characteristics.

This conclusion might be thought to amount to the proposition that "human affairs are not all that one might have hoped" or perhaps "there is a tragic dimension to the human condition." Human beings cannot live together without political society and political authority, but salient and indeed highly valued characteristics of human beings should render both of these objectionable to them. This conclusion may be thought jejeune, trite, or at least morally and politically irrelevant. One can of course mount these objections against authority and citizenship, but pursuing them yields no program, no course of action, no even partial solution to the difficulties the recognition of which prompts the objections.

I suggest that reactions such as these are inappropriate. True, if the difficulties and objections I have been discussing are as general and as deeply grounded as I have suggested, they will not be entirely resolved or eliminated by awareness of them or by action informed by such awareness. But such an awareness may temper hopes, deflect quixotic initiatives, and contribute to the sobriety necessary if the difficulties are to be kept within tolerable proportions.

These perhaps unwelcome reflections presume what numerous theorists of authority and citizenship fervently deny, namely, that there are indeed insuperable theoretical and practical obstacles to overcoming the difficulties that have been my focus. So far from treating my objections as trivial or irrelevant, leading modern theorists of authority and citizenship have labored to overcome them. The conclusions I have just been anticipating would be justified only if their efforts could be shown to be unsuccessful.

The attempts that require consideration can be subsumed under the two broad categories that I have denominated Hobbesean and Rousseauist. The first seeks (in various ways) to render authority acceptable to political equals by limiting the activities, including the activities of citizens, of those who share in it. The second seeks to make authority effective in pursuing lofty ends and purposes by democratizing it radically, that is, by insisting that its possession and exercise be equally and continuously shared among all citizens who are within its jurisdiction.

Michael Oakeshott

I will focus my examination of developments in the Hobbesean tradition on Michael Oakeshott's attempt to achieve a purified version of an F-P theory of authority. I noted that Hobbes's theory maintains a vital connection between authority and an end or purpose alleged to be of overwhelming importance to all human beings. Hobbesean subjects authorize and subscribe to the authority of the Sovereign in order to achieve the peace and security that, in his judgment, can be attained in no other way. I argued, however, that this feature of Hobbes's argument puts authority in constant jeopardy. Rational subjects can be expected to maintain their subscription only insofar as doing so actually contributes to the end for which they instituted authority.

It is a major objective of Oakeshott's theorizing to secure the authority of political society against this jeopardy. He seeks to remedy this defect in Hobbes's theory by jettisoning the notion that political authority exists for the sake of achieving some end or purpose. In pursuing this objective, Oakeshott formulates a severely uncompromising version of the F-P theory of authority. As in all versions, the key notions (in addition to equality among those who subscribe to authority) are rules, offices, and procedures created by rules.

> The authority of rulings and of administrative requisitions is recognized in terms of the rules which permit them to be made and which specify their jurisdiction. The authority of an office lies in the rules which constitute it and endow it with powers and duties and is to be recognized in terms of those rules. The authority of the occupant of an office lies in the rules which constitute it and endow it with powers and duties and is to be recognized in terms of those rules. The authority of the occupant of an office, his right to exercise its powers, is the license he acquires in coming to occupy it according to the rules of a prescribed procedure of appointment or succession. The authority of legislators to make, to amend, or to repeal . . . [law] is recognized in the rules which specify the conditions to be subscribed to in order to occupy the office, and the . . . [law] they declare is recognizable as authentic law in having been enacted in subscription to a prescribed procedure and in the exercise of powers conferred in this procedure.[33]

Rules are constitutive of authority: to understand authority is to understand rules; to subscribe to authority is to subscribe to and to know how to act in relation to rules.

Thus far Oakeshott's formulation differs from other F-P theories only in the single-minded, relentless reliance it places on the notion of rules. The special quality of his version, and its distinctive interest

[33]Oakeshott, *On Human Conduct*, pp. 150–51.

for present purposes, resides in its insistence that the system of rules which constitutes political authority must be understood entirely without reference to desires and interests, ends and purposes, or even beliefs and values shared among those who make, enforce, and subscribe to those rules. The rules of civil authority are said by him to be purely "adverbial" in character; these rules speak exclusively to the manner in which individual citizens act on beliefs and values, pursue ends and purposes, to the choice of which authority, its rules, and the civil society they constitute are altogether indifferent.[34] Speaking of rules of this kind, Oakeshott says: "A rule (and *a fortiori* something less exacting, like a maxim) can never tell a performer what choice he shall make; it announces only conditions to be subscribed to in making choices." The criminal law "does not forbid killing or lighting a fire, it forbids killing 'murderously' or lighting a fire 'arsonically.' " The system of rules that makes up the practice of political authority in a civil society should be understood as "an instrument to be played upon, not a tune to be played."[35]

It is not difficult to understand the motivation behind Oakeshott's development of this view. If the rules that constitute a practice of authority do not serve assignable interests or objectives, then it is impossible to decide whether to subscribe to them by deciding whether one approves the objectives they are intended to serve or by deciding whether in one's judgment the rules actually contribute to their intended objectives. Instrumental, utilitarian, or any other teleological reasoning is categorially and hence categorically excluded from the practice of authority. Members or citizens in a civil political association invested with authority relate to one another exclusively as subscribers to adverbial rules. For this reason, the question of whether they share ends or purposes, interests or objectives, beliefs or values, is irrelevant to whether they will be able to maintain authority. Or to put the point more positively, the common subscription to the procedural or adverbial rules that constitute political authority makes it possible for them to pursue their individual or group ends and interests, to sustain and act on their beliefs and values, without falling into destructive conflict.

[34]Ibid., pp. 116–17. In this discussion I leave aside Oakeshott's importantly different account of authority in what he calls an "enterprise association" or *universitas* as opposed to civil association or *societas*. He develops the distinction between the two modes of association and their authority in the second and third essays of *On Human Conduct*.

[35]Ibid., p. 58.

It should be noted that this understanding of authority accords an important place to, places a deep reliance on, something that might just as well be called citizenship. Citizens must maintain and act on, indeed are properly characterized by, a "disciplined imagination." There will be a standing temptation to use political authority to advance some substantive project or purpose, to achieve some anticipated and wished-for outcome. If a rule that contributes to such an objective can be invested with authority so that all citizens acquire an obligation to accept and obey it, then (as long as authority remains effective in commanding obedience) those who favor the objective will have materially advanced their cause. But to succumb to this temptation is to put authority and hence civil life in jeopardy. The turn to authority to pursue the objective indicates that there is disagreement concerning it, that those who favor the objective have failed to convince their fellow citizens of its merits. Investing a rule that serves the objective with authority adds nothing to the arguments for the objective itself. It asks, or rather purports to require, those who do not share it to accommodate themselves to it for some other reason—most likely to sustain authority. But there will be very good reasons for them to refuse to do so. In their view authority will have become a weapon in the service of the partisan objectives. To submit to it will be simply and straightforwardly to submit to a tyranny in the classical sense of rule in the perceived interests of the rulers and contrary to the perceived interests of the ruled. Thus citizens in the true sense are persons who understand the distinctions between adverbial rules on the one hand and substantive rules on the other and who act to assure that only the former are invested with the authority of the civil society.

This understanding of citizenship and its relationship to authority is directly relevant to the difficulties in that relationship that I have been considering. It is compatible with the essential features of the understanding that all citizens will participate in the offices that adopt and promulgate adverbial rules. (Which is not to say that Oakeshott himself favors a notably inclusive or democratized conception of citizenship, and it is certainly not to say that he favors active citizenship in the sense of a role that occupies large quantities of the time and energies of citizens.) Moreover, if authority is never used to pursue controversial or divisive objectives, there will be no instances in which subscription to it will qualify or compromise the equality, freedom, autonomy, or dignity of individual citizens. On this understanding, the very fact that citizenship is inseparable from authority appears to mean that citizenship guarantees the equality that has been the supposition of theories of authority since Aristotle.

Oakeshott has given up on Hobbes's expectation that agreement could be achieved concerning the overriding importance of peace and defense, agreement sufficient to engender and sustain a stable and effective system of authority in a political society. In place of agreement on that (or, allegedly, any other) end or purpose, he proposes to substitute subscription to adverbial rules said to be indifferent to all ends and purposes. For reasons already considered, this proposal is both apposite and meritorious. Short of reverting to a fully Platonic conception of substantive-purpose authority, there can be no authority without distinctions between procedure on the one hand and substance on the other, between formal credentials and material desirabilities.

But Oakeshott's distinctions cannot do anything like all of the work he asks of them. A rule that prohibits killing "murderously" or lighting fires "arsonically" is a rule against murder or arson; it is a rule that prohibits a class of actions through the taking of which agents seek imagined and wished-for ends and purposes. Most generally, subscription to authority is itself human action and, as with all species of this genus, is done for a reason, to achieve some objective.[36] If there is no agreement whatsoever concerning the objectives of subscription, the subscription can be maintained only by sacrificing equality among subscribers. A civil society on the Oakeshottian model might well diminish the conflict between authority and citizenship, but it could not eliminate that conflict. Although I will not be able to defend it here, I assert that the same is true of the numerous more mechanical devices proposed for the same purpose by other theorists in the F-P tradition.

Rousseau and the Ideal of High Citizenship

Oakeshott seeks to render authority and citizenship compatible by severely limiting the objectives or purposes of each. The limitations he seeks are to be achieved through understanding and self-discipline on the part of participants in civil society. They must

[36]Oakeshott himself gives us an excellent analysis of these features of human conduct. See ibid., esp. the first essay.

appreciate what is distinctive about such a society and they must think and act in ways consonant with that appreciation. In this respect he differs from Hobbes and from most other thinkers who, like himself, have been concerned to limit the activities of those in authority. Hobbes relies on rulers to limit their own uses of their authority, looking to subjects primarily for obedience and for restraint in respect to the reasons for it. Others who have sought limitations on authority have placed little faith in either ruler or ruled, looking rather to a variety of devices such as constitutions, bills of rights, divisions of authority of various kinds, countervailing forces in society, and so forth. In the perspective given by these comparisons, we might even characterize Oakeshott as a theorist of high citizenship.

Writers in what I have called the Rousseauean mode nevertheless firmly reject Oakeshott's outlook. Citizens may play a role in his conception of civil society, but that role is woefully limited, woefully negative in character. Citizens act to protect their equality as individuals; they act to prevent political society from imposing collective goals and preferences on individuals who do not share them. This of course means that political society will almost certainly be debarred from acting to eliminate the innumerable and highly destructive inequalities that coexist with the essential but unsatisfactorily thin equality that obtains among its members by virtue of the fact that they are human agents. More important, it means that citizenship is not a role in and through which individuals pursue, in company with one another, the moral excellences (however encompassing) of which they are capable. For Rousseau the theory and practice of authority and citizenship takes "men as they are" but seeks to achieve "laws as they might be" in order not only that "justice and utility may in no case be divided" but that man's "faculties" will be "so stimulated and developed, his ideas so extended, his feelings so ennobled, and his whole soul so uplifted" that he attains to a "moral liberty."[37] For Oakeshott, the objective of the theory and practice of *citizenship and authority* is to take human beings as they are—and leave them that way.

Crucial to the position of Rousseau and his followers are a pair of assumptions that at least appear to be highly plausible. The first of these is that the possession and exercise of authority enlarges and

[37]Rousseau, *Social Contract,* I, viii.

enhances one's capacity for effective decision and action. To possess the authority to do X is to have a kind of right to take that action. It is to have a warrant for doing X that is established in one's community, a warrant that other members of the community have an obligation to respect. Thus acquiring authority is in principle equivalent to eliminating or freeing oneself from a whole array of limitations on and obstacles to action that might be posed by the objections of other parties. The latter might disagree or object, but they are bound by their subscription to go along or stand aside. The second assumption gives a communal or collectivist cast to the first. At bottom it is the notion that authority will not be objectionable to those who possess and exercise it. If a system of authority enhances the possibility of effective action, and if we exercise authority under that system, then we should welcome the system of authority.

The objections to authority, in other words, always, and reasonably enough it would seem, come from those who do not have it. From these assumptions there is drawn what seems to be the impeccable inference that authority could be made welcome to all by the device of extending its possession and exercise to the entirety of those who make up the community in which it is established. If each and every member of the community participated fully in the possession and exercise of whatever authority is established in it, the efficacy of collective action would be enhanced and no member would have reason to complain about either the existence or the use of authority. If authority is thoroughly democratized, it becomes acceptable in a society of equals. More positively, by virtue of their status as members of the citizenry, each citizen is in the attractive position of possessing and exercising authority, and hence the attractive aspects of both citizenship and authority complement rather than conflict one with the other.

Of course no proponent of democratized authority and/or high citizenship has ever seriously envisaged distributing authority to *all* members of any political society. The assumption of political equality has without exception been withheld from children and from certain classes of criminals and those judged to be mentally deficient or deranged, and it has been extended only hesitatingly and grudgingly to those of alien religious conviction, to the unpropertied, and above all to women. These large qualifications aside, from the perspective of this essay much of the theory of high citizenship can be viewed as taking a highly favorable attitude toward authority

and attempting, through citizenship, to extend the supposed benefits of its possession and exercise. Whereas the line of thought
running from Hobbes to Oakeshott views authority as contributing
certain essential but narrowly confined advantages, the Aristotelian
and more especially the Rousseauean tradition looks upon it as,
potentially, a highly desirable feature of human affairs. If authority
is suitably arranged and distributed, those who possess and exercise
it can be ennobled by the experience.[38]

The key assumption that political authority enhances individual
and collective action seems to be challenged by much of our experience with systems of authority. Systems in which authority is firmly
established, seldom if ever resisted or challenged, are nevertheless
characterized by dispute and division, often by deadlock that is
broken, if at all, by compromises satisfying to no one. Rather than
facilitating action, the existence of established political authority
motivates and organizes opposition to it.

Rousseaueans are likely to argue that this evidence, although
abundant, is irrelevant to their argument because it is as it were an
artifact of the very views that their argument confutes. Those who
have failed to appreciate the potential advantages of political authority, those whose thinking is dominated by experience with
authority improperly arranged and distributed, have deliberately
incapacitated the systems of authority in or under which they live.
The claims of the Rousseauean theory can be tested only in systems
that have eliminated artificial limitations on and complications in
the exercise of authority and have established an organic connection between authority and high citizenship.

It will be instructive to pause here to note points of agreement
between Hobbes and the Rousseaueans. At least as concerned as the
latter with the efficacy of authority, Hobbes argued that it would be
maximized where (a) its scope and (b) its location or possession
were as little in doubt, as little subject to debate, as could be.
Dispute about (a) would be excluded by making the authority of the
Sovereign unlimited, without qualification of any kind, the solution
Hobbes comes very close to adopting. So far as Hobbes can see,
dispute about (b) can be eliminated by investing all authority in one
person *and* by treating that person as "representing" all those over

[38]For suggestive reflections that bear on this theme from a somewhat different
angle of approach, see Nannerl Keohane, *Philosophy and the State in France*
(Princeton: Princeton University Press, 1980), esp. her interpretation of Rousseau as
continuing and in a sense completing the tradition of absolutist thought in France.

whom the authority is to be exercised; it can be kept minimal by investing it in a small number of persons also treated as "representing" all of the others; or it can be maximized by distributing it throughout the populace (making, of course, unavailable the valuable notion of representation). Hobbes of course favors the first over the second and abhors the third.

Hobbes's handling of (a) is often and on the whole correctly attributed to Rousseau himself and to other recognizably Rousseauean positions. Without going into controversial exegetical details, theorists of high citizenship hope for too much from authority to allow them to be comfortable with notions of constitutional, institutional, and other limitations on it.

As to (b), Rousseaueans also share Hobbes's concern with plurality, diversity, and conflict among the possessors of authority. Of course they must reject monarchy (albeit there is the Legislator!), aristocracy (albeit there are the noncitizens!), and all notions of representation that permit one party or set of parties to act on behalf of—that is, in place but in the name of and in a manner binding on—another party of parties. In fact, therefore, a Rousseauean polity necessarily distributes authority in what Hobbes thinks is the worst possible way—that is, among a great many individuals each of whom, by virtue of occupying the office of citizen, can do as she wishes with her measure of political authority. How, then, are confusion and stalemate to be avoided, efficacy of action to be achieved?

Despite the obvious differences between Rousseau and Hobbes, commentators concerned with this question have discerned in Rousseau and other theorists of high citizenship notions akin to the "unity" that Hobbes claims is produced when Leviathan is created by the "authorization" of its "subjects."[39] But Rousseau's rejection of representation means that this unity can not be "artificial" in the sense of Hobbes's "*unity* of the represener, not the *unity* of the represented."[40] For this reason, and perhaps owing to the prominence of obscure notions such as general will in theories of high citizenship, it has frequently been suggested that the desired "efficacy" would be achieved at the expense of plurality and individuality—that is, by fostering an all too "real unity" consisting of stultifying conformism maintained by democratic tyranny.

[39]Hobbes, *Leviathan,* chap. 17.
[40]Ibid., chap. 16.

We should note at once that a requirement of *some* degree of consensus, of broad if not unqualified agreement on at least some matters, is a feature of any theory of authority and any theory of citizenship. Even Hobbes and Oakeshott, who are as anxious to minimize this requirement as any thinkers known to me, recognize that the requirement must be satisfied in some measure. As a bare minimum, there must be agreement that *this* and not *that* is an office invested with authority, that *these* and not *those* are the rules and procedures by and through which authority is exercised. But even this much agreement cannot be achieved or sustained unless there is also something close to consensus on some number of further values and beliefs. For Hobbes, peace and security must be accorded overweening importance and there must be a shared belief that they can be achieved and maintained only if there is political authority. For Oakeshott the comparable value seems to be the desirability of "abating" somewhat the "contingency" that conditions all human conduct,[41] this objective or value being conjoined with the belief that contingency is best abated by fidelity to an adverbially defined civility constituting a practice of authority. I elaborate somewhat on this point below, but it is manifest that to criticize the ideal of high citizenship for supposing consensus on *something* is frivolous if not captious.

Second, it would clearly be a mistake to interpret the major theorists of high citizenship as *pre*suming deep and extensive consensus. They do presuppose the degree of commonality represented by acceptance of the natural moral equality that forbids a politics of personal authority. They argue, however, that further and more substantive commonalities will develop in the course and as a consequence of a life of shared citizenship. Citizenship is a remedy for the fragmentation, division, and conflict that exists in its absence. Rousseau's work is especially striking in this regard, containing both biting denunciations of the selfishness, competitiveness, and antagonism rife in his society and paeans to the mutuality that could be expected if Frenchmen became genuine citizens. The same contrast between reality and potentiality is sharply drawn by contemporary theorists of high citizenship such as Arendt, Barber, and Pateman. Whether inspired by classical city-states, eighteenth-century Geneva, Swiss cantons, or Yugoslavian factories, these theorists describe high citizenship as a kind of bootstrap operation;

[41]Oakeshott, *On Human Conduct*, p. 180.

active, continuing involvement in the life of a suitably organized political association will itself create such commonalities as are necessary to politics in this mode. To the objection that their ideal is irrelevant because the conditions of its realization are nowhere satisfied, they rejoin that serious pursuit of the ideal will itself create those conditions.

Third, there is no reason to think that there is any very large inventory of items on which consensus is specifically required. The scope of the consensus that is expected varies depending on the theorist's conception of the aspects of life that are fit subjects for political deliberation and interaction. There is, for example, no need for Aristotelian or Arendtian *citizens* to agree on the principles of a household economy. Critics who represent the ideal as requiring or aspiring to an encompassing uniformity simply misrepresent it.

These interpretations can be restated to give a better focus to the question of whether high citizenship contributes distinctively to easing the authority-citizenship relationship. The theory of high citizenship presents an ideal that is primarily procedural. It does not celebrate political outcomes or states of affairs—for example, those in which everyone agrees with the substance of all decisions, or those in which everyone ought to agree because the decisions are correct, just, or otherwise meritorious. True, some proponents of the ideal have believed that decisions made by an active citizenry will, as a generalization, be better decisions better supported. If true, these generalizations provide ancillary support for the kind of politics the theory promotes. But it would be imprudent to argue for high citizenship primarily on these grounds, even less prudent to argue that citizens should obey laws for these reasons. The first argument tends either to make authority irrelevant or to disqualify citizen involvement wherever the generalization fails to hold. On the second argument authority becomes equivalent to that about which consensus obtains and hence is again either superfluous when available or unavailable when needed.

In its most persuasive formulations, then, the theory of high citizenship favors a particular kind of political process because it generates and sustains distinctive characteristics and attitudes among the citizenry. Perhaps the most appropriate general term for the characteristics and attitudes the theory hopes to engender is identification: self-identification as citizen and shared identifications as members of a citizenry pursuing the good of the collectivity of citizens. In place of fragmenting, conflict-generating attitudes such as self-interestedness and competitiveness, it encourages cooperation and trustful acceptance of interdependencies. As sharers in the authority of the polity, citizens engage in deliberations addressed not to the question of which interests will prevail (albeit most decisions will in fact benefit some interests and disserve others) but what they as conjoint authorities should best do. They are to think of authority not as a weapon to be fought over but as a communal asset to be wisely used.

As citizens develop these characteristics their disagreements become "friendly" in the sense of a "friendly amendment" to a motion, one offered in the spirit of a contribution to a common enterprise. Thus those who oppose proposals, who argue and vote unavailingly against them, can not only accept but identify with their adoption. They can do so not only because they have participated in the process that yielded that outcome but because they identify with the spirit that animates it and with the enterprise of which that spirit is the vital center.

Understood in this manner, high citizenship is more than an attractive ideal. It captures qualities that are, in some measure, almost certainly indispensable to any encompassing, politically organized association. Most pertinent here, it specifies features without which no such association could develop or sustain authority. Authority is a kind of reason for action: to acknowledge the authority of a rule is to acknowledge that there is a reason for conforming to it. But it is a reason of a very special kind. Although it cannot be entirely divorced from the content of the rules in which it is invested, neither can it be equated with or reduced to the merits of those rules. It is therefore a conceptual as well as a practical impossibility to sustain subscription to authority in the absence of considerations—including considerations in addition to assessments of the substantive merits of the rules—which support the judgment that the authority of a rule is a reason for obeying it. In the entire absence of identifications of the kinds promoted by the theory of high citizenship such considerations would be unavailable.

Should we not enlist ourselves in the cause of high citizenship?

Conclusion: Citizens and Individuals

My own answer to this question is a qualified negative. It is negative primarily because the ideal of high citizenship accommodates itself too readily to political authority. Stated somewhat iron-ically, my answer is negative primarily because the theory of high citizenship is too successful in the task that I, in company with some of its most distinguished proponents, set for it, the task of reconcil-ing citizenship and authority.

Early in this essay I argued that citizenship is inseparable from authority. I then asked whether this is reason to be suspicious of citizenship as well as of authority. The theory of high citizenship returns a negative answer to my question. It encourages citizens to identify with authority.

This response has its share of attractions. If authority became what the ideal of high citizenship portrays it to be, why shouldn't we as citizens identify with it? It is of course appropriate to be wary of authority in conflict-ridden societies in which authority is pater-nalistic at its best and tyrannical at its more usual worst. Because these have been and continue to be the circumstances of most human beings, resistance to the alternative understanding proposed by the theory of high citizenship is more than understandable. Unfortunately, that resistance perpetuates the very circumstance that prompts and sustains it. Authority will cease to be suspect only when we create for ourselves a politics of high citizenship in which we no longer have reason to suspect it.

In my judgment, however, authority is *on principle* suspect, on principle objectionable. It is more objectionable under some cir-cumstances than others, but it is *always* objectionable. The reasons it is always objectionable can be stated in a number of ways and could take us into a moderately technical literature.[42] At bottom, its objectionable qualities reside in a fact we have encountered several times, namely, that (certain special cases aside) it has a role to play only when we disagree concerning the merits of the actions we should and should not take, the policies we should and should not adopt. Where there is consensus concerning what should and should not be done we simply act or refrain from acting on reasons specific to the actions in question. But if we disagree or are uncertain (but nevertheless judge that a decision must be made) authority may be invoked as a reason for accepting a particular decision. Thus as a

---

[42]See, for example, Richard B. Friedman, "On the Concept of Authority in Political Philosophy," in Flathman, *Concepts in Social and Political Philosophy;* Joseph P. Raz, *Practical Reason and Norms* (London: Hutchinson, 1975) and "On Legitimate Authority," in *Philosophical Law,* ed. Richard Bronaugh (Westport, Conn.: Greenwood Press, 1978).

logical matter (the psychology of the situation may of course be less clear-cut) either authority has no work to do or it works to give us a reason for an action that we would not otherwise (that is, in the absence of authority) take. To subscribe to authority is to commit oneself to take actions that one would not take if considered exclusively on the merits of the actions themselves.[43] Under suitable circumstances, there may on balance be convincing reasons for such a commitment; I at least do not see how a reflective person could make that commitment without regret.

Neither the theory of high citizenship nor any other theory alters this characteristic of authority. Insofar as action is taken in the absence of consensus, or is continued after that consensus has disappeared, some citizens will be required to accommodate to policies with the content of which they disagree. If or insofar as the idea of high citizenship is realized, however, this fact will not so much as give them pause; they will not find it objectionable or even mildly regrettable. Having come to identify themselves as citizens and hence as sharers in authority, when a decision has been made they will focus not on its content but on the fact that authority of which they are a part has made it. Identifying themselves as they do with authority, they cannot regard that which is invested with authority as infringing on or derogating from them.

The politics of high citizenship may begin in plurality and disagreement, but (insofar as it acts in a determinate manner on any specific question) it *must* end in unchallengeable agreement (concerning that question). But of course agreement cannot alter (what as likely as not will be) the fact that there are excellent reasons against the decision or policy. In short, the politics of high citizenship would not change the fundamental character of authority; it would change the attitudes of citizens toward authority.[44]

[43]More precisely, it is to commit oneself to the proposition that one may (if authority is in fact invoked) acquire obligations to take actions that one would not take on their merits. The obligation, of course, need not be regarded—in my judgment, ought not to be regarded—as an invariably decisive reason for action.

[44]Much of this argument can be abbreviated by reference to the complications mentioned in n. 43, above. If we regard the obligation to obey authority as less than an invariably decisive reason for action, we in effect open up space for civil disobedience. If I have correctly construed the ideal of high citizenship, in a politics that fully realized that ideal civil disobedience could never be justified. Or rather, civil disobedience would be both a logical and a psychological impossibility. I have argued elsewhere that a defensible theory of political authority must provide a place for justifiable civil disobedience. See my *Practice of Political Authority*, pt. II.

I said that my answer to the question "Should high citizenship be our ideal?" is a qualified negative. It remains to say something about why, from the perspectives of this essay, the negative is qualified, about why our attitude toward citizenship and politics should be chastened not withdrawalist.

I argued that Plato's theory is incoherent because it relies on *an* authority while denying a condition thereof, that is, denying the availability of persons who are not themselves authorities but who have sufficient knowledge or understanding to accord that standing to others, to recognize and acknowledge the authority of the pronouncements or performances of others. This argument can be restated as follows: Plato makes unintelligible the relationships among authority, its pronouncements and performances, and those to whom those pronouncements are addressed (for whom they are to bear authority or be authoritative).

Although typically (not invariably and seldom clearly) employing the concept of *in* authority, withdrawalist and "low" citizenship theories are in constant danger of an analogous incoherence (and its practical consequences). The characteristic pronouncements or performances of *in* authorities are laws and commands promulgated to those who have authorized or otherwise subscribed to the system of authority in question (who are in the jurisdiction of that system of authority). With the qualification that they depersonalize authority by making it a property of offices and rules, these theories claim (as in Hobbes and Oakeshott) or tacitly allow (as in much of the "low" theory of citizenship) that there is an intelligible relationship among the three elements analogous to those that compose *an* authority relationships *à la* Plato, that is, offices invested with authority, laws and commands issuing from those offices, and the citizens or subjects to whom the laws and commands are promulgated. If those laws and commands are *intra vires,* that fact about them is said (by these and numerous other theories) to create—or rather to constitute—an obligation, the obligation of obedience to the laws and commands, for everyone in the jurisdiction. For present purposes let us concede (what deserves challenge) that abstractly (conceptually) these relationships are intelligible.

Insofar as they are successful in discouraging the interactions between officeholders and citizens or subjects, withdrawalist and low citizenship theories reduce the relationships in question to the terms just stated, that is, they reduce "politics" to authority, law, and to the obligation of obedience. While all forms of "legal absolutism" and numerous explications of *in* authority construe the obligation to obey as independent of the merits of laws, these theories go further and argue that citizens or subjects should disavow (as in Hobbes) or suppress to the greatest possible extent (as in most of the theories cited in note 1, above) concern with the reasons for or merits of laws and commands. It may be (as in Hobbes but rarely in other theories of political withdrawalism and low citizenship) deemed valuable for them to understand why authority and law are necessary, but it is not valuable, may be harmful, for them to consider or even to be made aware of the reasons for and against the adoption (as distinct from the enforcement once adopted and until repealed) of this, that, or the next law.

The strongest formulation of the argument I am advancing against these theories (strongest, that is, if we continue to assume the intelligibility of the conceptual relationships discussed just above) is that this position is incoherent because citizens and subjects who do not understand the reasons for a law *cannot* discharge their obligation to obey it; they cannot do so because knowing what counts as obeying a rule, knowing *what* the rule demands or forbids, requires understanding the reasons for it. Although I think there is a convincing version of this argument, because presenting it here would take us far afield, I instead make the (for present purposes sufficient) arguments that (a) such an understanding is *often* necessary to knowing how to obey (or disobey) a rule and (b) that in any case in the absence of such understanding the occurrence of obedience or disobedience becomes random, ceases to be explainable and to that extent expectable in terms of thought and action within politics.

This charge, frequently stated in terms of volatility or a tendency to lurch from sullen but otherwise lifeless submission to destructive disorder, is often brought against, as it were, the other side of the equation, that is, against authoritarianism and the unwillingness of authoritarian rulers and their apologists to justify or even explain the reasons for their laws and commands. By eschewing or discrediting concern with and involvement in the political processes that produce laws and commands, withdrawalism and theories of low citizenship make it difficult if not impossible for those subject to authority to augment or enrich the (at best) thin intelligibility of their relation to political authority as such by an understanding of

the reasons for and against the laws and commands they are expected to obey.

Stripped of what is often their arrogant and aggrandizing moral-
ism and perfectionism, the promise of theories of high citizenship is
that they will eliminate this randomness, will give intelligibility and
the possibility of stability to the relationship between political authority, law, and obedience and disobedience. For the reasons I have
given, this promise is worse than false. There is no unproblematic
theory of authority, no sure way to maintain intelligibility—let
alone yet more attractive or satisfying connections—among the
components of authority relationships. But as programs for public
life, withdrawalism and low citizenship give up on the attempt to
sustain these relationships in so much as a tolerable condition.[45]

There is no formula for making political life tolerable, but there
are two languages that may assist us as we make the continuing and
inherently problematic effort to do so. The more prosaic of these
features the distinction between persons—or better, individuals—
and their statuses and roles. "Citizen" is one status (office) that
most of us occupy, citizenship one of the roles that we play. As
individuals we are also parents, plumbers, and professors, con-
sumers, co-workers, and colleagues. As individuals, one of our
concerns is to try to understand and maintain in a satisfactory
condition the relationships among our several statuses and roles.
Doing so requires something by no means easy to achieve or maintain, that disciplined imagination of which Michael Oakeshott has
written. Theories of high citizenship privilege the status and role of
citizenship at the expense of all others (and of individuality); theories of low citizenship privilege all others at the expense of citizenship (and the protections and other advantages that it, properly
understood, can afford to individuality).

Our self-awareness as individuals may afford critical perspective
on the several partial and more specialized roles that we play,
including the role of citizen. As Aristotle's sometimes poetic discus-

---

[45]I say programs because theories of *politics*, that is, attempts to theorize the
present form of human association which is both encompassing and coercive, must
maintain accommodations for individual and group exceptionalism and idiosyn-
crasy. But individuals and groups who want to universalize or even generalize their
withdrawalism are obliged, it seems to me, to adopt philosophical anarchism.
Nothing in this essay is intended to discredit or diminish the immense attractiveness
of the latter view.

sions of the relationship between a good man and a good citizen may also be interpreted as suggesting, such perspective may allow us to understand that citizenship implicates us in the perhaps necessary but nevertheless objectionable mode of relationship that is subscription to political authority. Such an understanding yields no argument for withdrawing from citizenship and politics, a course that could put our individuality and hence all of our roles in jeopardy. It does give us reason to conduct ourselves as citizens in a manner befitting our individuality; it gives us reason to adopt a chastened view of citizenship.

4

Liberalism and the
Human Good of Freedom

Among the complaints commonly brought against liberalism, one of the most familiar is that it accords unjustifiable importance to individual freedom. In ideological terms, socialists object that liberalism subordinates equality to freedom, conservatives that it promotes license in the name of freedom, communitarians that it destroys communal ties and engenders unresolvable conflict. In more philosophical formulations, the liberal emphasis on freedom is traced to an ahistorical metaphysical atomism and an empiricism or positivism that are at once jejeune and pernicious. Reflected in an untenable conception of freedom as "negative," as no more than the absence of the crudest obstacles and impediments to physical movement, these ill-considered commitments are said to explain the dangerous incoherence of liberal political and moral thought.

These charges are frequently overdrawn. Insofar as they are directed against the politically organized societies most frequently characterized as liberal (as "liberal democracies"), they of course exaggerate the individual freedom actually available in those societies. In part, these exaggerations consist of overlooking or underestimating interferences with freedom that are condemned (however vigorously and effectively) by the public philosophies that predominate in liberal democracies. But the critics of liberalism also describe incorrectly the place of freedom in influential versions of liberal ideology. It is true that "freedom" and its cognates are prominent in the political discourse of self-styled liberal democracies. It is also true that certain freedoms have been accorded a privileged position in the public law of a number of liberal democracies. But any moderately close examination of the influential versions of liberal ideology makes it clear that their authors and exponents are not only receptive to but anxious to promote extensive de jure limitations on individual freedom. As libertarians (against whom the charges I mentioned are perhaps more plausibly leveled) complain, freedom is no more than one of a number of liberal values, and liberal publicists have readily found justifications for subordinating freedom to conflicting and competing considerations.

The same observations hold concerning the more abstract and systematic formulations of political and moral philosophers who by self-designation or wide agreement are of a liberal tendency. Just as few among the critics of liberalism declare themselves against freedom properly understood and ordered, so many theorists who by self-declaration or common designation are liberals deny that they hold the views their critics attribute to them. Here again language that arouses the ire of critics is frequently enough encountered; "freedom" and "liberty" are certainly prominent in the work, say, of Locke, Kant, and Constant; Mill, Green, and Hobhouse; Rawls, Dworkin and Ackerman. But Locke's argument for religious toleration, said by Rawls to be a (if not the) decisive moment in the formulation of liberal doctrine,[1] has been shown to rely crucially on a view about faith that is out of keeping with the secularism characteristic of liberalism and in any case accords religious freedom no more than instrumental significance. Moreover, Locke's theory of political society, so far from being atomistic, privatistic, or even notably impersonal and adversarial, accords a central position to a notion of mutual trust.[2] As to Kant, while some of the charges I noted may seem justified concerning his specifically political and legal views, attention to the wider moral and epistemological theory that informs those views calls those charges into serious question.[3]

Benjamin Constant was certainly a vigorous champion of "modern" (roughly "negative") freedom against the "ancient," more communal or "positive" variety, and he may be a better object of

[1]John Rawls, "Justice as Fairness: Political Not Metaphysical," *Philosophy and Public Affairs* 14 (1985):249.

[2]John Dunn, *The Political Thought of John Locke* (Cambridge: Cambridge University Press, 1969), esp. chap. 4; *Rethinking Modern Political Theory* (Cambridge: Cambridge University Press, 1985), esp. chap. 2.

[3]I am indebted here to conversations with George Armstrong Kelly and Bonnie Honig.

antiliberal polemic than practitioners of that art have realized. If we leave aside the reasons for his relative neglect (at least in the anglophone literature), recent studies show him to have been a man of complex views and perhaps less opposed to "ancient" beliefs and values as such than to indiscriminate conflation of beliefs and values that are and should be kept distinct.[4] Again, classical utilitarianism, long treated as a form of liberalism, systematically and indeed insistently subordinates individual freedom to utility or the greatest happiness. J. S. Mill, for many the paradigmatic liberal, is famous for a spirited defense of freedom of thought and expression; but well-documented recent interpretations of his thought,[5] including accounts that absolve him of the cruder antifreedom features that have led recent liberals to disown Bentham and Mill's father, argue persuasively that Mill favored those freedoms primarily because they contribute to self-realization—an idealist or perfectionist concept whose salience in the self-announced liberalism of Green and Hobbhouse has often embarrassed liberals as well as their critics.

To bring this hurried assemblage of reminders up to some present writers, we note that Ronald Dworkin insists that equality, not freedom, is the "nerve" of liberal thought and denies that there can be any right to liberty.[6] John Rawls opposes the idea that there is a "presumption in favor of something called 'liberty'" and instead argues for a short list of "basic liberties" on the ground that they are necessary to justice or "fair cooperation."[7] Bruce Ackerman's conception of "neutrality" or "neutral dialogue" leads him to insist on a strong form of egalitarianism that would severely restrict a number of freedoms highly valued and strongly protected in self-styled liberal democracies.[8]

Whatever the merits of these particular qualifications on free-

[4]See, for example, Guy H. Dodge, *Benjamin Constant's Philosophy of Liberalism* (Chapel Hill: University of North Carolina Press, 1980); Stephen Holmes, *Benjamin Constant and the Making of Modern Liberalism* (New Haven: Yale University Press, 1984).

[5]See John Gray, *Mill on Liberty: A Defence* (London: Routledge & Kegan Paul, 1983); Fred Berger, *Happiness, Justice, and Freedom: The Moral and Political Philosophy of John Stuart Mill* (Berkeley: University of California Press, 1984).

[6]Ronald Dworkin, *A Matter of Principle* (Cambridge: Harvard University Press, 1985), p. 183; *Taking Rights Seriously* (Cambridge: Harvard University Press, 1977), esp. chap. 12.

[7]Rawls, "Justice as Fairness," pp. 232ff. and passim.

[8]Bruce Ackerman, *Social Justice in the Liberal State* (New Haven: Yale University Press, 1980).

dom, it is impossible to deny that individual freedom must be limited in various ways. The most obvious reason for this conclusion is that freedoms often conflict with one another, so that as a practical matter either there will be some sort of standoff or one freedom must take precedence over another or others. Because freedom and its values will be on both or all sides of such conflicts, the conflicts cannot be resolved without appeal to considerations other than freedom itself.[9] Beliefs and values not reducible to convictions about freedom necessarily enter into thought and action about freedom. Moreover, the recurrence in our tradition of distinctions such as between freedom and license is powerful evidence that further limitations will be thought necessary. In bare principle it is not impossible that "license" and related notions could be restricted to cases in which one or more sets of freedoms are in conflict; in even barer principle it is perhaps conceivable that conflicts between and among freedoms might be resolved in terms of some notion of maximizing freedom. But the latter combination of ideas may well be incoherent,[10] and notions such as license are in fact regularly and potently invoked in the name of numerous beliefs and values other than freedom itself. In attending to these matters, liberal theorists have done what any theorist must do.

We will be better placed to accommodate freedoms to one another and to harmonize freedom with other concerns if we have a clearly formulated view of why freedom is valuable. Critics of liberalism write as if "it" already includes such a formulation. If taken to mean that there is a view that is at once well articulated and widely accepted among those of a liberal persuasion, this suggestion is manifestly false; it would perhaps be more accurate to say that freedom has often been verbally honored but seldom clearly located or effectively defended in liberal thought; it is in any case undeniable that a number of the liberal writers who have considered the matter more closely have put freedom in a subordinate, perhaps a less than secure, position.

We find ourselves, then, in a complex and perhaps anomalous situation. Vociferous opponents of liberalism attribute to it an uncritical and unjustifiable commitment to individual freedom, an attribution that finds some support in the rhetoric of self-styled

[9]See H. L. A. Hart, *Essays in Jurisprudence and Philosophy* (Oxford: Clarendon Press, 1983), esp. chaps. 9 and 10.
[10]Cf. Dworkin, *A Matter of Principle*, p. 189.

liberal practices, ideologies, and theories, much less warrant in the details of those practices, ideologies, and theories. Thus (a) if liberalism does (or, consistent with other of its commitments, should) accord individual freedom the place its critics allege, it (b) might deserve the condemnations the latter direct against it. On the other hand, if (c) freedom deserves something akin to the place that critics allege liberals accord it, then liberals are subject, rather, to the criticism that (d) they do not clearly, or (e) clearly do not, accord freedom the place their detractors say they accord it.

Of these possibilities, I am disposed to (a) and (c), disposed against (b), and I argue accordingly in the remainder of this essay. I have already indicated my sympathy for (d) and (e), but for two reasons that are connected with each other and that influence my mode of argument concerning (a), (b), and (c), I will not offer further support for them here. First, (d) and (e) are propositions in intellectual history and in historical and contemporary political sociology. Confirming or disconfirming them would require detailed exegetical and otherwise empirical investigations well beyond the scope of this essay. Second and more important, to confirm or disconfirm (d) and (e) as propositions about *liberal* practices, ideologies, and theories would require that I abandon evasive phrases such as "self-declared" and "generally agreed" and specify the permissible range of the concepts "liberal," "liberalism," and the like. An account of the views about freedom of Bentham, or Mill, or Rawls, however well documented and convincing, would count for or against (d) and (e) only if it had also been established that they are (in the respects in question) properly regarded as liberal theorists. Even if it is in principle possible and desirable to settle this question (I have serious doubts on both but especially on the second score), it is obvious that I cannot hope to settle it here. Accordingly, I argue as best I can for a conception of the value of freedom. I call my conception "liberal" and I summon certain considerations in support of that designation and on behalf of the claim that the conception is an improvement over those offered by other self-identified liberals. But for present purposes the merits of the conception must be more important than the merits of calling it liberal.

Two further caveats before starting off. First, throughout I assume and employ a "negative" concept of "freedom" and "unfreedom." "Freedom" and "unfreedom" are predicates of human actions. Roughly, actions are taken by (and hence talk of both freedom and unfreedom presupposes) persons who are "agents," that is, persons who, in the setting of a community with a shared language and the elements that Wittgenstein and others have identified as necessary to such a language, form and hold beliefs; form desires and interests, objectives and purposes, that are influenced by their beliefs; frame intentions to act to satisfy their desires, interests, and so forth; and attempt to act on their intentions. Agents and actions are free insofar as their attempts to act are not prevented, impeded, or deflected from their objectives by the actions of other agents, and are unfree insofar as they are prevented, impeded, or deflected by the actions (including deliberate refusals to act) of other agents. In the absence of agency or action there is no "freedom-evaluability," nothing of which either freedom or unfreedom can be predicated. I have elsewhere defended this use of the concepts against arguments proceeding from various "positive" construals of them (and against the view that there are no significant differences between negative and positive formulations), and I can only refer readers who are skeptical on these points to that discussion.[11]

Second, the view of freedom I advance is general in character and therefore cannot itself dictate resolutions of particular conflicts among freedoms or between freedoms and other desiderata. If coherent and convincing, a general view of the value of freedom can influence and in some measure discipline the continuing task of arriving at circumstantial and revisable accommodations and harmonizations, but it cannot itself perform or displace that task. This feature of general theories is not infrequently overlooked or denied by theoreticians who claim that specific distributions of freedoms or of restrictions upon them are required by their theories. A subsidiary theme of this essay, connected in ways that I do not myself fully understand with my argument about the value of freedom, is that liberals (even if they can agree on few other things) ought to stand against such conceptions of the theory-practice relationship.

I

Among other things that they are, human beings are desiring, interest-pursuing, end-seeking, purposive creatures. Partly because

[11]Richard E. Flathman, *The Philosophy and Politics of Freedom*, pt. 1 (Chicago: University of Chicago Press, 1987).

of the character of their interests and desires, ends and purposes, and partly because of characteristics of the environment in which they live, in most cases they must take action to achieve their ends. Given these characteristics of human beings and their environment, freedom of action is a high-order human good, a condition or state of affairs on which human beings will, and in reason should, place high value. The value of freedom is not tied to a particular inventory of interests and desires, ends and purposes. The content or substance of human interests and desires varies from one person to the next and often changes substantially during the life history of a single person. Freedom is a good of great general value because it is necessary to the satisfaction of a great many interests and desires, the achievement of many ends and purposes, and contributive to the satisfaction and achievement of yet many more. Unfreedom is a serious evil because it prevents or inhibits achievements and satisfactions and produces frustration, distress, and harm.

There is a certain commonsensical quality to the foregoing remarks. If or insofar as we understand human beings in the ways I have employed, it seems obvious that a substantial freedom, a generous area of discretionary action, will be something valued by them and valuable to them. On the face of things, it is not easy to see how it could be denied that human beings have these characteristics or that, having them, freedom will be valuable to them.

In fact, however, there is nothing necessary, nothing rationally undeniable or indisputable about this reasoning or its conclusions. Empirically, we know of people who have very few desires, purposes, and the like, and of others who, owing to the combination of the character of their desires and the fact that their circumstances are especially favorable or unfavorable to satisfying them, have been understandably (if shortsightedly) indifferent to freedom. We are also familiar with thought experiments that imagine changes in human beings and their environment which would, if implemented, require us to qualify or abandon the reasoning. Finally, human beings and the human environment have features other than or additional to those on which my reasoning relies. Readers of these essays do not need to be told of the many attempts to ground normative thinking about freedom in considerations quite different from those I have urged.

It will emerge that the most important type of objection is the last one mentioned. But the more (or at least initially more) empirical objections require consideration in their own right, and examination will show that they merge into the difficulty last mentioned.

My initial response to the objection that the above reasoning misrepresents the facts on which it relies is as follows: perhaps the project of developing a general argument for freedom as opposed to particular freedoms is misbegotten. Perhaps such arguments will either be so abstract as to be vacuous or so hedged with qualifications as to be useless. But if there are to be such arguments, and if such arguments are to be based in part on facts about human beings, they will have to rest upon generalizations, not upon universal truths. The significant question about the reasoning I sketched is not whether we can identify exceptions to the generalizations I advanced about human beings and their circumstances; rather the question is whether exceptions occur so frequently as to make it clumsy and distracting to rely on the generalizations in forming a general orientation toward or perspective concerning freedom. If we accept the reasoning I sketched, we will approach concrete issues concerning freedom with a certain set of expectations and with concepts and principles in which and with which to assess what we actually encounter. If our expectations are confuted, if our talk of the importance of freedom to satisfying desires and interests, achieving ends and purposes, regularly elicits incomprehension or hostility, what was intended to be a simplifying and facilitating move will complicate and divert our reasoning and our judging. Rather than being able to subsume particulars under agreed categories and principles, we will have to defend the generalizations on which our categories and principles depend. But if this happens only rarely or exceptionally we will (so far as the objection I am considering is concerned) be justified in taking our bearings from those generalizations so long as we remain alert to the possibility of exceptions to them.

There is every reason to believe that the reasoning I sketched would be irrelevant or distracting in numerous societies and cultures. Implicit in that reasoning is an understanding that I earlier called the liberal principle, or LP: namely, that it is prima facie a good thing for individuals to form, to act on, and more or less regularly to satisfy (their) interests and desires, their ends and purposes.[12] But this idea has or has had little or no acceptance, little or

12Richard E. Flathman, *The Practice of Rights* (Cambridge: Cambridge University Press, 1976), pp. 7–8, 44–47, 167–81.

no standing, in numerous cultures and societies. Some cultures have regarded desires and interests, particularly desires and interests of individual persons, as prima facie or even categorically bad or wrong. The first, perhaps even the exclusive, concern has been to abide by the divine laws and commands, to discharge duties assigned by the collectivity, to pursue the common good, advance the mission of the church, the class, or the party. Individual interests are to be subordinated if not rooted out. If individual freedom has been valued at all in such societies (and characteristically such societies prize the authority of the collectivity over its individual members, the freedom of the collectivity vis-à-vis other collectivities), it has been not for the reasons I sketched above but because individual freedom (or the freedom of certain select types of individuals) enhances extra- or supra-individual goods and ideals. If one argued for individual freedom on the grounds I sketched, one would be arguing against—not from—the prevailing conceptions of, the prevailing beliefs about and values concerning, human beings.

The foregoing remarks underscore the underdefended character of the reasoning I presented for the value of freedom. The factual generalizations I advanced may be true of only some cultures and societies. But even if they are quite generally *true,* they will be accepted as elements in an argument for freedom only in societies in which they are positively valorized. A premise in my reasoning is axiological in character and attributes positive value to the state of affairs described by the empirical generalizations I advanced about human beings and their circumstances. LP is one possible formulation of such an axiological premise or principle: human beings do, or should, not only recognize but accept that they are desiring, interest-seeking, end-pursuing, purposive creatures whose well-being consists in important part in being able to pursue and satisfy their individual interests and desires, ends and purposes, and whose well-being is therefore enhanced by circumstances that are conducive to their doing so.

It is clear that premises of this character have been entirely rejected (or never considered) in some human societies and have been accepted only with severe qualification in numerous others. But it seems equally clear that premises of this character have been promoted to the standing of principles by persons influential in the shaping of modern Western societies and are in fact widely influential among the members of those societies. The fact that my sketch, abbreviated as it is, is intelligible and even commonsensical can perhaps be taken to testify to the correctness of these assumptions. The sketch is intelligible because it proceeds from, is a modest elaboration on, thinking that is widely received in modern Western societies.

My sketch is nevertheless eminently disputable, disputable from within the confines of thinking widely received in the societies in question here. It can be controverted without adopting ascetical, perfectionist, or collectivist views more radical than those influential in the societies in question. One way to dispute it is to argue that it provides too weak an argument for freedom. By making the value of freedom instrumental to the good that is the pursuit and satisfaction of interests and desires, ends and purposes, it leaves freedom's value hostage to psychological and cultural contingencies. The value of freedom may be augmented by considerations such as those I have adduced, but its deeper grounding is, or should be made, more secure. Freedom is an inherent or intrinsic, not an instrumental, good. Or at least its value in human life is due to features of human beings that are less variable, less culture specific or dependent (and more noble, elevated, or at least dignified?) than "interestedness," "desirousness," and purposiveness.

Intrinsic, inherent, and related terms are sometimes used as epistemological concepts signaling a direct or unmediated intuition or other apprehension of truths about which evidence or argumentation other than the experience of the intuition itself are impossible or irrelevant. The deepest difficulties with this notion need not be rehearsed here. It suffices to say that, as a moral and political matter, this view engenders dogmatism and helps not at all in resolving questions about conflicts among freedoms and between freedom and various other goods.

Leaving aside arguments about freedom as opposed to determinism (metaphysical freedom) and about physical movement as distinct from action, it will nevertheless repay us to consider one further version of the idea that freedom is an intrinsic, not merely an instrumental, good. The argument in question is that both the fact of and a high regard for freedom of action is one of the deepest conventions of and, in that Wittgensteinian sense, a starting point of thought and action in our culture. It is intrinsic to our moral and political practice in the normative sense that any practice that is deeply incompatible with or generally destructive of freedom of action is therefore, without the need of further evidence or argumentation, deemed unacceptable. We do not argue for the value of freedom: our moral and political argumentation starts from, is premised on, its value. This view is consistent with dispute as to what counts as freedom and unfreedom, as to whether this or that arrangement or action serves or disserves freedom, and whether freedom in this or that respect should properly be subordinated or sacrificed, here and now, to some other value or good. But arguments against freedom as such, and hence arguments for policies and practices that are categorically or even generally antifreedom, are not countenanced.

Something like this sense of freedom as an intrinsic good is involved in Stanley Benn's discussion of the principle of noninterference (PNI).[13] Insofar as we have made it a *principle* that the burden of justification falls on anyone who proposes to interfere in or with the actions of other persons, our day-to-day reasoning *begins* with the idea or belief that freedom is a high-order good. Interferences with freedom must be justified in the face of or despite the fact that they contravene or diminish that good. The fact that we entertain and accept such justifications shows that freedom is not an absolute in the sense of a good that takes precedence whenever it is involved or at issue. But it is an intrinsic good in the sense that it is a feature of our practices that must be understood in order to comprehend those practices and one that must be accepted in order to participate intelligently and defensibly or respectably in them. An observer who did not grasp what might be called the constitutive character of the good would fail to understand much of what goes on among us; the actions and arguments of participants who did not grasp the standing of that good would almost certainly—that is, apart from quite remarkable coincidences—meet with antagonism or incomprehension from other participants.

Unlike the first construal of "intrinsic" I considered, this one does not exclude the *possibility* of arguments for the value of freedom. Of course the claim that the good of freedom is intrinsic in this sense suggests that such arguments will rarely be encountered in explicit form: for the most part arguments for the good will be unnecessary in the sense that they will be redundant. It may even be difficult for

---

[13]Stanley Benn, "Freedom, Autonomy, and the Concept of a Person," *Proceedings of the Aristotelian Society* 76 (1976):109–30.

participants to think of considerations, independent of the good, in terms of which to argue for its standing as such. But this difficulty is social-psychological, not logical or epistemological in character, and there are reasons for thinking that it is valuable to do what we can to overcome it.

Leaving aside reasons that hold for all of our beliefs and values (for example Socrates' view that the unexamined life is not worth living, J. S. Mill's view that people who do not know, or who have lost sight of, the reasons for their beliefs and values do not fully know *what* they believe and value), two such reasons are especially pertinent. The first is grounded in the fact that freedom of action as a high-order value is rejected in many cultures and societies. If it is true that the value is deeply embedded in modern Western societies, it is important that those who reject or challenge it understand that, and why, this is the case. It may be a kind of response to such challenges to say, "This is what we think; this is how we do things hereabouts." It may even be that disagreements about the value of freedom of action, as with differences of religious belief, run so deep that mutual understanding and accommodation is the best that, or even more than, can be hoped. But even this modest objective is furthered if the parties to the disagreements can articulate for themselves and to others the grounds on which their views rest.

The second reason is grounded in two facts. I have already mentioned the first of these, namely, that we experience freedom and its value and disvalue by exercising various freedoms, and these freedoms sometimes conflict with one another and with other of our values. Conflicts among freedoms could be resolved by appeal to the value of freedom per se only if we could make sense of the notion of maximizing freedom, and in any case such an appeal would resolve conflicts with other values only if we elevated freedom to the top of a strictly hierarchical value structure (to first position on a lexically ordered list of values), that is, only if we made freedom an absolute as well as an intrinsic value. Having more rather than less clearly delineated general reasons for valuing freedom of action will not settle, certainly it will not still, all questions about the comparative importance of freedom or of various freedoms. But it would be irrationalist or antirationalist to assume that no such reasons are available or that having such reasons will be of no use in resolving such issues (or at least in remaining civil with one another as we attempt such resolutions and as we live with our no more than partial successes). The second of these facts is that there is lively controversy in the literature of moral and political philosophy concerning why freedom should be valued and how its value should be compared with a variety of other desiderata. In addition to being intellectually engaging in its own right, this controversy reflects—albeit no doubt imperfectly—issues, positions, and arguments that are prominent outside of philosophical books and journals.

To summarize this stretch of discussion, it is plausible to treat freedom of agency as an intrinsic good in our moral and political practices in the sense that its being a good is a datum in or of those practices. If so, the fact that it is no less than a datum is vital to understanding and to participation in those practices. The fact that it is, qua *intrinsic* good, no more than a datum means that the question of why freedom of agency should be valued (and hence, finally, whether and how much it should be valued) invites our reflection. Because this version of the idea that freedom is an intrinsic good is the only one that is both plausible and pertinent to our present concerns, I can summarize the discussion of that beguiling idea by restating my original contention: freedom of agency is a contingent and an instrumental good, albeit one that is contingent on factual generalizations about human beings that are difficult to dispute and instrumental to values that are widely shared and deeply established in modern Western societies.

II

I henceforth refer to the belief-cum-principle that freedom is a high-order good as the general presumption in favor of freedom, or GPF. On the reasoning I have thus far given (as distinct from my claim that something like this belief-cum-principle is a datum of our culture), GPF is an inference from (not an entailment of) the evaluations expressed by principles such as PNI or LP. If we accept these evaluations, we have reasons to endorse and to act on GPF. For present purposes the question then becomes whether we can further strengthen the case for GPF as a general presumption or principle of thought and action.

Disposed as I am to defend GPF, I will treat this question as how best to argue for it. But of course pursuing this objective requires identifying and assessing the merits of arguments against the principle.

Continuing to work with the sketch I first set out, the chief task is further to defend LP or some principle analogous to it. I say this because the other main elements in the argument, generalizations about human beings and their circumstances and about features of our culture, are less likely to be disputed. Of course there is no shortage of objections to self-interest and its pursuit or to desires and desirousness (albeit arguments against end seeking and purposiveness are rare, a point to which I return below). But most such objections, certainly within our culture, are to the effect that human beings *should not* do these things or *should* subordinate the doing of these things to other of their activities, other of their characteristics. People who advance such arguments typically allow that the generalizations are (all too) accurate concerning human beings as we in fact encounter them in our culture. Their contention is that these characteristics are unfortunate and that the freedom to indulge them is anything but a good thing.

The first task, accordingly, is to defend the idea that it is good for human beings to form, to act on, and to satisfy interests and desires. If this idea can be defended, the further ideas—that freedom of action is a high-order human good and that a heavy burden of justification should fall on those who propose to limit, qualify, or interfere with it—will be easier to defend.

The most uncompromising opposition to LP comes from proponents of various forms of asceticism or self-denial. In considering this source of objections we should first note that at least some of their force is blunted by attention to the elements out of which LP is formed and to the formulation of LP itself.

Asceticism is at its apparently most potent (at least in its secularized forms) when it objects to desires and desire satisfaction, particularly when it interprets desires as passions that "well up in," "take over," and otherwise supplant or obliterate the more rational, the more disciplined, the higher human faculties. Surrendering to these passions, "wallowing in them" in the sense of letting them and their satisfaction become the sole or primary raison d'être of one's existence, is "de-grading"; instead of living up to one's "grade," one's capacities or potential as given by God, or nature, or the culture into which one is born, the desirous, sensual, hedonistic person sinks to or below the level of nonhuman animals. Insofar as the sensualist can be said to have an aim or project, that project is self-defeating. Desires beget desires in a "bad infinite" that may spiral down to "polymorphous perversity" and that in any case excludes the possibility of more than ephemeral, more than un-satisfying satisfactions.

This picture is implausible if desires and action on desires are properly understood.[14] Beliefs that are subject to correction and if corrected will alter the desire, identification of objects that will satisfy the desire, choice of courses of action likely to attain those objects—all of these are features of desires and actions to satisfy them. None of this prevents desires from being unseemly, debased, or repugnant to others, and it certainly does not guarantee that the actions taken to achieve them will be acceptable to others. But the idea that forming and acting to satisfy desires is itself an abandon-ment of the true or higher human capacities is largely a misunder-standing. The unqualified, necessarily debased sensuality attacked by asceticisms from fourth-century anchorites to Schopenhauer is in the realm of behavior, not desires and action on desires. There may be a case for freedom of such behavior, but it is not the same case as the case for freedom of action.

The second element in LP—namely, interests and attempts to serve them—is most commonly attacked not on the ascetical ground that it is degenerate but rather that it is narrowly calculating, egois-tic, and socially divisive. The "interested" person uses her capacities for discernment, judgment, and evaluation, but she does so with no more than instrumental regard for others and hence, on some for-mulations of anti-interest argumentation, shortsightedly from the standpoint of her own larger or longer-term interests. As the last clause reminds us, however, the objection that actions motivated by interests are selfish in antisocial or immoral ways, or even impru-dent, is contingent on the character of certain interests and certain strategies for satisfying them. Notions such as Tocqueville's "en-lightened self-interest" and J. S. Mill's "permanent interests of man as a progressive being" (and of course yet wider uses of the concept such as in the philosophies of Ralph Barton Perry and Jürgen Habermas) make it clear that these objections have no application against much thought and action standardly characterized as "self-interested."

It is no part of my intention to deny that much that occurs in human affairs in the name of desires, interests, and their pursuit and satisfaction is objectionable and—albeit this is a further point—

[14]I rely here on an analysis of desires and interests presented in part 1 of Flath-man, *The Philosophy and Politics of Freedom.*

justifiably prevented. But recognizing this provides no reason for objecting to LP. LP says that it is prima facie a good thing for human beings to have, to act on, and to satisfy desires and interests. If categorical objections to desires and interests (or "desirous" and "interested" conduct) are without merit, it remains open to us to adopt LP and the presumption it establishes in favor of human desires and interests and then to consider arguments that this or that desire or interest, as pursued in these or those circumstances, is nevertheless objectionable. Nor does this stance or strategy debar the conclusion that certain subclasses of desires and interests are generally objectionable and to be discouraged. If we are committed to LP we will, of course, view such reversals of the burden of proof with suspicion; but the logic of the principle itself, featuring as it does both "prima facie" and the comparative notion of "good," requires that we remain open to the possibility that they will sometimes be justified.

Aside from the last comments about LP, my remarks thus far are modest elaborations of the point that the concepts "desire" and "interest" are situated in the Wittgensteinian sense that they are part of a conceptual system governed by widely accepted conventions and rules. Although capacious in that they accommodate a wide range of beliefs and objects, they are concepts, not mere words or markers, "somethings," not "anythings." The desires and interests that we can form and pursue are restricted in ways either misunderstood or ignored by ascetical critics.

The conventions and rules that govern "desire" and "interest" are, of course, open textured and subject to change. They are part of language-games and forms of life that are internally complex and changeable and that are influenced by activities and developments more or less independent from them. I am not suggesting that there is a fixed inventory of possible interests and desires or that either the fear of declension or the hope of an ascension in their usual or predominant character is *necessarily* misplaced or misbegotten. But attention to secular tendencies in the language-games of desire and interest will further disqualify the more fervid concerns that they sometimes arouse.

According to Albert Hirschman, the concepts of interests and self-interest came into prominence in Western thought in contrast with and as means of controlling the very notions—that is, "passions,"—to which ascetical and anti-interest writers are prone to assimilate them. Further abbreviating a complex story that Hirschman himself has severely compressed, as confidence declined that reason (and, one should add, faith and its discipline) could control the violent and destructive passions, the idea developed that interests could help to tame them, to domesticate them sufficiently to make peaceful social life possible. Denoting "an element of reflection and calculation with respect to the manner in which [human] aspirations were to be pursued,"[15] interests came to be regarded as more potent sources of motivation than abstract reason and yet less divisive and destructive than passions. "Once passion was deemed destructive and reason ineffectual, the view that human action could be exhaustively described [in their terms] meant an exceedingly somber outlook for humanity. A message of hope was . . . conveyed by the wedging of interest in between the two traditional categories. . . . Interest was seen to partake in effect of the better nature of each, as the passion of self-love upgraded and contained by reason, and as reason given direction and force by passion."[16]

On the view of interests Hirschman describes, severely ascetical forms of anti-interest argumentation are not only archaic but self-defeating in that they demean and condemn the forms of motivation-cum-reason for action most likely to prevent degeneration to the unbridled and destructive sensuality that those who advance such arguments fear and despise. Strikingly, the "element of reflection and calculation" of which Hirschman writes corresponds closely to features still "denoted" by "desire" as well as by "interest."

In an analysis that endorses but extends Hirschman's, Stephen Holmes develops further themes pertinent here. Focusing primarily on seventeenth- and eighteenth-century materials, Holmes argues that interests were distinguished from and preferred to notions of privilege and paternalism. The allegedly more elevated character of the latter bases for and motivations to action came to be viewed as a device for giving a spurious legitimacy to social and political arrangements that were oppressive insofar as they were effective and increasingly ineffective in maintaining peace and order:

> Liberals turned a friendly eye toward self-interest to discredit the degrading ranks of prestige and chains of dependency characterizing the old regime. . . . By focusing on [desires and] interests, and by

[15]Albert Hirschman, *The Passions and the Interests* (Princeton: Princeton University Press, 1979), p. 32.
[16]Ibid., p. 43.

attributing paramount importance to self-preservation, Hobbes strove to put an end to the English Civil Wars. His aim was not to promote the interests of the merchant class, though that may have been a side-effect of what he did. By discrediting [for political purposes] the ideals of glory and salvation, he hoped to encourage peace.[17]

Holmes's remark about the merchant class alludes to objections to interests and interest-oriented conduct that became familiar after the period he is discussing; but the arresting feature of the contrasts he is most concerned to draw is that they are between, on the one hand, the desires and interests promoted by liberals and by Hobbes and, on the other, forms of thought and action that *in fact* are self-indulgent and self-defeating in just the ways *attributed to* desires and interests by severe critics of the latter. Holmes's liberals distinguish claims based on shareable and, in principle, mutually reconcilable desires and interests from entitlements of place and privilege which are insisted (by their holders and defenders) to be incommensurable with such desires and interests. Because the entitlements are regarded by their claimants as intrinsically superior, they can be accommodated to or harmonized with the ordinary run of desires and interests only in the weak sense that the latter might be given consideration after the superior entitlements have been fully honored. Holmes's Hobbes distinguishes desires and interests, which can be pursued and satisfied by all members of a society, from ideals of character and conduct, which their partisans at least tacitly concede to be unshareable or at least undistributable. In fact, however, the privileges the liberals attacked are self-, class-, or caste-indulgent in at least two senses: (a) they are *excessive* in demanding a gross superfluity of wealth and power, and (b) they are unjustifiably *exclusive* in that they are restricted to a small and assignable number of persons or to specific classes or castes with fixed memberships. Because of these characteristics, claims to the privileges are self-defeating: if satisfied they corrupt their beneficiaries at the same time that they harm those from whom the benefits are extracted; the corruption of the former and the oppression of the latter delegitimate the claims to them so that the claims must either be abandoned or enforced by tyrannical means that are costly in themselves and that sooner or later incite revolts that destroy the system of privileges. The ideals of character that Hobbes attacks are

---

[17]Holmes, *Benjamin Constant and the Making of Modern Liberalism*, p. 253.

(again from a political standpoint) self-indulgent in the sense of having an exclusivity closely analogous to that already discussed (they are aristocratic ideals) and self-defeating because conduct in pursuit of them is incompatible with a society stable enough to allow such conduct to flourish. By comparison with both the privileges and the ideals, the *allegedly* self-indulgent and self-destructive desires and interests are shareable and are supportive of a peaceful and stable social and political order.

The particular passions, privileges, and ideals at issue in the controversies Hirschman and Holmes report play a smaller part in the debates of our own time. But in form these early defenses of desires and interests are responsive to any attempt to discredit them either as self-indulgent or self-defeating. Because such attempts remain common in our time, the defenses are pertinent to present concerns.[18] The timeliness of yet wider moral and political views that were part of the thinking Holmes discusses is evident from a further passage from his work. When asserted against views such as Maistre's that "human individuality" is a "nullity" from God's point of view, "self-interest was a dimension of self-affirmation." Yet more broadly, it was important to the thinking of Constant and others of his time that interests "are distributed without regard to birth: they are just as independent of the social status of your family as they are of your religious beliefs. To act upon interest is to claim the status of an equal—of a masterless man."[19] Here we have much more than a defense of desires and interests against various traditional charges, much more than a claim that interests and desires do not have various unacceptable characteristics and consequences. In these formulations, developing, pursuing, and satisfying interests and desires are positive goods, are characteristics that deserve to be valued, protected, and promoted. They are made central to conceptions of individuality, of equality, and of freedom and hence are fundamental to a society suitable to human beings as liberals had come to conceive of them. We are not to apologize for our "desirousness" and "interestedness"; we are to insist on them.

These last views are in effect arguments for LP (or at least PNI) and GPF. They say that human beings have certain pronounced characteristics, and they make connections between those charac-

---

[18]Cf. Holmes: "Even today, antiliberal attacks on self-interest express nostalgia for systems of deference, authority, and condescension" (ibid.).

[19]Ibid., pp. 252–53.

teristics and values that should be central to society. If analysis of "desires" and "interests" helps to defend these notions against certain persistent forms of attack, the linkage between them and equality and freedom not only legitimates but positively promotes them. Combining Hirschman and Holmes, we can say that the thinkers Holmes discusses were doing two things at once. They were promoting equality among and the freedom of individuals in a society that had begun to accept these values, but in which opposition to the values remained strong. In order to do so, they drew on the emerging legitimacy of desires and interests to affirm a notion of the individual for whom equality and freedom were appropriate. By tying the two sets of notions together, they gave support to both. And the resulting combination constitutes an argument for LP and GPF.

Of course this combination and hence this argument for LP and GPF can be and has been resisted. If Rawls and others are correct that an at least implicit commitment to freedom and equality is the distinctive feature of moral and political thought and practice in modern Western societies, then one of the pairs that form the combination has been generally accepted. And while it can hardly be denied that desires and interests are widely regarded as *legitimate,* and are viewed yet more positively than this term suggests by many people in these societies, more and less vehement antidesires and anti-interests views remain familiar among us. Perhaps some who hold such views are also opposed to freedom and equality, but it is implausible to think that this is always or even commonly the case. We cannot assume that arguments for LP and GPF which depend on the combination just discussed will be generally convincing.

Let us *reculer pour mieux sauter.* Let us assume that Hirschman is correct in his claim that desires and interests have been recognized as prominent characteristics of the members of our societies and that these characteristics have been legitimated to the extent that generalized stigma no longer attaches to them. Forming, pursuing, and satisfying desires and interests may not have attained to the standing of prima facie goods, but they have shed the disrepute that once attached to them. (Or at least let us assume that the arguments supporting generalized hostility to desires and interests have been shown to be without merit and hence that in reason generalized stigma ought not to attach to them.)

On these assumptions, a number of further arguments can be made for LP and GPF as normative principles. These arguments can be introduced by making a comparison. Consider the phenomenon of children, wives, employees, soldiers, and so forth who are told to "think for themselves," "take initiative," "be independent," and the like, but whose every thought and initiative is disapproved and rejected. Such people quickly learn either to dismiss as insincere the advice and await the forthcoming directives (perhaps simulating thought, initiative, and independence) or to rebel against the disapprovals and rejections and pursue their chosen courses as best they can. Either way, the practical incompatibilities among the demands made upon them are a source of severe and often damaging confusion and frustration.

There is a strong and positive analogy between this phenomenon and the situation that would obtain in a society that legitimated the formation and pursuit of desires and interests but that rejected LP (or at least PNI) and GPF. Encouraging an employee to think for herself and to take initiative does not commit superiors to agree with her every thought or to applaud the particulars of all the initiatives she takes. But doing the former in good faith creates, or rather carries with it, several presumptions. The most obvious of these are the presumptions that the superior believes that the employee is in fact capable of the kind of conduct in question (at least latently so) and that the superior genuinely encourages or perhaps authorizes her to engage in it. Taken together, these two presumptions carry a third, a guarded formulation (akin to PNI) of which is as follows: if the superior disapproves or rejects the employee's thoughts and initiatives, she must justify doing so and must do so in terms responsive to the particulars of the thoughts and initiatives in question. We might say that the superior must present such justifications in order to avoid engendering dissonance, exasperation, and the like in the employee. But since it is only very likely and not certain that these consequences will be produced, we should first say that in practical reasoning anyone who understands the first two presumptions will also accept the third.

The parallels between the first two presumptions and my Hirschmanesque assumptions about the recognition and legitimacy of desires and interests is clear enough (a possible difference being that *legitimacy* may be a weaker term than *encourages* or even *authorizes* in the second presumption). In the guarded form in which I stated the third presumption, something like Benn's PNI is more closely parallel to it than is LP. This is because neither PNI nor the third presumption as stated imply or even suggest a disposition positively to approve, or even an expectation that one very likely will approve, the content of the thoughts and initiatives. The idea is more formalistic; having licensed or authorized the thinking or the initiative taking, the superior is obliged to justify disapprovals and rejections of their content; having recognized and legitimated a tendency to form and pursue desires and interests, society is obliged to justify interferences with manifestations of that tendency.

The less guarded formulation of the third presumption parallels the more positive idea expressed by LP—that forming, pursuing, and satisfying desires and interests is prima facie a good. Having judged the employee capable of thinking for herself and of taking initiative, and genuinely approving of her doing so, the superior is disposed to approve her thought and her initiative or at least maintains a grounded expectation that she will approve of them. Rather than a mere, perhaps even a somewhat grudging, formal authorization, the superior has wholeheartedly and out of genuine conviction encouraged the thinking and the initiating. (The more positive formulation of the third presumption goes better with "genuinely approved" than with "legitimated" in the second presumption.) Her reasons for having done so create and support a disposition or expectation to approve the actual content of the thinking or of the initiatives. Society's reasons for recognizing and genuinely approving the formation, pursuit, and satisfaction of desires and interests carry over to and inform its response to the desires and interests actually formed and pursued. "Prima facie" does not mean "initially and formally but readily subject to justified exception"; it means "for good general reasons that are expected to hold in most cases albeit subject to the possibility of justified exceptions."

My claim, then, is that the legitimation of desires and interests charted by Hirschman and Holmes itself supports an argument that goes beyond legitimation. In the weaker forms that stop at rebutting generalized objections to desires and interests, the legitimation of the latter supports PNI and GPF. It does so in the internalist sense that those who understand and accept the legitimation and the reasons for it will understand and accept PNI-GPF and also in the consequentialist sense that accepting legitimation but rejecting PNI-GPF will very likely create confusion, frustration, and conflict. In

the stronger formulations involving genuine approval of desirousness and interestedness (for example, those formulations that link
desires and interests closely to freedom and equality), legitimation
itself supports LP in both the internalist and the consequentialist
renderings of "supports." In short, to reject PNI-GPF or LP-GPF,
one would have to adopt some version of the views that come to be
rejected in the period studied by Hirschman and Holmes and that
comport very badly with the present logic of "desires" and "interests." At a minimum we are entitled to conclude that generalized
anti-interest and antidesire arguments are either confused or deeply
radical in the sense of rejecting an interwoven and mutually rein-
forcing set of beliefs and values which is very firmly established in
modern Western societies. In a society that recognizes and has
legitimated desires and interests, LP is appropriate at least as a
principle of mutual toleration or a weak principle of equality. In a
society that genuinely respects individuality and diversity, certainly
in one with a genuine enthusiasm for them, it recommends itself
much more strongly. If desires and interests are in fact among our
salient characteristics, and if we genuinely accept and value this fact
about ourselves, we will accord one another's desires and interests
the presumptions expressed in and required by LP.

III

If it is easy to list moralists who object to desires and interests, it is
difficult to identify any who object to "end-seekingness" and purposiveness. Neither "end" nor "purpose" has been associated with
passion, impulses, and other subjectivist or even "animal" notions
that are prominent features of the literature concerning desires and
interests. It is true that virtue-, duty-, and rights-oriented theorists
argue that the pursuit of the ends and purposes we form should be
disciplined by principles and rules of conduct that are in some sense
independent of those ends and purposes. It is also true that teleological and consequentialist theories that reject or seem unable to
accommodate such disciplining principles and rules have been much
criticized. But virtue theorists identify the virtues they promote as
qualities of character that are necessary or strongly conducive to the
achievement of certain end states judged to be suitable to human
beings at their best; most deontologists have allowed that the con-

straints of duties and of rights, even if in some sense self-justifying, are constraints on end-seeking, purposive activities and would have no application to creatures who do not engage in such activities.[20]

The fact that LP includes ends and purposes among the prima facie goods means that, formally or conceptually, it has room for, it can accommodate, the as it were positive concerns or objectives just mentioned. When combined with the foregoing arguments about desires and interests this suggests that, formally, LP should prompt few if any objections. Indeed, in respect to the more individualist of the rights-oriented deontological theories, we can make the stronger claim that something akin to LP is presupposed by them. Rights are discretionary, not mandatory; they leave it to the right bearer to determine whether to take the class of actions that the right protects. At a minimum, this allows that agents may make these determinations on the basis of their ends and purposes as they see them. If end-seeking, purposive conduct were not at least a prima facie good, it is difficult to see how such discretion could be justified. In this perspective, decisions to establish rights are based on judgments that certain classes of ends and purposes are especially important and deserve not merely the protection afforded by LP and GPF (the protection afforded by a right in the sense of a "liberty" in Hohfeld's schema),[21] but the further protection afforded by a right (a "claim-right" or "right in the strict sense" in the Hohfeldian vocabulary).

But proponents of the doctrines just mentioned typically argue not for end seeking or purposiveness as such, but for particular, more or less definite ends or purposes that they regard as embodying the ideals or excellences of human life. In the moderately technical language now current, proponents of these doctrines are advocates of perfectionism.[22] Accordingly, the fact that LP includes an endorsement of "ends" and "purposes" in abstract, generic terms is not likely to heighten their enthusiasm for it. Perfectionists cannot

---

[20]See esp. John Rawls, "The Basic Liberties and Their Priority," in *The Tanner Lectures on Human Values,* vol. 3, ed. S. M. McMurrin (Salt Lake City: University of Utah Press, 1982), p. 49; "Kantian Constructivism in Moral Theory," *Journal of Philosophy* 77 (1980):530.

[21]See Wesley N. Hohfeld, *Fundamental Legal Conceptions* (New Haven: Yale University Press, 1919).

[22]I believe that the concept acquired its present prominence because of its central place in Rawls's work. See *A Theory of Justice* (Cambridge: Harvard University Press, 1971), esp. p. 25 and sec. 50.

deny that LP as an axiological principle formally *encompasses* the ends and purposes they favor. Nor can they deny that an argument for freedom of action grounded in LP will provide support for freedom to pursue those ends and purposes. But they will surely object that the support it offers for those freedoms is much too weak, and they surely will also object that it offers at least initial support for freedoms that are insupportable. The axiological principles of society should *coincide with* the inventory of substantive ends and purposes that perfectionists favor (or at least the axiological principles should exclude all ends, purposes, and other reasons for action that conflict with pursuit of the ends and purposes perfectionists favor).

As a first step in assessing these objections, it will be helpful to consider the case of freedom of religious belief and practice. For people who are indifferent about religion, the religious desires and interests, ends and purposes that people in fact have and pursue are as eligible for the standing of prima facie goods as any other. Moreover, according a wide freedom for religious practice may diminish conflicts that might prevent or inhibit other activities supported by LP.

But what about people who are convinced that their beliefs, whether pro or antireligion, are true not merely in the sense that they themselves hold them but simply or unqualifiedly? Consider the atheist who is satisfied that she has conclusive arguments against the existence of a divine being and who is also convinced that all forms of religiosity are worse than vulgar superstition. Or consider the believer who is "morally certain" of the truth of her specifically religious beliefs and who is equally convinced that irreligiosity and religious diversity make so much as decency impossible in human society. For such people religious freedom will seem much worse than a poor thing. How can it be, even prima facie, a good thing to maintain practices that are false and harmful? How can society allow, let alone endorse as a good, ends and purposes that lead to action destructive of human well-being?

Of course atheists and believers can accept a generous religious freedom as a lesser evil. If it has proven to be genuinely impossible to win general acceptance of the beliefs and practices that are true and good, we retreat to that arrangement to protect such truth and goodness as obtains among us, and we regretfully pay the price of tolerating beliefs and practices known by us to be false and harmful.

But we do not pretend that what we know to be false is prima facie true or that what we know to be harmful is prima facie good. Indeed, we do not pretend that the arrangement that protects the false and the harmful is anything better than an unfortunate necessity, an evil that we accept because it is least among the evils with which we are confronted. (Somewhat more positively, the arrangement might be defended as a way of buying time. By protecting the good practices that exist among us we preserve the possibility that example and argument will win converts enough to permit us to advance to something better.)

Perfectionist positions in respect to moral and political questions are analogous to (albeit not necessarily fully parallel with) the position of the atheist and believer as just discussed. There are ends and purposes that are good simply or all things considered, not merely prima facie. There are others that are clearly wrong or harmful or evil. In the latter cases the burden of justification falls on anyone who proposes to pursue those ends and purposes, not on those who object to them. How we should go about promoting good ends and purposes, and how dispositions and attempts to pursue bad or evil ones should be discouraged or prevented, are of course further questions. But actions and arrangements that are means to achieving good ends take at least initial justification from that fact about them, and actions and arrangements that are means of preventing the pursuit or achievement of evil ends take initial justification from that fact about them. Insofar as perfectionists have concerned themselves with freedom, freedom to pursue good ends is easily justified; certainly freedom to pursue evil ends is objectionable and restrictions on such freedom are easily justified.

As with strongly convinced atheists and with religious believers in respect to freedom of religion, convinced moral and political perfectionists might accept or accommodate themselves to a view of freedom that maintains wide latitude in the pursuit of individual ends and purposes. They could accept moral and political toleration as a lesser evil or as a temporizing device. Society averts its glance, at least its organized, collective glance, from much that is undoubtedly objectionable and even harmful, reserving its collective notice and its collective, authoritative action to the most directly and seriously harmful activities of its members. Nevertheless, within the compass of their perfectionism—that is, in respect to the ends and purposes that they judge to be undeniably evil or harmful—a moral and political perfectionist must regard such arrangements as no better than arrangements of toleration. They can no more cherish or delight in such arrangements and the freedoms of action they recommend than the deeply committed atheist or believer can cherish or delight in freedom of religious belief and practice.

IV

My remarks about ends and purposes are overly schematic in respects that would have to be remedied in a full discussion. For one thing, there are numerous versions of perfectionism, and it would be wrong to suggest that they all involve the same stance toward or the same implications concerning LP and GPF. (Consider, for example, the difference among T. H. Green and Friedrich Nietzsche, Alasdair MacIntyre and Hannah Arendt. Each of these writers is plausibly regarded as a perfectionist in Rawls's sense, but their conceptions of the good or ideal to be pursued, their conceptualizations of freedom, and their assessments of the value of freedom or various freedoms to achieving the good or ideal, vary widely.) For another, there are well-developed positions that reject both LP-GPF and perfectionism.

I cannot discuss these variations in detail, but I suggest that they share an objectionable feature, namely, privileging certain ends or purposes so strongly as to categorically exclude the possibility of justifying actions (and hence freedom to take those actions) which conflict with the preferred ends and purposes. I conclude by developing and briefly defending this suggestion by reference to a view, that of John Rawls, which sharply challenges my argument but does so from a position that shares many of the assumptions from which I have been arguing and a number of the conclusions I have drawn.

Although allowing that his theory includes "ideal-regarding" as distinct from "want-regarding" principles,[23] Rawls rejects perfectionism in the sense of views that claim there is a single substantive conception of the good that ought to be accepted by all persons and that should be adopted and implemented by politically organized societies.[24] But he also rejects, or rather sharply qualifies, LP and

[23]Ibid., pp. 326–27.
[24]Ibid., pp. 326ff., 414ff.

GPF, arguing against them that interests and desires that conflict with the principles of justice deserve no consideration and that freedom to pursue such interests and desires can never be justified.[25]

It is important to recognize that Rawls's principles of justice hold only in respect to the "basic structure" of politically organized society, and that outside of the ambit of that structure he endorses a position very close to the one I have presented here. As the term itself tells us, however, the basic structure includes the principles, institutions, and practices fundamental to social life, those that do more than any others to influence the thought and action, the purposes and prospects of everyone in society.[26] Seen in this light, the categorical restrictions that his theory imposes on LP and GPF are by no means marginal or inconsequential.

For reasons already discussed, we cannot treat freedom of action to pursue interests and desires, ends and purposes, as a good that can never be subordinated to any other objectives or principles. Rawls's theory is not objectionable because it argues for justice-based rankings of and restrictions on freedoms. Nor, in my view, is the content of Rawls's proposed principles of justice seriously objectionable. In its abstract formulation the first of those principles is at least akin to GPF in that it is a principle of equal liberty, and Rawls's elaboration of it yields a familiar and to my mind quite eligible short list of basic liberties.[27] The second principle is more disputable (and much disputed), but it is worth noting not only that it is subordinate to the first principle but that it is defended in part as necessary to making the first principle effective.[28]

The difficulty, rather, is that Rawls rigorously excludes the possibility of revisions in, and/or circumstantially justified departures from, the rankings of and restrictions on freedoms of action that his theory proposes. The principles of justice are in lexical order, and justice itself is accorded strict, invariable priority over all other considerations. The justice-based basic liberties have the standing not merely of constitutional rights, but of pre- or extraconstitutional principles that could be revised, reconsidered, or justifiably

---

[25]See ibid., p. 31, for an especially severe statement. Cf. Rawls, "The Basic Liberties and Their Priority," p. 171; and "Kantian Constructivism in Moral Theory," p. 527.

[26]See Rawls, *A Theory of Justice*, pp. 7, 259.

[27]See Rawls, "The Basic Liberties and Their Priority."

[28]See ibid., esp. sec. 7.

violated only (so long as "reasonably favorable conditions" obtain) as a part of the deeply radical activity of rethinking the entire basic structure of society. We are to privilege some and restrict other freedoms not merely by accepting social and moral conventions, by adopting constitutions and promulgating laws, but in the much stronger sense of committing ourselves unqualifiedly and into the indefinite future to principles and institutions that embody them which we will thereafter regard as beyond justifiable violation and all but beyond reconsideration.

My argument for LP and GPF is of course an argument against any such commitment. If human beings and their circumstances are as I have described them, and if modern Western culture has (at the least) recognized and legitimated those characteristics and features, then Rawls's scheme presents itself as severe, uncompromising, and perhaps alien. For limited but crucial purposes openness to and celebration of the possibilities of freedom of action are replaced by unyielding rejection of large classes of interests and desires and of actions taken to serve and to satisfy them; within the realm of social justice impulses and tendencies to diversity and change are not only subject (as they must be) to disapproval and prohibition by (disputable and revisable) public judgment and by the (contestable) decisions of (replaceable) public officials, but categorically excluded by principles that are to be regarded as immune to reconsideration in or through the processes and procedures of moral, constitutional, and political discussion and debate. In its most basic respects the realm of freedom is not to be settled, unsettled, and settled and unsettled anew; it is to be settled once and for all. We are to deprive ourselves of the freedom that is arguably the most fundamental of all, the freedom to go on deliberating the scope of our freedom.

Rawls advances a number of arguments of an affirmative character for his principles of justice and for the extraordinary standing he assigns them. He proposes a conception of moral personality featuring two "moral powers" (a sense of justice and the capacity to form a conception of good) and two corresponding "highest-order interests" (roughly, interests in developing and using the two moral powers),[29] and he argues for a "thin" theory of the good according to which there are certain "primary" or all-purpose instrumental goods that are necessary to the satisfaction of the highest-order

[29]Rawls, "Kantian Constructivism in Moral Theory," sec. 7; "Justice as Fairness," pp. 233–34.

interests and in particular to realizing any and all conceptions of the good.[30] In this perspective, the rigorism of his position presents itself as a function of his conception of moral personality and its needs.

These affirmative arguments for the absolute weight of justice and the strict lexical ordering of the two principles of justice may or may not be vulnerable to Rawls's own strictures against perfectionist views. (As noted, Rawls allows that his theory includes ideals, but claims that it is not perfectionist because it does not advance a substantively determinate conception of the good to be adopted by everyone.) For present purposes the more important point is twofold. First, we could accept Rawls's conception of moral personality and its needs and yet reject his rigorism. Accepting the former would dispose us to the basic structure Rawls proposes, and we might in fact create and sustain a constitutional system instantiating that structure. But we would insist that the features of that structure must remain open to reconsideration both in the sense that the principles might be revised so as to better serve the needs to which the structure is instrumental and in the further sense that particular circumstances might justify refusals to act in the manner specified by the principles. (The principles would be regarded as constitutional, not pre- or extraconstitutional, and there would be a constitutional procedure for amending the constitution; civil disobedience and what I have elsewhere called "civil encroachment" on rights[31] would have an accepted place in constitutional and political theory.)

Second, Rawls acknowledges the possibility just canvassed, at least in the sense that he advances another, negative, argument for his rigorism, an argument that appeals less to the affirmative merits of his conception of moral personality and his principles of justice than to the consequences of adopting a less rigorist approach.[32] The sort of mobile, amenable, latitudinarianism proposed here, he argues, depends on an unworkable form of "intuitionism," on the unwarranted assumption that conflicts such as those among freedoms and between freedoms and other values can be successfully

[30]Rawls, *A Theory of Justice,* sec. 15; "Kantian Constructivism in Moral Theory," pp. 525–27; "The Basic Liberties and Their Priority," pp. 21ff.

[31]Chap. 5 in this volume.

[32]Rawls, *A Theory of Justice,* sec. 7, pp. 315ff.; "The Basic Liberties and Their Priority," pp. 10, 26, 32, 74; and "Justice as Fairness," p. 258.

resolved circumstantially, that is, by resort to the unsystematized (or less systematized) moral and political intuitions that have developed out of our socialization, acculturation, and education. Of course in Rawls's own thinking this negative argument is connected with the affirmative one just discussed; the (in Rawls's mind) predictable failure of reliance on intuitions is objectionable first and foremost because of the effects it would have (has) on the moral powers and the highest-order interests that go with them. But the force of the negative argument need not depend on acceptance of the affirmative one. One need not subscribe to Rawls's conception of moral personality or his theory of the good in order to object to intractable conflict, arbitrary imposition, and the other barriers to fair cooperation that, according to Rawls, are certain to attend unconstrained intuitionism. By introducing this negative argument Rawls encourages the thought that the case for rigorism is separable from the case for his principles of justice. While it is surely not his view that *any* rigorist scheme would be preferable to intuitionism, his objections to the latter constitute his most general challenge to the view I have advanced here.

The affirmative arguments for the latter view presented in sections I–III of this essay require rejection of neither Rawls's conception of moral personality nor his principles of justice. Those arguments do require that we recognize the conception as a moral ideal, one that may or may not be judged superior to other ideals. They also require that we view the principles of justice as instrumental to the ideal and hence revisable and defeasible, even if allegiance to the ideal is general and constant. Those arguments promote an openness to possibilities not only as regards life-styles and patterns of conduct outside of the basic structure but concerning social and political structures, arrangements, and practices. Although hardly agnostic about general human characteristics and values, even in this respect they are culture-specific, not transcendental or universalist, and they otherwise express a moderate skepticism intended (among other things) to protect freedom from overweening philosophical and ideological claims, from kinds of dogmatism that issue (as my arguments themselves do) from the urge to general theory. True, they leave the question of whether in other respects freedom will be adequately secured to interactions among moral and political agents taken as we find them in the settings in which they live their lives. If—as I think—this is a liberal conception of the role of political philosophy in political practice, it is indeed likely that political practices informed by it will continue to feature the disagreement and conflict that Rawls regrets and seeks to contain. But even if it is within the powers of political philosophy to institute the fuller accord and greater harmony that Rawls seeks (which is of course unlikely), it would be objectionable for it to do so.

5

Moderating Rights

Rights might be regarded as an objectionable and even a dangerous feature of moral, political, and legal arrangements. It is an element of all (Hohfeldian) types of rights that Able's having right X entails requirements or prohibitions for Baker. These restrictions hold against Baker at Able's discretion, that is, unless Able excuses Baker from respecting them. Nor are the restrictions merely decorative. We must presume that they are established because of the expectation that Baker would otherwise be disposed to interfere with the action Able's right warrants her in taking.[1] Thus as writers as early as Spinoza have stressed, rights are powers—one might even say weapons—which Able may use against Baker. Of course, as a practical matter these "weapons" are frequently ineffective. Baker may willfully ignore her obligations and prevent Able from enjoying her entitlements.[2] But such occurrences, as common and as unfortunate as they are, do not materially ease the task of justifying rights. It is only insofar as rights are effective, and hence only

Earlier versions of this paper were presented to sessions of the Western Canada Chapter of the Conference for the Study of Political Thought, the Inter-American Congress of Philosophy, a National Endowment for the Humanities Seminar at the Johns Hopkins University, and to graduate seminars in political philosophy at Johns Hopkins. I am grateful to participants in these sessions, and especially to my colleague David Sachs, for their comments and suggestions.
[1]Wesley N. Hohfeld, *Fundamental Legal Conceptions,* ed. W. W. Cook (New Haven: Yale University Press, 1919). I have discussed Hohfeld's distinctions and defended the claim about Able's discretion in *The Practice of Rights* (New York: Cambridge University Press, 1976), esp. chap. 2.

[2]This theme is stressed in Stuart Scheingold, *The Politics of Rights* (New Haven: Yale University Press, 1974).

insofar as anyone will have reason to defend them, that they are weapons in Able's hands.

It is true and important that rights may also influence, channel, and even limit Able's actions. There is first the point, inadequately appreciated by communalist critics of rights (such as Alasdair MacIntyre),[3] that rights integrate individuals into the society or polity in which the rights are established.[4] In addition, to give Able a right to do X may make it less likely that Able will do some more objectionable action Y. To give workers a right to strike may reduce the likelihood that they will wreck factories. It may be asking too much to expect factory owners to relish the constant threat of strikes. But they might prefer this circumstance to more anarchic conditions with which it might be compared.

But if rights are "taming" or "domesticating" devices, or devices employed in the hope of achieving some valued end or goal that can be defined independently of the rights themselves and used to discipline the exercise of the rights, they may also encourage excesses of a sort that Hobbes and others have associated with a "wild" or "savage" condition. This is in part because many rights are "open-ended" or "unlimited" in at least the respect that if Able has a right to do or to have X she can do X as often as she wishes and she can have, as far as her right is concerned, as much of X as she can get. If our union has the legal right to strike, we can legally do so as often as we think will serve our interests. Or to take the generic instance that most dramatically illustrates the dangers of this feature of rights, my right to hold property allows me to imitate such exemplars as Lord Thomson and the Rockefellers. I can accumulate so much capital that I cannot spend as fast as I "make," acquire so many newspapers as to monopolize the flow of information to millions of people, own vast estates that sit unused for months or years at a stretch, and exclude whole generations from experiencing art objects of unique beauty by hoarding them in private places. In Blackstone's perhaps flamboyant but by no means uninfluential formulation, by virtue of her right, Able acquires "sole and despotic dominion . . . over the external things of the world, in total exclusion of . . . any other individual in the universe."[5]

---

[3] Alasdair MacIntyre, *After Virtue* (Notre Dame: University of Notre Dame Press, 1981).

[4] See Flathman, *Practice of Rights,* esp. chap. 9.

[5] William Blackstone, *Commentaries on the Laws of England,* bk. II, chap. 1, 2d paragraph.

This extreme version of rights theory can be put in the cadence of a once notorious slogan—"Extremism is the exercise of rights is no vice." As thus understood, some critics see the practice of rights as lacking in principles of moderation. Thus, we have a number of familiar plaints about rights: the "Weimar plaint" about extremists using their political rights to sabotage a civil order; the "Dickens plaint" about the well-heeled grinding down the impoverished by holding them to the letter of their obligations vis-à-vis contractual rights; the "Rachel Carson" or "Sierra Club plaint" about property holders treating their rights as licenses to despoil the commons.

Arrangements that give one person or group such powerful weapons in competitions and conflicts with others, that give one person or group so much as an approximation to "sole and despotic dominion" over the goods available to humankind, are, on the face of things, objectionable and dangerous arrangements.[6] It may be possible to justify such arrangements. But they are arrangements that cry out for explicit, systematic, and—I would add—cautious justifications.

So at least it would seem from the foregoing, admittedly discursive remarks. And yet, to quote Blackstone once more, "There is nothing which so generally strikes the imagination and engages the affections of mankind" as do rights.[7] Of course, there has long been lively dispute as to what should be established and maintained as rights, who should have those rights, how they should be interpreted, and so forth. But the idea that rights as such, rights of any sort, may be lacking justification seems to be in danger of losing its foothold to the steadily rising waters of general enthusiasm for them. Rights are widely and deeply admired and the thought that they—the institution or device itself—might be without justification is entertained only by those who are radically alienated from, deeply disaffected by, beliefs and values fundamental to most contemporary Western societies and cultures.

The impressions just sketched are reinforced by recent writing about rights in moral, political, and legal philosophy. Numerous philosophers have not only accepted but celebrated what I have

---

[6]In slightly less polemical terms: from a deontological perspective, while rights do much to protect, support, or even guarantee the freedom of Able, they thereby impinge on, interfere with, or restrict the freedom of Baker. From an axiological or classical utilitarian perspective, rights may guarantee that Able can act so as to maximize her personal utility as she conceives it, but they thereby put the greatest good or aggregate utility at risk.

[7]Blackstone, *Commentaries*.

characterized as the immoderate characteristics of rights. Of course they do not use this language. But they insist on what in less polemical language might be called the distinctively independent standing and stringency of at least certain rights. That is, they insist both that certain rights are independent of considerations such as ends and purposes, and that they constitute warrants for doing or having some X that parties other than the right holder either cannot override at all (that are, for all other parties, dispositive, all things considered, reasons for the right holder doing or having X) or can override only by appeal to some other, conflicting right. In the most unqualified of the recent presentations of such views—that is, Robert Nozick's—rights are asserted as moral givens and it is argued that all other moral and political issues must be resolved within the "side constraints" set by those rights.[8] Other recent versions of natural or human rights theory—for example, Hart's and Gewirth's[9]—offer a derivation for rights, but the most basic of the rights derived are treated as moral, legal, and even political "trumps" that properly defeat or even exclude all apparently competing considerations.[10] If we don't understand and accept that rights are trumps, we simply haven't grasped and accepted the idea of rights. Sophisticated as the expressions of the "affections" of these theorists may be, there is no denying that their affections are deeply "engaged" by (what they understand to be) the idea of rights.

In this essay I continue my efforts to qualify these tendencies of thought.[11] I do not do so from an antirights position such as MacIntyre's communitarianism or numerous of the versions of Marxism. Nor is it my intention to argue from or for any of the versions of utilitarianism that so thoroughly subordinate rights as to deprive them of distinctive character or significance. Although skeptical about the justifiability of a number of the rights most prominent in our society (especially some forms of the right to property), I regard the practice of rights as among the valuable features of legal, politi-

[8]Robert Nozick, *Anarchy, State, and Utopia* (New York: Basic Books, 1974).

[9]H. L. A. Hart, "Are There Any Natural Rights?" *Philosophical Review* 64 (1955):175ff.; Alan Gewirth, *Reason and Morality* (Chicago: University of Chicago Press, 1978).

[10]See Ronald Dworkin, *Taking Rights Seriously* (Cambridge: Harvard University Press, 1977).

[11]See Flathman, *Practice of Rights,* and my paper "Rights, Utility, and Civil Disobedience," in *Ethics, Economics, and the Law,* ed. J. Roland Pennock and John W. Chapman, *Nomos* 24 (New York: New York University Press, 1982).

cal, and moral life in modern Western societies. Although wanting to delineate and defend a more qualified view of the logic of rights than is presented in the insistently deontological accounts to which I have referred, I share the view that rights are distinctive and distinctively stringent entities. In the language of my title, I want to moderate not to abolish, and I want the entities that I moderate to be recognizable as rights.

The question that I address, then, is whether it is possible to accommodate the independence and distinctive stringency of rights while nevertheless avoiding the "immoderation" that seems to be attendant on them.

I

I begin with a passage from a recent paper by T. M. Scanlon, one that is promising from the standpoint of moderating rights but that will be regarded as most unpromising indeed by many theorists of rights. "In attacking utilitarianism, one is inclined to appeal to individual rights, which mere considerations of social utility cannot justify us in overriding. But rights themselves need to be justified somehow, and how other than by appeal to the human interests their recognition promotes and protects. . . . Further, unless rights are to be taken as defined by rather implausible rigid formulae, it seems that we must invoke what looks very much like the consideration of consequences in order to determine what they rule out and what they allow."[12] On this view, a right will be established and maintained only if it is consonant with or perhaps even contributive to the satisfaction of human interests that can be identified without reference to the right. In interpreting and enforcing established rights in particular circumstances, consideration will be given to the consequences, presumably for human interests, of moderating rights at least in the sense of coordinating their exercise and enforcement with a variety of other considerations that are valued in the society or group in which they are established.

It must be admitted, however, that Scanlon's formulation confronts us with formidable difficulties. Scanlon is saying that a theory of rights must be consequentialist and in some sense teleological. In

[12]T. M. Scanlon, "Rights, Goals and Fairness," in *Public and Private Morality*, ed. Stuart Hampshire (New York: Cambridge University Press, 1978), p. 93.

our time most theorists would take this to mean that such a theory will be utilitarian. But among numerous difficulties imputed to utilitarianism, one of them is just that no genuine form of that doctrine can provide a theoretically secure place for, or even a coherent account of, rights. Accepting for the moment a dichotomy widely regarded as exhaustive of the forms of utilitarianism, in its unqualified act-utilitarian versions utilitarianism tends to lose hold of the concept of rights, and wittingly or otherwise, to end up in the antirights camp. Rule-utilitarianism, by contrast, finds itself losing hold of its consequentialism and sliding toward a deontological position in order to "take rights seriously." If the program implicit in Scanlon's remarks is necessarily utilitarian, there are well rehearsed reasons for thinking that it cannot be carried through.

The most insistent formulations of these reasons have been presented by theorists who identify with the tradition of natural rights or human rights thinking. In the least qualified versions of this position, of which the most notable of the recent, secularized formulations is Robert Nozick's,[13] it is asserted that rights simply are the starting points, the unfounded foundations, of morality (and of those parts of law and politics that are or should be subordinate to morality). Because they are not founded on or derived from anything independent of themselves, there can be no question of justifying or disproving, modifying or even interpreting, them in anything like the manner Scanlon suggests. And because they are starting points in this strong sense, they are stopping points in an equally strong sense. The entire independence and the absolute stringency of at least those rights that are "natural" is guaranteed.

The usual objection to this version of the natural rights position is that it is merely dogmatic; deprived of the religious suppositions that gave it credibility at earlier periods, it now presents itself as a form of intuitionism which, as with all others, provides no basis for resolving any disagreements or conflicts that may arise among intuitions.[14] Other formulations—for example, H. L. A. Hart's and Alan Gewirth's—attempt to escape this objection;[15] they offer

---

[13]See Nozick, *Anarchy, State, and Utopia.*

[14]Cf. Thomas Nagel's criticisms of Nozick in "Libertarianism without Foundations," *Yale Law Journal* 85 (1975):136. There are other ways in which Nozick's argument might be construed, one of which makes it more closely akin to views of G. E. M. Anscombe which I take up and largely endorse below.

[15]See Hart, "Are There Any Natural Rights?"; Gewirth, *Reason and Morality.*

elaborate arguments intended to validate the belief that certain fundamental rights are independent of and properly dominant over considerations of the kinds adduced by Scanlon.[16] If convincing, these arguments would provide nonarbitrary grounds on which to determine the content and distribution of at least the most basic rights as well as philosophical justification for rejecting views that subordinate rights to (or even coordinate them with) other kinds of considerations. In short, if arguments such as Hart's and Gewirth's go through, Scanlon's enterprise is doomed to failure. In the terms I have been using, the philosophical project of moderating rights would be shown to be misbegotten. The understandings that I have wrongheadedly characterized as immoderate would be in fact deep truths.

In my judgment the arguments in question are unconvincing. In summary, I contend that there are two possibilities: either (1) the claims are merely dogmatic (as in Nozick's case); or (2) the natural rights are justified by appeal to some beliefs or values independent of the rights and it is both logically possible and practically probable that those considerations (whatever they may be) will be ill served by the distinctive institution or practice of *rights*. In the only philosophically interesting case—that is, (2)—it of course follows that no argument has been given for the entire independence and un-qualified stringency of the so-called natural rights.

I will not elaborate these rejoinders and objections here. Because I find them convincing (there are of course numerous other such rejoinders to natural rights theory), I am prepared to pursue my project of finding a philosophical basis for "moderating" rights. But the difficulties with theories of natural and human rights do not obviate the fact, known to us as participants in the practice of rights (if not simply as speakers of languages that include the concept of rights), that rights are distinctive and distinctively stringent moral, legal, and political entities. Whatever our assessment of theories of human or natural rights, rights are widely regarded as potent entities and are valued and sought for that reason. There are numerous settings in which Able's showing that she has a right to do or to have X will settle the disputes that prompted her to invoke that right. If

---

[16]In Hart's case rights are dominant only in the realm or dimension of morality that is their home. He allows that there is another realm, the home of concepts such as the common good and the general welfare, the pursuit and service of interests and purposes, which has its own independence and integrity.

we denied these facts, or lacked a tolerably orderly account of them, we would not be in a position to determine whether we had moderated rather than distorted or failed to accommodate them.

A brief but incisive paper by G. E. M. Anscombe will help us in this regard.[17] She gives an account of the features of rights (and of rules and promises) which have been my concern, namely, their independence and their stringency. Her discussion of the stringency of rights begins with a puzzle about them. How can it be that the fact that you have a right (or the fact that I have made a promise, or that there is a prescriptive rule) creates an obligation for me; that owing to your right I *must* act in a certain manner or *must* refrain from a certain action or actions? These "musts" and "can'ts," which certainly are a characteristic of rights, are puzzling in part because they are obviously not the "musts" of physical necessity or impossibility. They are typically if not invariably invoked when it is obvious that in fact I *can* do or refuse to do the required or forbidden action. They are further puzzling because the necessity or impossibility seems to result from or be created by nothing more than a certain form or combination of words. But "how on earth can it be the meaning of a sign that by giving it one purports to create a necessity of doing something—a necessity whose source is the sign itself, and whose nature depends on the sign."[18]

In attempting to resolve these puzzles, Anscombe takes up Hume's view that the necessities attendant on promises (and rights and certain rules) are "naturally unintelligible" and can only arise and be understood as part of a system of human conventions. For Hume this means two things: first, there is no natural object or event that is known to us by perception and for which (or for the image or sensation of which) the words *promise, right,* and *rule* stand; second, even if there were such an object or event it (our perception of it) could not of itself give rise to that "inclination to perform," that sense that one must perform, which is perhaps the most distinctive feature of promises, rights, and rules. Both the "object" and what we call the sense of duty or obligation attendant on it are artifacts of human decision and agreement.

In respect to Hume's first point, Anscombe extends her argument to all "words and their relation to their meanings." All uses of

[17]G. E. M. Anscombe, "Rules, Rights, and Promises," *Midwest Studies in Philosophy* 3 (1978):318–23.
[18]Ibid., pp. 320–21.

words involve something conventional—namely, rules and rule following. For this reason, language can never be "naturally" intelligible in Hume's sense. When we realize the ways in which the very meaningfulness of language depends on rules, we appreciate that words themselves, words as such, cannot be the source of that "inclination" or sense of duty which attaches to rights, promises, and prescriptive rules. Quite apart from psychological considerations such as Hume invoked, we could make no sense of the notion of duty or any particular duty. Of course words are typically used in the course of and as a vital part of creating, discharging, and enforcing duties. But what matters, what generates and allows us to understand the "inclination" or duty, is not particular words or marks, signs or symbols, but the rules or—as Hume would say—conventions followed by those who use the words. It is because the activities of making and keeping promises, establishing, exercising, and respecting rights, adopting, obeying, and enforcing laws, are rule-governed that there is that sense of necessity, of stringency, attached to them.

To understand the stringency of rights, then, we must examine their place in rule-governed activities and practices. Doing so reminds us that there are a very large number of activities that involve "musts" and "can'ts" which have nothing to do with physical or natural limitations and necessities—which are asserted and acted on just when and in part because in their absence we would be at liberty to do or refrain from doing the forbidden or required action. Such "modal pairs"[19] are a feature of every human activity that involves language. Any number of activities, moreover, involve rules over and above those governing the language used in the course of and as a part of engaging in them.

Let us pause to note that in this perspective the "musts" and "can'ts" that are a prominent part of rights present themselves as less distinctive, more ordinary, than they have been made to appear by moral and political philosophers. "It is part of human intelligence to be able to learn the response to . . . [these "musts" and "must nots"] without which they wouldn't exist as linguistic instruments and without which these things [and many others!]: rules, etiquette, rights, infringements, promises, pieties and impieties

---

[19]Anscombe employs the notion of modals in analyzing pairs such as "necessary, possible," "must, need not."

would not exist either."[20] They "are understood by those of normal intelligence as they are trained in the practices of reason."[21] In their generic character they are puzzling—or rather mysterious—only in the exceedingly deep sense in which we might find human intelligence and the practices of reason mysterious.

The foregoing observations indicate that Anscombe's analysis of modals is pertinent to the independence as well as the stringency of rights. This is also true of a further aspect of her discussion to which I now turn. It is very often the case that "musts" and "can'ts" are "accompanied by what sounds like a reason."[22] In the case of rights, the statement that Baker must do X or can't do Y is commonly followed by a phrase such as "it's Able's." "You must pay Able $50, she is entitled to it under the terms of your contract with her." The second clause in each of these statements is a reason for the "can't" and the "must." But it is a reason of a special kind, "a 'reason' in the sense of a *logos,* a thought. . . . If we ask what the thought is, and for what it is a reason, we'll find that we can't explain them separately. We can't explain the 'You can't' on its own; in any independent sense it is simply not true that he can't (unless 'they' physically stop him). But neither does 'It's N's' . . . have its peculiar sense independent of the relation to 'You can't.' "[23] A "can't" or a "must" and its logos are interdependent or interwoven. If we separate them, try to understand or assess either of them alone, they lose their "peculiar sense," the sense they have in the activity or practice of which they are part. "If you say 'You can't move your king, he'd be in check', 'He'd be in check' gives the special *logos* falling under the general *logos* type: a rule of a game."[24] If you say to a police officer, "You must permit Able to speak, it's her right under the First Amendment," "it's her right" gives the special logos of a constitutional right falling under the more general logos types "a right" and "a constitutional right limiting public authority." Those who know chess will understand that, and why, "You can't move your king"; anyone familiar with rights and with constitutional practice in, say, the United States will grasp that, and why, the police officer must permit Able to speak.

[20]Anscombe, "Rules, Rights, and Promises," p. 321.
[21]Ibid., p. 323.
[22]Ibid., p. 321.
[23]Ibid., p. 322.
[24]Ibid.

Persons unfamiliar with these games and practices will be puzzled by both.

As I suggested, this notion of a reason in the special sense of a logos deepens the respects in which rights (but, again, also many other arrangements and practices) are stringent and independent. There is a reason not to move the king and not to prevent Able's speech; these "musts" and "can'ts" are not arbitrary. But in both cases the reason is internal to the game or practice and is so interwoven with "its own" "must" or "can't" as to be inseparable from it. The point, of course, is that it is not to be thought that the notion of a "reason" in the general sense of "something independent [of the particular practice and the 'must' or 'can't' in question] which someone puts forward as his reason for what he does"[25] is sufficient to understand or assess the "musts" and "can'ts" of rights. The logos of a right only "appears to be a reason" in this wider sense (the sense exemplified by, say, "serves human interests," "maximizes utility," or "is necessary to human freedom and well being"). Being distinct from reasons in the wider sense, the reasons for (or better, the reasons of) the "musts" and "can'ts" of rights at once embody and manifest the independent standing and stringency of the latter.

II

Anscombe's account is a description of rights not a derivation, explanation, or justification of or for them. She assembles reminders of features of rights that are familiar to us as participants in practices and relations that involve rights. Her intention in assembling these reminders is not to advance a general theory but to dissolve or at least diminish any puzzlement that may overtake us if we attempt to derive, explain, or give a general justification for rights. Rights are no more puzzling than a large genus of other features of human affairs with which they share a number of characteristics; what might be the puzzling character of a particular right disappears when we attend to its specific characteristics or differentiae, above all its logos.

If, as I believe, Anscombe's account is essentially accurate, it yields tests that have to be satisfied if we are to "moderate" *rights*. A

[25]Ibid.

theory that failed to incorporate "musts" and "can'ts" and their internal relationships with a logos would simply not be a theory of rights as we know them. With these tests in mind, I return to the project of coordinating rights with other desiderata and thereby—or to that extent—moderating them. I continue my pursuit of this objective in two stages. First, I consider features of utilitarian theories, particularly John Stuart Mill's as recently construed by David Lyons, which, despite being teleological and consequentialist, seem more consonant with Anscombe's description than Scanlon's. Second, I draw comparisons between rights on the one hand and authority and the theory and practice of civil disobedience on the other. Authority has many of the characteristics Anscombe finds in rights and for this reason might seem equally unamenable to accommodation in and thereby moderation by theories such as Scanlon's and Lyons's Mill. Yet the theory and practice of civil disobedience, which typically if not invariably gives substantial weight to teleological and consequentialist considerations (or at least to considerations "independent" of authority, laws, and rights), has been judged by many—including many philosophers—to accommodate the basic characteristics of authority while effecting valuable analogous understandings concerning rights. In short, I argue that there is available a version of teleological and consequentialist theory which can meet the tests posed by Anscombe's description of rights and which, if accepted and acted on, would moderate rights in much the way that civil disobedience moderates authority.

If described in what is by now orthodox terminology, Lyons's recent essays concerning Mill interpret him as a "rule" or "restricted" utilitarian rather than a proponent of the "act" or "unrestricted" version of that theory.[26] But in my view, Lyons's account calls attention to aspects of Mill's theory which are inadequately appreciated in recent reformulations of utilitarianism as well as in exegetical and historical studies. The most important point, which has strong affinities with the view of Anscombe just discussed, is made through a comparison with the much less subtle utilitarianism of G. E. Moore.

[26]David Lyons, "Human Rights and the General Welfare," *Philosophy and Public Affairs* 6 (1977):113–29; "Mill's Theory of Justice," in *Values and Morals*, ed. A. I. Goldman and J. Kim (Dordrecht: Reidel, 1978); "Utility and Rights," in *Ethics, Economics, and the Law*, ed. Pennock and Chapman. My discussion of this last paper is based in part on the original draft version, primarily on the published version. References are to the latter unless otherwise indicated.

In Moore's view, all moral questions are properly decided by determining which among the available courses of action will "promote intrinsic value to the maximum degree possible." The principle "Always act so as to maximize intrinsic value" replaces equally forward-looking and undifferentiating imperatives such as "Act so as to maximize pleasure and minimize pain" and "Act so as to achieve the greatest happiness of the greatest number." According to Lyons, Mill's advice is that we "begin" our practical moral judging and deciding "at the other end." As with his predecessors and successors in the utilitarian tradition, Mill is a teleological theorist who aims to achieve certain objectives or end states. But he does not use these basic purposes as engines of a reductionism that wipes out the many differences among moral concepts, questions, and issues. In Lyon's words, "He considers . . . what forms of judgment must be accommodated by a moral theory and then applies his basic values within the . . . constraints" established by those forms of judgment."[27]

The key phrases here are "forms of judgment" and "must be accommodated." Examples of forms of judgment are the concepts, arrangements, and practices of justice, obligation, and rights. In the paper of primary interest here, Lyons concentrates on the form of judgment that is a legally established right. His discussion stresses the settled characteristics, the defined limits and implications of this "form." By virtue of Mary's right (which is to the exclusive use of a garage that comes with a house she has rented and the private driveway leading to the garage), there are a number of actions that she can take (or not) entirely at her discretion; certain restrictions and obligations fall to everyone other than Mary unless she releases them from them; and there are more or less clearly defined exceptions to what she can and they must and must not do (for example, ambulances can use or block the driveway without Mary's permission when responding to emergencies). In Anscombe's terms, "because the driveway is hers (to use)," Mary not only can but may act in certain ways, and for the same "reason" certain "musts" and "can'ts" hold for or apply to other persons.

The notion that these forms "must be accommodated" is complex, involving at least two different (albeit related) senses of "musts." The first of these is conceptual. We might say that the form of judgment determines the appropriate descriptions or char-

---

[27]Lyons, "Utility and Rights," draft version, p. 28.

acterizations of the actions of Mary and others in respect to the driveway. Whatever else might be said about those actions, some of them are the exercise or enforcement of the right, others the violation of the right or the discharge of obligations in respect to the right. Persons who fail to recognize the correctness and acknowledge the relevance of these descriptions quite literally "do not know what they are talking about."

This "must" holds regardless of one's attitude toward or assessment of the right. Jane might think that Mary's right is indefensible and should be abolished—even that all rights should be abolished. And she might decide to "respect" the right only if forced to do so. If she convinced others of these views, she might succeed in getting the right abolished. But *what* Jane is against is not some pattern of movement or conduct that can be identified without reference to rights; what she is against is the right. If Joan doesn't understand the notion of a right, if say, she is from a culture that lacks rights, she might object to the fact that Mary is the only one who uses the driveway. But Joan would not be against the same thing that Jane is against.

According to Lyons, Mill recognized such conceptual "musts" and built recognition of them into his theory. He may not have been aware of the number and diversity of such "musts," but insofar as he was aware of them he made it a criterion of the adequacy of his theory that it accommodate them.

The second sense of "must" is more clearly and directly normative. Rights must be accommodated by a moral theory when, and because, they are justified by whatever criteria of assessment the theory employs. Accordingly, there are some theories that neither must nor can accommodate any rights whatsoever. I suggested above that this is true, at least as regards rights of individuals, of certain forms of communitarianism and Marxism. It is also widely held to be true of "extreme" utilitarianism. Proponents of these theories who find themselves in a society in which some number of rights are morally or legally established are conceptually bound by the first kind of "must." And there might be tactical, instrumental, or prudential grounds on which they would sometimes or even regularly choose to conduct themselves in ways consonant with or required by those rights. But they could not regard themselves as morally or legally entitled to the havings or doings protected by the rights or as bound to the obligations that correlate with the rights of others. Whenever "violating" those rights served their basic values they would be bound by their theory to do so.

On Lyons's interpretation, Millian rule-utilitarianism attempts to accommodate the normative "must" of at least some rights. But it succeeds in doing so—even in respect to legal rights—only in a limited and finally inadequate sense. It does generate what by its own criteria are convincing justifications for the institution or practice of rights as one of the features of some societies and for establishing some specific rights. Confronted with the view that there should be no rights whatever, or with arguments against familiar rights such as to habeas corpus, trial by a jury of one's peers, various rights to property, and so forth, Millian-style utilitarians are able to make rejoinders that are forceful and consistent with the basic features of their theory. In respect to justifying institutions and practices, Millian utilitarians can easily march in the ranks of the pro-rights company.

The difficulty with Millian theory, Lyons argues, presents itself when the justification for the institution of rights or for a particular right must be brought to bear on conduct within the confines of the institution and concerning a particular right. Why should such a utilitarian respect a right in circumstances in which refusing to do so would better serve the general welfare? The justification for (as distinct from the conceptual grasp of) the institution and each of the rights of which it consists is its contribution to the general welfare. If refusal to comply with its requirements yields greater utility, the utilitarian is bound by his theory to refuse. In Lyons's view, this means that rights lose their standing as independent and distinctively stringent normative considerations.

Or rather this is a widely held view of the upshot of rule-utilitarianism. Lyons's analysis, although finally endorsing this assessment, is more complex. He considers the possibility that the utilitarian reasons for the right or other "form of judgment" give the utilitarian "reason to conform to the rules of the institution" in particular cases. It is possible that the usual objection against utilitarianism (as I just summarized it) ignores "the direct practical implications that the justification of social rules or institutions has for a utilitarian." If we take this view of it, "utilitarianism gives rise . . . to conflicting considerations." It would remain true, however, that utilitarian arguments for the institution of rights or for specific rights "would not show that direct utilitarian arguments concerning [particular cases of] conduct are excluded." They "would show only that such arguments must be weighed within utilitarianism against arguments flowing from the utilitarian justification of those institutions."[28] And in Lyons's view to show this much is not enough to defend utilitarianism. There is nothing in the theory that requires a right-thinking utilitarian to resolve such conflicts in favor of respecting the right.

Lyons's conclusion suggests that utilitarianism could be said to accommodate rights only if it did "exclude" direct utilitarian arguments from reasoning about particular cases of rights. Perhaps this is his view about the class "direct utilitarian arguments." But Lyons is not a natural or human rights theorist *à la* Nozick or Gewirth. He allows the possibility of morally defensible violations of morally justified rights, and he does not restrict this possibility to cases in which there is a conflict between or among morally justified rights. Thus, an adequate moral theory, one that successfully accommodated rights, would not have to—or rather could not—"exclude" all considerations external to or independent of rights themselves (of their logos) or the justification for them. Accordingly, Lyons's objection to utilitarianism is not that it allows the possibility of morally justified violations of rights; rather, it is that the theory makes it too easy to justify such violations. Although not an "absolute," a right "provides *an argumentative threshold* against objections to my . . . [*exercising*] it, as well as a presumption against others' interference."[29] Even on the most sympathetic interpretations of the most refined versions of utilitarianism, that theory cannot accommodate this feature and hence it cannot accommodate the "form of judgment" that is a right. Thus, we cannot look to utilitarianism as a way of at once accommodating and moderating rights.

Lyons claims that this conclusion is required by "the common understanding" of rights, particularly the notion that justifications for violations of rights must cross an "argumentative threshold." As should be evident from my reliance on Anscombe, I have no quarrel with the idea that there is such a common understanding and that a theory of rights should encompass and be responsive to it (albeit having grasped that understanding, a theorist might want to chal-

[28]Ibid., p. 129.
[29]Ibid., p. 111; italics Lyons's.

lenge it). Nor do I see any reason to deny that the common understanding includes something like what Lyon calls an argumentative threshold. If there were no such threshold, if any argument whatever justified violating any right, the obligations attendant on rights would amount to no more than the requirement that one give reasons for those of one's acts or omissions that affect the right holder in respect to the subject or content of her rights. The difficulty with the notion of an argumentative threshold as Lyons deploys it is that it requires no more than this. For this reason the notion is not so much wrong as it is unhelpful. It is, perhaps, conceivable that we could give it greater specifity in respect to *this,* *that,* or the next right. If we did so, and if concomitantly we performed a Millian utilitarian "calculus" as to whether we should respect or violate the right in the circumstances in question, it might turn out that the latter always—or very frequently—led us to conclusions at variance with the former and hence with the "common understanding." Even these operations would not establish Lyons's conclusion that Millian utilitarianism *must* diverge from what the common understanding requires. But in any case Lyons has performed no such operations. His discussion of the common understanding and the implications of Millian utilitarianism are in equally general terms—terms far too general to support his conclusion.

I myself have no intention of performing a series of operations such as I have just tried to imagine. (Indeed, the notion that one could settle the question of whether utilitarianism can accommodate rights by such an apparently inductive procedure is, for more than one reason, at least faintly absurd.) Rather, with Anscombe's more elaborate account of the common understanding of rights in mind, I will use a discussion of authority and civil disobedience to expand somewhat on features that Lyons attributes to Millian utilitarianism, particularly its understanding and handling of relationships among the conceptual features of forms of judgment, justifications for such forms of judgment, and reasoning about conduct within the setting of forms of judgment. I do not hope *to prove* that this understanding is correct. But I hope to show that it is more plausible than Lyons—to say nothing of more militantly anti-utilitarian writers—allows.

My first point can be viewed as an objection to Lyons's way of distinguishing between conceptual and normative reasons why forms of judgment must be accommodated. In the example on which Lyons relies, the practical question to be decided is whether an "official" (evidently an executive official such as a policeman or sheriff as opposed to a judge) who is of Millian utilitarian persuasion should acknowledge and discharge an obligation to enforce Mary's legal right to the exclusive use of the driveway. Lyons explicitly makes two assumptions about his official and implicitly makes a third. The first is that the official has no doubt that Mary's right is legally established—for example, in his mind there is no question about the constitutionality of the right. Second, he assumes that the official believes that the right is justified by the normative standard of Millian utilitarianism. To use Lyons's terminology, in the official's view the right is not merely a legal right, it is a legal right with "normative force." The third, unstated assumption is that the system or practice of authority under which he holds his position as an official, and the particular provisions of that practice which authorize him to enforce Mary's rights, are also justified by Millian utilitarian criteria. The rules and conventions that establish and partly constitute his authority are not merely legal or constitutional rules, they are legal and constitutional rules with "normative force."

Owing to the first assumption, if the official understands the forms of judgment in which the question of enforcement arises, he thereby knows that the question before him is whether, qua official exercising authority, he ought to enforce a right. Lyons is correct that as a Millian utilitarian the official will be concerned that his actions maximize the general welfare or happiness. Unlike the Moorean utilitarian, however, he will understand that the question is whether the general happiness will be served by his decision, qua official, to enforce or to overlook violations of *a right*. If he doesn't formulate the question in these terms, if he doesn't use these descriptions of himself and of the issues before him, he "doesn't know what he is talking about."

Putting the matter this way specifies and extends considerations that, as Lyons allows (albeit inadequately), are very likely to support a decision to enforce Mary's right. The official's belief that the right and the authority have normative force *is* the belief that the general welfare is served by the existence of these arrangements and practices. Lyons is correct that this belief does not itself require (the propositions that state this belief do not entail) the conclusion that the general welfare will best be served by enforcing the right in every particular circumstance. But first, and in the spirit of Lyons's account and of the accounts that most anti-utilitarians give of this point, if the official's belief is based on utilitarian criteria, we must assume that it developed out of and has been sustained by experience with cases involving rights and authority. If the belief is in fact well grounded, it is to be expected that it will hold for most future cases as well. If the official thought that it was an altogether open question whether the general welfare would be served by enforcing rights, if he thought that it was as likely as not that the general welfare would be served by allowing violations of rights, he would thereby demonstrate that he did not in fact hold the belief that Lyons attributes to him.

But this way of putting the matter, while perhaps appropriate concerning Benthamite reasoning, fails to appreciate a distinctive characteristic of Millian utilitarianism as Lyons describes it. We can appreciate the position better if we return to Anscombe's discussion and a Wittgensteinian thought that is consonant with it. It is a feature of rights that they "must" be respected. This feature, as we might put it, is a rule of the larger practice of rights of which any particular right is a part. And if, to introduce the Wittgensteinian thought, "rule becomes exception and exception rule; or if both become phenomena of roughly equal frequency—this would make our normal language games lose their point."[30] Of course exceptions are made to rules; of course "musts" and "must nots" are not always performed. But the notion of rules and of rule-governed practices such as rights and authority cannot be understood in merely contingent, probabilistic terms—in terms of nothing more than the likelihood that participants will find the arguments for following the rules convincing in this case or that. Someone who thought of them in such terms would misunderstand them. If Lyons is correct that Millian utilitarianism understands and seeks to accommodate such forms of judgment, then someone who thought of them in the manner assumed in Lyons's attack would not be a Millian utilitarian.

There is a more specific point here that will lead into the discussion of civil disobedience and the ways in which a Millian utilitarian

---

[30]Ludwig Wittgenstein, *Philosophical Investigations* (New York: Macmillan, 1953), I, 142.

would go about deciding whether to violate a right. It is a conceptual fact that officials (in the sense of Lyons's example) act only within their authority. Acts not within their authority are either private and hence without official standing or (if done "under color of" their authority) *ultra vires* and subject at least to nullification and very often to punishment.[31] It is a further conceptual fact that legal rights set limits on the authority of all officials. An action that violates a legal right is therefore either *ultra vires* or not an official action.[32] If an official is to act officially, she can do no other than respect rights. Hence, in this case the "musts" and "can'ts" are yet stronger than those described by Anscombe. In Wittgenstein's terms, in this case *there can be no* exceptions to the rule.[33]

III

We must not lose sight of the point on which Anscombe agrees with Hume. All of these "artificial" or conventional "musts" and "can'ts" are to be understood by contrast with physical necessities and impossibilities. The considerations I have been discussing do not settle what a Millian utilitarian (or anyone else) who among other things is an official *will* do; they only settle what, conceptually speaking, any person qua official can do.

Neither do they properly *settle* what a Millian utilitarian who among other things is an official ought on balance and morally speaking to do. It is unquestionably part of the common under-

---

[31] I follow Lyons in ignoring complications presented by the fact that his official is considering whether to enforce a right against encroachments by others. My discussion in the text holds without qualification for cases in which the official is considering an action that would itself violate the right. But I leave aside questions about the discretion that police officers, sheriffs, and the like have in deciding whether to enforce a person's rights against encroachment by other private citizens. It is not always the case that failure, or even refusal, to do so is *ultra vires*.

[32] This is the one respect known to me in which rights truly are "trumps" or "side constraints." Of course anyone familiar with the processes of interpreting the scope of rights will realize the extent to which this truth is a formalism. (I would not say a mere formalism.)

[33] We might think of this aspect of the relationship between authority and right as what Wittgenstein calls a "paradigm" in a language game. See Wittgenstein, *Philosophical Investigations*, I, 50, where he is discussing the role of the hermetically sealed meter bar in Paris. But note his further comment: "But this, of course, is not to ascribe any extraordinary property to it [the meter bar], but only to mark its peculiar role in the language-game of measuring with a metre-rule" (ibid.).

standing that an act by an official which violates a legal right is null and void. Millian utilitarianism accommodates this feature. Moreover, anyone who believes that the institutions of authority and legal rights, as they exist in her society, are valuable features of moral and political life, has excellent reasons for avoiding all *ultra vires* acts, and particularly for avoiding acts that are *ultra vires* because they violate legal rights. The combination of these distinguishable but by no means unrelated considerations amounts to a powerful argument that officials ought to respect and enforce rights. It is not too much to say that anyone who denies this does not *understand* the practices of authority and rights as we know them. On Lyons's account, Mill understood them.

Lyons is nevertheless correct; on a Millian utilitarian view understanding and accepting these practices does not and cannot properly *settle* the moral question of whether a person who is an official ought to enforce or respect a particular legal right in a specific set of circumstances.

Is Lyons, therefore, also correct that Millian utilitarianism fails to accommodate legal (and hence also moral) rights? Assuming that the foregoing discussion presents a correct account of Millian utilitarian reasoning, does that reasoning violate the common understanding concerning rights?

Imagine that someone claims to believe that authority is in principle a justifiable institution by Millian utilitarian criteria and also to believe that a particular instance of that institution, the authority of the government under which she lives, is justified by those criteria. She claims, that is, to subscribe to that authority. She nevertheless insists that it is both conceptually and normatively proper for her to obey (or to enforce if an official), admittedly *intra vires* laws and commands only when doing so, in the circumstances under which the question arises in practical form, maximizes the general welfare. This combination of views, most of us would hold, is incoherent; the last claim contradicts, and as a practical matter nullifies, the claims that precede it.

It might be thought that this incoherence could be avoided in one of only two ways. Our utilitarian must either commit herself to the view sometimes known as legal absolutism or she must forthrightly embrace philosophical anarchism. Either the authority of a law is a sufficient, a conclusive, reason for acting as the law requires or it is irrelevant to the question of how to act and acts must be chosen and justified on their (directly utilitarian) merits.

Neither legal absolutism nor anarchism, however, seems to me to map the "common understanding" of this matter. Many people see merit in the institution of authority and recognize that subscription to it commits them to treating the authority of laws or commands not only as a logos in Anscombe's sense but as a weighty, indeed ordinarily a decisive, reason—in Anscombe's wider sense—for acting as the laws and commands require. But they also believe that they ought to subject the content of laws and commands to critical scrutiny. More important here, a not inconsiderable number also hold that they are sometimes morally justified in disobeying or refusing to enforce substantively objectionable laws while continuing to avow, both sincerely and cogently, subscription to the authority of the government that promulgated the laws.

The views just sketched will be recognized as rudiments of the theory of civil disobedience. This theory, it seems to me, addresses the same question (albeit in a somewhat different institutional setting) Lyons raises about the compatibility of Millian utilitarianism with legal rights. Mill claims to understand and to accept as justified the institution of rights and obligations as they present themselves in the societies about which he is thinking; civil disobedients claim to understand and to accept as justified the institution of authority as it presents itself via the governments under which they live. Mill recognizes that accepting rights and their attendant obligations entails regarding these as weighty, ordinarily decisive reasons for action; civil disobedients take the same view of the practical import of their acceptance of authority. But both Mill and civil disobedients hold out the possibility, at once logical or conceptual and normative, of refusing to draw the practical inferences that (they not only concede but insist) are strongly supported by the reasoning that justifies the institution. In this respect, Mill and civil disobedients agree with Anscombe. Someone who doesn't understand that "it's N's right" or "it's a law" is the logos of a "must" or a "can't" does not understand the institutions of rights and of law. But: "Of course, *once these linguistic* practices exist, we can detach the two parts from one another and 'It's N's' can appear as an independent reason, for example, a reason why one will not do something."[34] Lyons's view that this feature of Mill's theory vitiates Mill's claim to accommodate rights and their correlative obligations implies that Anscombe does not accommodate rights and that civil disobedients

[34]Anscombe, "Rules, Rights, and Promises," p. 322; italics Anscombe's.

cannot, consistent with their overall position, accommodate authority.

I am inclined to agree with this conclusion as regards act-utilitarianism (which, as Lyons points out,[35] does not settle the question of whether act-utilitarianism is the theory we ought to adopt). But the conclusion seems wrong concerning the more complex, conceptually sensitive, mode of utilitarianism he finds in Mill. Let us return to the theory of civil disobedience to see whether it can help to arbitrate this disagreement.

Civil disobedients do not merely avow or claim, abstractly as it were, to respect authority. They take some pains to show that their commitment to authority carries specifiable import for their thought and action. The several versions of the doctrine pursue this objective in varying ways, but most of them do so at least by:[36]

1. treating questions about subscription and obedience, nonsubscription and disobedience, as distinct and distinctively important questions—as questions that have their own conceptual form and that involve reasoning of the kinds Anscombe has described.
2. accepting that there are circumstances in which a well-grounded adverse judgment about the substantive merits of a law or command does not provide a sufficient justification for disobedience. The familiar distinction between a single seriously objectionable law and a recurring pattern of such laws is perhaps the most dramatic manifestation of this view, but in almost all versions of the theory it is accompanied by less categorical maxims that counsel restraint and circumspection when deciding whether to engage in civil disobedience.
3. accepting a variety of constraints on the modes of conduct that will be employed in the course of disobedient action. Among the more important of these are that the action will be done openly not conspiratorially and without the use of physical violence.
4. insisting that their own adverse judgments about laws and command do not deprive officials of the authority to attach and enforce legal sanctions for disobedience to or refusal to enforce them. "You broke a law" remains the logos of "You must pay a

[35]Lyons, "Utility and Rights" (original version), p. 7.
[36]The following summary is taken, with minor modifications, from my *Practice of Political Authority* (Chicago: University of Chicago Press, 1980), pp. 121–22.

fine" or "You must go to jail." Adverse judgments about laws and commands, in other words, do not themselves (directly) deprive the latter of their authority. The only implication that follows from such judgments is that the obligation to obey or to enforce them, which ordinarily follows (the civil disobedient insists) from the fact of their authority, is called into question as a conclusive reason for obeying them. It remains a reason for obedience to which serious-minded persons must give considerable weight (which it does not do, for example, for the anarchist or the revolutionary). But if the judgment that the laws are strongly objectionable coincides with a number of other judgments about matters such as the likely consequences of the acts of disobedience, including the likely effects of acts of disobedience on the viability of the practice of authority, that judgment is accepted as contributing to a justification for disobedience.

On this understanding, justifying disobedience will not be notably easy. Authority remains a potent concept, one that yields "musts" and "can'ts" that cannot be understood or assessed apart from the rule-governed practice in which it has its sense. In these ways the theory and practice of civil disobedience can be said to accommodate authority and law. The familiar criticism that civil disobedients either do not understand authority or aim to destroy it (that they are in fact revolutionaries or anarchists) is belied by the details of their thought and action. In the light of its details, the criticisms to which I allude tell us more about what the critics would like—for reasons that are independent in Anscombe's sense—authority and law to be than they tell us about what that understanding is and what is consonant with it. The question arises whether this is not equally true of critics of "civil encroachment" concerning established rights.

There are two morals to be drawn from these considerations, one primarily conceptual and theoretical, the other more broadly moral and political. As to the first, authority is parallel with rights at least in the Anscombian sense that both involve rules that are understood to create "musts" and "can'ts" that are interwoven with reasons in the sense of a logos. In other words, both are independent and stringent. As evidenced by the fact that it concerns, involves, and defends illegal acts, the theory and practice of civil disobedience introduces such independent reasons into the practice of authority; it appeals to such reasons as grounds for diminishing the stringency of the "musts" and "can'ts." Although controversy continues concerning it, it has been widely accepted that civil disobedience is nevertheless conceptually and theoretically compatible with authority. (Note that insofar as we are talking about legal rights, a practice of authority that countenances civil disobedience has very likely also countenanced instances of civil encroachment on rights. Many—though not all—acts of civil disobedience encroach on legal rights.)

Rights and authority are not fully parallel. And the only undeniable commonality between civil disobedience and Millian utilitarianism is that both entertain considerations "independent" of practices and institutions in the course of thought and action within and concerning them. Thus, even the entire disappearance of controversy concerning civil disobedience would not *prove* that Millian utilitarianism is conceptually and theoretically compatible with the common understanding of rights. But neither has Lyons (or, to my knowledge, anyone else) *proven* the contrary. The purpose of the comparison I have introduced is to give greater plausibility to the view that Millian utilitarianism can accommodate rights.

If I have succeeded in this—to turn to the moral and political upshot of my story—it may now be possible to address more directly the question of whether we *ought* to understand rights so as to admit of the kind of thought and action Mill recommends. *Should* we be open, should we be receptive, to the idea that Baker might consider, for purposes of deciding whether to respect or enforce a right of Able's, the possibility that the exercise of that right is unjustifiable in the circumstances at hand?

My suggestion is that we should. I suggest that openness to such thinking and acting would moderate rights in much the same manner that openness to civil disobedience moderates authority. Practices of authority that are open to civil disobedience afford participants a range of socially approved responses not otherwise available in the same sense. Presented with a law or command that is at once legally valid and substantively objectionable, participants in the practice are not forced to choose among obedience, merely criminal disobedience, or revolutionary action. Other participants recognize the differences between civil disobedience and the last two alternatives; their responses to disobedients reflect that recognition. Most important, argumentation about the merits of the law or command not only continue after its adoption or promulgation but take on added forcefulness and drama. It is more difficult for those who support the adopted law or command to say, "Well, that's settled, let's go on to other things." It is even more difficult for them to say, "We won that one, let's go out and win another." In these ways, civil disobedience enhances the seriousness of moral and political discussion—perhaps especially the seriousness attached to the arguments of those not in positions of authority and power.

In a practice of rights open to "civil encroachment" and perhaps even "civil nonenforcement," alternatives would be comparably enlarged and enhanced. Presented with Able's right claim, Baker could concede that the right was well established and generally well justified and yet experience social acceptance or legitimacy as she attempted to dissuade—perhaps even to prevent—Able from exercising the right in the circumstances at hand. If the right was legal, Baker would have to "take the consequences" of refusing to respect or enforce it. But those consequences would not necessarily include the moral opprobrium—and hence the sense of wrong doing, guilt, and shame—that strict deontological theories attach to violations of rights.

Of course, such a practice would also eliminate or qualify some alternatives that would be assured by understandings of rights according to which they are yet more strongly independent and stringent. In particular, in such a practice it would be more difficult for Able to "stand on her rights," to dismiss or brush aside arguments that they should not be exercised in this or that circumstance. She would have to anticipate not only Baker's persistence but the possibility that Baker might enjoy sympathy and support from others in the community. Rights would alter the character of discussion about what should and should not be done, but validly asserting a right would not necessarily end that discussion.

The terms *civil encroachment* and *civil nonenforcement* are not in general use and may seem menacing. Understood as I have described them, however, the thinking and even the acting to which they refer are familiar enough and no reason for disquiet. I have argued that Millian utilitarianism and civil encroachment have in common the willingness to entertain "independent" reasons in deciding how to act in respect to rights. On this view, civil encroachment is a mode of action opened up and sometimes justified by

Millian utilitarian thinking.[37] I have further argued that Millian utilitarianism is consonant with the common understanding of rights. If I am correct in these contentions, an increased willingness to consider civil encroachment would not itself represent a change in—certainly not a threat to—the practice of rights. If anything were menaced by such a development it would be misunderstandings that encourage extremism in the exercise of rights and give rights an undeservedly bad name. If I am correct in thinking that extremism in the exercise of at least some rights is prevalent, an increased incidence of announced and defended civil encroachment might benefit the practice of rights in much the manner that civil disobedience has benefited the practice of authority.

[37]Of course there are other modes of thinking—those that appeal to religious considerations would be an example—which entertain and invoke "independent" reasons. Millian utilitarianism is only one of a number of possible bases for civil encroachment.

6

The Theory of Rights and
the Practice of Abortion

Is there a convincing argument for a *right* to abortion on demand? A variety of particular forms of such a right are now legally established in this and a large number of other legal systems, and it is known that these rights have been successfully exercised millions of times. Yet defenders of such a right are not in agreement as to the patterns of reasoning that best support it, and a large number of people continue to believe that abortion itself, and certainly a right to abortion on demand, are utterly indefensible. I hope to contribute to the discussion of this difficult matter by drawing explicitly on aspects of existing theory concerning rights. I will try to show that explicit attention to the idea that there should be a right to abortion on demand serves to clarify controversy over abortion and helps to produce a strong argument in favor of what has become (in an astonishingly short period of time given the centuries of opposition to it) accepted legal and moral practice over much of the globe.

It must be stressed at once that the question "Should there be a right to abortion on demand?" is not equivalent to the question of whether abortion is (ever) morally, legally, or otherwise justified or defensible. True, if abortion could not be justified at all, there could hardly be a justified right to it. But it is possible that abortion could sometimes be justifiable and yet that there would be no adequate justification for according or establishing any rights to have abortions. Abortions might be permitted under certain circumstances but in every case the decision for or against them would be made by some authority. (It could even be the case that abortions were mandatory; which would imply that there was a duty to have one but no right to do so.) Rights are distinctive moral and/or jural entities, and having and exercising, protecting and respecting, violating and infringing on them are distinctive modes of action. It is impossible to derive a sufficient justification for any particular right from the distinctive characteristics of rights as such, but justifications for all particular rights are, tautologically but not trivially, justifications for rights and not something else. Hence such justifications must take the distinguishing characteristics of rights into account.

What Is a Right?

There are a number of distinct types of rights that will have to be distinguished if we are to make headway with our question about the right to an abortion on demand. There are nevertheless certain generalizations that hold across the major subtypes, and we will begin by discussing them.

We can think of the rights we actually have (as opposed to those that are merely proposed or that we may think we ought to have) as warrants for actions. These warrants are supplied by rules that are established in some society, group, or association. Once established the rules themselves warrant the holders (A's) of the rights they create in taking a certain class or type of action (X) and they place other persons (B's), who can be expected to object to A's doing X, under various kinds of restrictions, prohibitions, or requirements in respect to A's doing X. When A sets out to do X and B comes forward to object, A can conclusively establish a kind of propriety for her doing X, and a kind of inapplicability for B's objection, by producing the constitutional provision, statute, court decision, feature of the moral code, and so forth that constitutes the warrant for her claimed right to do X. Such warrants hold against—that is, serve to defeat—a more or less clearly specified range of the known or anticipated objections to A's doing X. Thus to have a right to do X in a particular jurisdiction, community, or group is to have a distinctive degree of assurance, in advance as well as during and after the fact of acting, that doing X will be held to be proper by some criterion possessed of authoritative standing in that jurisdiction or society. Doing X will be held to be correct or blameless despite the fact that members of the society vigorously object to it.

Two features of this account of rights deserve further emphasis. First, when a society or group establishes a right it in effect adopts an official or collective or authoritative position concerning a more or less clearly identified class of actions and objections to that action. It commits itself, in advance of specific instances of the action qua exercises of the right (and hence in advance of knowing the consequences of particular instances of the exercise of the right), to the position that the class of actions will be permitted (and at least to that extent encouraged). The unfolding of experience may convince that this commitment is mistaken and may lead to alteration or repeal of the rule that established the right. But until such time as the rule has been changed, the action will be entitled to protection whenever proposed or taken by a holder of the right. Such commitments, moreover, are all but invariably made in the awareness that the actual exercise of the right will commonly be controversial, that there will be persons who strongly object to A's doing X. If it could be expected that A's doing X would be universally welcomed or at least accepted, there would be no point to establishing a right to do X.

The second feature that deserves emphasis is implicit in the first. The commitment just described is in effect a commitment to accept and to protect the decisions of right holders to do X or not. With rare exceptions that are irrelevant here, to have a right to do X is to be at liberty to do X or not as one sees fit. If A decides that it will be to her advantage to do X, the fact that there is an established right to do X itself warrants her in proceeding to do it. If she chooses to reveal her reasons for doing X and others find them objectionable or even repugnant, they may think badly of her as a person and she may suffer some ill consequences as a result. But given that she has a legal right to do X, others cannot properly hold that her doing X was, is, or would be illegal; given that she has a moral right, others cannot hold that it was, is, or would be immoral. The practice of according rights is one of the, probably the, single most dramatic respect in which societies accord autonomy of action to individual agents.

Types of Rights

The last sentence will require elaboration when I reach the question of the justification for including the practice of rights among the arrangements and institutions that structure our legal and moral lives. It will also prove to be a crucial consideration in my proposed justification for a right to abortion on demand. But before taking up these matters I must pause to note some significant distinctions among types of rights, distinctions that concern the particulars of the warrants supplied by various rights. Because the distinctions in question are familiar and largely uncontroversial, and because I can barely touch the interesting theoretical questions that arise concerning them, this part of our discussion will be brief.

The all but canonical work here is by Wesley N. Hohfeld.[1] Responding primarily to legal materials (statutes, court opinions, legal commentaries), Hohfeld developed distinctions among four recurrent uses of "a right" and "rights." He drew the distinctions in terms of what he called the "correlates" and the "opposites" of each of the uses. The correlate is the jural attribute that attaches to some *B* by virtue of *A*'s having a right of a particular type. The opposite applies to *A* herself and is what the term says, namely, the opposite of having the right that *A* actually has. (On examination the notion of the opposite of a right commonly proves to be elusive.) In schematic form the four types are as follows:

Type of right	Correlate	Opposite
1. liberty	no-right	duty
2. right strict sense	duty	no-right
3. power	liability	disability
4. immunity	disability	liability

Probably the most familiar of these types is the second, rights in the strict sense. If *B* validly contracts to pay *A* $400 per month for the use of *A*'s apartment, *A* thereby acquires a right in the strict sense to that payment and *B* a correlative duty to make the payment. The important point is that there is no such thing as a right of this type without an identifiable *B* or *B*'s with a specified obligation in respect to that right. In the language used above, the combination of the rules concerning contracts and the fact that some *B* has entered into a valid contract with some *A* warrants *A* in demanding that *B* pay and (assuming no defeating conditions intervene) puts *B* under a definite obligation to meet that demand.

Both the difficulty and much of the interest of the first type, rights

[1]See Wesley N. Hohfeld, *Fundamental Legal Conceptions*, ed. W. W. Cook (New Haven: Yale University Press, 1919).

in the sense of liberties, lie in the correlate that Hohfeld dubbed a "no-right." As the category name indicates, if *A* has a right to *X* in this sense she has a liberty, is at liberty, to do *X*. But what exactly does this imply for other persons? Presumably the *B*'s have a duty to respect the right. But of what does respecting the right consist? My own interpretation, which I have elaborated elsewhere,[2] is that *B*'s no-right merely(!) means that she must not contend that it was, is, or would be wrong for *A* to do *X*. If the liberty is a legal one, *B* must not contend that *A*'s doing *X* is illegal; if the *X* is a moral liberty, *B* cannot properly contend that *A*'s doing *X* is morally wrong or blameworthy. Unlike rights in the strict sense, however, *A*'s liberties do not warrant her in demanding, and *B*'s no-rights do not obligate her to perform, any affirmative action to aid or facilitate *A*'s doing *X*. Indeed the combination of *A*'s liberty and *B*'s no-right does not itself prohibit *B* from acting in ways that may, as a practical matter, make it difficult or impossible for *A* to succeed in doing *X*. To take a familiar example, if *A*'s right to freedom of speech under the United States Constitution is a liberty, *B* (the Congress, a police officer, an ordinary citizen) may not contend (or act on the contention) that it would be illegal for *A* to exercise that right. But *B* need not supply *A* with a soapbox, a public address system, or time on national television. Indeed *A*'s liberty does not itself prohibit *B* from beating a bongo drum so that *A*'s speech cannot be heard.[3]

How Can Rights Be Justified?
The Liberal Principle

The bearing of the foregoing on the question of a right to abortion on demand is not far to seek. To accord a right of any sort to

[2]See Richard E. Flathman, *The Practice of Rights* (New York: Cambridge University Press, 1976). A number of the questions taken up in this chapter are discussed in greater detail in this work.

[3]Rights in the sense of powers and immunities have less relevance to issues about abortion, and I will simply give an example of each to make the distinctions somewhat clearer than they are in the above schema. A standard example of a right in the sense of a power is the legal capacity to make a will. It would be impossible to make a will apart from the constitutive rules of will making. But *A*'s power to make a will imposes no obligations on *B*. What it does is make *B* liable to become a beneficiary of *A*'s will should *A* choose to exercise her power to write one. When *A* actually makes a will that includes *B*, rights in the strict sense are likely to result. A

abortion on demand would be (is) to provide all those who have that right and who decide they want an abortion with a warrant for having one, a warrant that is established as conclusive against some specified range of objections against the desire and its satisfaction. If the right is a legal right in the sense of a liberty, according it bars all other persons (in the jurisdiction) from contending that having an abortion (under the conditions included in the definition of the right) is or would be illegal; if a moral liberty, it bars all other persons (in the moral community) from contending that having an abortion (under the conditions included in the definition of the right) is morally wrong or blameworthy. If the right is a legal or a moral right in the strict sense, it would be established that the desire to have, and having, an abortion is not only innocent but imposes some further obligations (for example, to perform the abortion if one is a qualified physician) on assignable B's. To accord a right to abortion on demand, in other words, is not merely to say that there is a reasonable case for abortion, that fair consideration will be given to allowing abortions under certain circumstances, or that others will respond tolerantly, charitably, or sympathetically to persons who wish to have or have had abortions. Rather, it is to put the legal or moral authority of the society or community on the side of those who want abortions and against the objections of those who oppose them.

Quite clearly, it would be impossible to justify according any species of right to abortion without detailed consideration of the characteristics and consequences of abortion itself, of the particular conditions under which the right would obtain, of the type of right under consideration, and (in the case of rights in the strict sense) of the specifics of the obligations that would correlate with the right. As with all rights without exception, sufficient justifications and disjustifications are impossible apart from the particulars of the right in question.

---

standard example of an immunity is represented by the Fifth Amendment provision prohibiting compulsory self-incrimination in certain classes of cases. Ordinarily the prosecutor, judge, congressional investigating committee, and the like have authority to require an accused person or witness to testify, and the latter are under a liability to be questioned and have an obligation to respond when questioned. But A's immunity qualifies that authority and its correlative liabilities and resultant obligations and puts the prosecutor, judge, congressional investigating committee under a disability to ask certain classes of questions.

It nevertheless remains the case that all rights are rights; that it is impossible to accord a right to a particular X without according a right. And because a right is a something, not an anything whatever, because rights are characterized by a more or less distinct and identifiable family of characteristics (albeit it would be impossible to state the necessary and sufficient conditions of something counting as a right), there are considerations of a more general nature which bear on the question of whether there should be any rights at all and on the question of whether, given that we know something about a particular X, there should be a *right* to that X.

Among the most prominent of the features characteristic of rights is the extent to which they protect and encourage freedom of action on the part of the individuals (or other agents) who hold them. The most obvious respect in which this is true is the one I have been discussing: in ways that vary according to the right in question, A's desire to act is protected against objections and other forms of resistance thrown up by persons who believe that they, others, or some thing or state of affairs will be disadvantaged or harmed by A's proposed action. This deserves to be regarded as a feature of the logic of the notion of rights. If no restrictions of any kind are placed on any B's, we simply are not dealing with a right.

This characteristic of the logic of a right is surrounded or accompanied by a number of others, one of which might be called the asymmetry between the positions of A and B. It is ordinarily for A to decide whether to exercise her rights or not. Whereas in most cases it is clearly wrong for B to fail to discharge her obligations vis-à-vis A's right, the notion that it is wrong for A not to exercise her rights is not well established. If a second party criticizes A for not exercising rights that A clearly has, A is usually justified in telling that party to mind her own business. A cannot unilaterally determine what rights she has, but her autonomy in deciding what to do with her rights is very great.

A second such feature concerns the rhetoric characteristic of rights discourse, especially the rhetorical style characteristic of the A's. It is not only common but generally thought unexceptionable for A's to claim, maintain, assert, demand, and insist on their rights. And it is seldom taken amiss, often applauded, if they do so insistently, forcefully, staunchly, boldly, and even zealously. A right is something to which one is entitled, something one can unabashedly and unapologetically assert against all challenges and challengers.

How can a practice with these characteristics be justified? What assumptions are being accepted in a society that not only sustains such a practice but gives it, as this society has done, an honored place among its institutions and arrangements? It is worth noting in this context that the practice of rights is by no means without its critics. There have been and are societies and cultures that find the self-assertive individualism characteristic of the practice of rights deeply objectionable. Indeed there is a persistent minority in this culture that reacts negatively to the very idea of rights. In most cases this view is associated with yearning for a greater degree of community, fraternity, and similar values in human relations. Persons who espouse it seek fellowship, integration, and cooperation; deep, intense, and intimate ties. And they find the practice of rights antithetical to these values. Rights are said to disaggregate and to fragment. They generate selfishness and competition rather than friendship, love, and a willingness to sacrifice for others and for the community.

A society or culture that sustains and celebrates individual rights has not necessarily rejected all of the values associated with concepts such as community. Its members may believe that there is an important, even a vital place for love, friendship, and fellowship; they may want to sustain relationships to which rights and their exercise are indeed inappropriate. But it is clear that a society or culture will not value the practice of rights as we know it unless it has a strong commitment to some kind of individualism; unless the preponderance of its members believe that free, autonomous individual action is at least one of the chief among their values, a value that social, political, and moral institutions and arrangements ought to honor and to serve.

It will be convenient to give this commitment or value a more explicit formulation and to provide it with a name. The name I propose is "the liberal principle" (LP) and the formula I will employ is as follows:

It is a prima facie good for individual persons to have and to be in a position to act on and to satisfy interests and desires, objectives, and purposes.

Although it is impossible to derive or defend this principle in anything like adequate detail here, three comments concerning it cannot be avoided.

First, I take it to be a part of our moral (as opposed to our merely genetic or biological) concept of a human being that all human beings in the moral sense (hereafter human persons or simply persons)[4] do have interests and desires, purposes and objectives, and are capable of acting on and pursuing them. This feature of the concept shows up in many ways, one of the more dramatic of which is the very special manner in which we expect one another to relate to persons who for some reason have failed fully to develop these characteristics or who have partially lost them. Consider the vastly greater care that is owed to such persons; the concern, solicitude, active helpfulness, and so forth that is expected in respect to them. By contrast, interactions among persons who suffer no such disabilities may appear to be almost reckless in the ways in which they presume that others can, as we sometimes say, "take care of themselves." (Which is part of the reason that persons with partial disabilities are, rightly, sensitive about inappropriate forms of "solicitude" which assume that the partially disabled person cannot "take care of herself" in respects in which, in fact, she is perfectly well able to do so.)[5] In short, the interested, purposive character of

[4]There is of course controversy concerning how this distinction should be drawn and what inferences can be made from and concerning it. I will be elaborating and defending my use of the distinction below. But that there is and must be some such distinction could hardly be controverted. For a vigorous defense of the distinction, see Michael Tooley, "Abortion and Infanticide," in *The Rights and Wrongs of Abortion,* ed. Marshall Cohen, Thomas Nagel, and Thomas Scanlon (Princeton: Princeton University Press, 1974).

[5]I will take the occasion provided by this turn in the discussion to remark on a point concerning abortion itself. It is commonly suggested that the pro-abortion position implies or otherwise invites insensitivity and worse toward life forms that, as with the fetus, lack characteristics of full human personhood or personality. I deal with aspects of this argument below. But it is worth emphasizing the point made in the text above, namely, that our duties to human persons who lack a part of the usual complement of characteristics are commonly and rightly thought to be much stronger, much more demanding, than those owed to persons with no disabilities. The judgment that a member of some class departs in some way from the usual characteristics of the class to which she or it belongs cannot itself settle the question of how she or it ought to be treated.

I permit myself one further aside of a somewhat polemical nature. I am inclined to think that the attitude of anti-abortionists toward women commonly presents an extreme case of the kind of recklessness toward normal human persons mentioned above. It is admitted that women are deeply affected by pregnancy, childbirth, and child rearing, and so forth. But it is assumed that "they can take care of themselves" in these regards, that is, that they do not require the help provided by such things as rights to abortion. This attitude might be acceptable, might even be a kind of

human persons is ordinarily presupposed or taken for granted. And where this presumption must be qualified in respect to the ability of an individual to act on her interests and desires, other persons are expected to give special attention to fostering and serving them.

These same considerations—and this is the second comment—go some distance toward supporting what is of course the chief moral thrust of LP, namely, that it is prima facie a good thing for persons to be able not just to have and to act on but to satisfy their interests and desires, achieve their purposes and objectives. A related consideration that offers further support concerns what can be called the transitive character of interests, desires, and so forth. All interests and desires are in or for some object or state of affairs, all purposes and objectives make essential reference to a condition or outcome that it is the person's purpose or objective to achieve. Hence to say (1) that persons have interests and desires, objectives and purposes, and (2) that this is a good thing is surely to imply (3) that it is, at least prima facie, a good thing to satisfy the interests and desires and achieve the objectives and purposes. To state (1) and (2) but to deny (3), although not formally a contradiction, is at least to write a recipe for intolerable frustration.

My third comment on LP will bring us closer to its bearing on the justification for rights. As is indicated by the qualifier "prima facie," the principle is not itself a sufficient justification for any action. If accepted, the principle establishes a presumption that individuals ought not to be criticized for or otherwise prevented from having, acting on, and satisfying interests and desires, objectives and purposes. All criticisms, prohibitions, and so forth must be justified in the light of the fact that they prevent or qualify the achievement of a prima facie good. But the presumption that the principle establishes is always subject to defeat. In respect to any action whatever (save the action of denying the principle itself) it may be possible to justify a criticism, a prohibition, or a constraint.

For this reason alone LP will not itself sufficiently justify any right and hence will not sufficiently justify any instance of the practice of rights. Any right, and hence the practice of rights in any instantiation, involves additions to the protection that LP provides for individual actions. It adds the notion that there are some actions

---

compliment, if they were in fact allowed to take care of themselves, that is, to handle sexual relations, pregnancy, and the like in their own way(s).

that are not simply prima facie good but are conclusively justified against some more or less definite range of objections. And rights in the strict sense add the further protection accorded by the particular obligations they assign to the B's. These additions require defense. They require defense, among other reasons, because they involve restrictions on the very good that LP celebrates. This is most obvious in respect to rights in the strict sense because the obligations that such rights entail serve to prevent the B's from acting on and satisfying those interests, desires, and so forth that prompt them to want to interfere with A's doing X. Thus adherents of LP have reason to be suspicious of the practice of rights and of all particular rights.

LP nevertheless provides a plausible foundation for the practice of rights. This is because the principle celebrates that very individualism and freedom of individual action for which rights provide further and more conclusive kinds of protection. (That is, given that there will be rules, laws, and restricting institutions and practices of some sort, the practice of rights celebrates such individualism more explicitly and directly than the other rules and practices with which we are familiar.) A society strongly committed to LP, it is true, will almost certainly be in need of fewer rights than one with a weak commitment to it. This is because its members will already have committed themselves to respect for the kind of individualism that rights protect. But it will also be well prepared for the practice of rights. If it finds that certain modes of individual action are particularly important and yet especially liable to interferences and objections, acceptance of the idea of according those actions the special protection that rights afford will come easily to it.

Can a Legal Right (Liberty) to Abortion on Demand be Justified?

Arguments for Such a Right: LP Applied

Manifestly, a very large number of women have had, now have, and can confidently be expected to develop an interest in or desire for an abortion; manifestly, at some point or points in their lives a great many women make it their objective or purpose to have an abortion. Thus if we approach the issue of abortion from the perspective given by a practice of rights thought of as supported by LP, it will follow immediately that being able to have an abortion when one is in fact desired is a prima facie good, the denial of which requires explicit and substantial justification. Because it is also known that there is likely to be opposition to having an abortion when desired, it is also at least initially plausible to think that there ought to be some species of right to have one.

The contrast between this perspective on the matter and what might be called the traditional approach to it is of course very great. The traditional approach (to abortion and to a great many other moral issues) is to assume that the individual's interests, desires, and so forth are suspect, are probably guilty in some way, and to search revelation, natural law or right, tradition, the needs of the moral or legal community, or some other body of transcendent truth for (the expected) evidence that satisfying, acting on, or even having the particular interests and desires in question is indeed blameworthy and is therefore to be prohibited, prevented, punished, exorcised. No one who has read the by now voluminous anti-abortion literature can fail to be impressed by this among its characteristics. It is increasingly common for anti-abortion writers to concede that back-alley abortions are unpleasant and regrettable, that unwanted children enter life under great disadvantages, perhaps that the burgeoning world population threatens all life with catastrophe. It is rare indeed to encounter the view that the interests and desires, objectives and purposes, that (after all) make up so much of the lives of human persons are themselves deserving of immense respect and support.

Given this circumstance, little or nothing of a practical sort could be accomplished simply by stating LP in abstract formulation and pointing in a general way to its obvious applications to the question of abortion. Even if we do not regard interests and desires as guilty, we are all too wont to denigrate them with adjectives such as *mere;* to think of them as fleeting, evanescent, and insignificant. Purposes and objectives that are "merely individual" are also thought to be eligible for this treatment. We have been taught to think that what matters in life is virtue and duty, the sacrifice of individual interests and objectives to high moral principles and transcendent truths, the subordination of the individual to the community, the nation, the church. Thus even so erudite and incisive a student of the abortion issue as Professor Noonan has argued that the pro-abortion movement has taken much of its strength from "a trend to reject all codes of morality" and "a desire to be free of a code of morality."[6]

But there is nothing "mere," "insignificant," "unprincipled," or a-, non-, or immoral about respect for the interests and desires, objectives and purposes of individual human persons. Nor is there anything abstract about the significance of LP in its application to the question of abortion. Admittedly some interests and purposes are more substantial, more lasting, more important than others. One of the advantages of approaching questions about rights from the perspective of LP is that the latter allows of a ranking of interests and desires and hence provides logical space for the judgment that some, but by no means all, of them deserve the special protections afforded by establishing rights to act on them. But it could hardly be suggested, especially by anti-abortionists, that a woman's interest in having an abortion is trivial or insignificant. Having elevated childbearing and rearing to the status of acts of the greatest possible sanctity, having treated motherhood and its duties as sublime and life-pervasive, anti-abortionists can hardly turn about and dismiss a woman's interests and desires in respect to them as transient and insubstantial.

Accordingly, I will resist the temptation to elaborate on the significance of the more obvious of the interests (for example, those that concern pregnancy and childbirth themselves) which a right to abortion on demand would protect. But there is one aspect of this matter, one that connects directly with the theory of rights, which requires discussion.

The value, to its possessor, of a right is not restricted to the protections it affords at the moment or moments of its exercise (in the sense of the actual doing of the protected act—in this case the actual having of the abortion). Its value projects back and out from that moment to the whole skein of thoughts and actions that precede it in more or less connected ways, and it projects forward into the continuing life of the actor after that moment. I personally have had relatively few occasions explicitly to assert and exercise my right to freedom of speech against specific challenges and challengers. But the knowledge that I have that *right* is a recurrent

[6]John T. Noonan, Jr., ed., *The Morality of Abortion* (Cambridge: Harvard University Press, 1970), p. xv.

influence on my activities. I think thoughts, make plans, attend to events in my society, consider modes of action, and so forth in ways that would be impossible or that would be done under very different circumstances if I were living in Chile, Uganda, or the Soviet Union. And my life following any exercise of the right has, if anything, been yet more markedly different than it would have been in the absence of the right.

Consider in this perspective the position of women in societies that have not established a right to abortion on demand. Consider in particular their position in respect to sexual relationships (and the entire constellation of potentially joyful experiences that radiate around such relationships) during those stretches of their lives in which they do not want to undertake the bearing and rearing of a child. It is no exaggeration to say that these relationships, which can be so beautiful, so sublime, so life-enriching and enhancing, are commonly sources of anxiety, sometimes of fear, sometimes of something close to terror. And for good reason. Assume "the worst" occurs and the woman becomes pregnant. If she is married and chooses to carry the fetus to term and to raise the child, her plans for her own life will certainly be significantly affected and may have to be entirely given up. If she seeks *permission* to have an abortion, she faces official interrogations, hearings, the making of judgments—in short, gross intrusions by strangers into the most intimate aspects of her life. For much of human history her alternative has been the debilitating and very likely dangerous ministrations of the illegal abortionist. And in either case, especially if she has the abortion, she must face the guilt and the shame that societies insistently impose on women who have not taken "due care." If she is unmarried, the entire experience is in all likelihood very much the worse, and its adverse effects might well continue through the remainder of her life.

Under these circumstances, which have been relieved but by no means eliminated owing to improvements in and the easy availability of contraceptive devices (relieved, that is, for those who have not been taught to feel ashamed of using such devices), the absence of a legal right (liberty) to abortion on demand projects its destructive consequences backward and forward in time (from the moment at which the right would actually be exercised) and inflicts those consequences on much of the woman's life.

The contrast between such a circumstance and one in which a

right to abortion has been established could hardly be sharper. In the latter case, women can enter into that whole array of life experiences that radiate out from sexual relations secure in the knowledge that control of the effects of those experiences on their lives is largely in their hands; secure also in the knowledge that they can exercise that control in dignity free of clumsy and unwelcome intrusions. I would not deny that it is possible to enter imaginatively and sympathetically into the differences between these two situations and nevertheless conclude against a legal right to abortion on demand. I do not see how it is possible for anyone who appreciates the enormous differences between them to deny that there is a powerful case for such a right.

Arguments Against a Legal Right (Liberty) to Abortion

There are of course a number of additional arguments that are commonly advanced by proponents of abortion on demand. Many of these concern social consequences—the ill consequences of prohibiting abortions and the good consequences of a right to it. Although cogent and indeed persuasive in many instances, the use of these arguments in support of an individual right would introduce complexities (having to do with the so-called utilitarianism of rights) which cannot be dealt with here.[7] Accordingly, and because I believe that the foregoing arguments constitute a strong case for a legal right (liberty) to abortion on demand, I leave the other arguments aside and turn to the case against such a right.

That there is such a case, and that it merits a serious response, has been implicitly conceded in the foregoing discussion. If opposition to a legal right to abortion on demand were without creditable foundations, if it were based entirely on prejudice, misinformation, manifestly faulty reasoning, and the like, mounting a detailed argument for such a right would by now have been shown to be an exercise in futility if not irrelevance. But this is manifestly not the case. There are substantial arguments against a legal right to abortion on demand and we will have to concede to them on some points.

[7]The most compelling among the additional arguments, and those that introduce the fewest complexities, concern the ways in which respect for the interests and desires, objectives and purposes, of women carries over to respect for the interests of other persons involved in or affected by the abortion decision.

Arguments Grounded in Characteristics of the Fetus as
Such (as Opposed to the Potential That the Fetus Carries)

The Fetus as Animate

The least complicated of the arguments against abortion are
based on principles such as the "sanctity of life" or "reverence for
life" (as, for example, in the well-known formulations of St. John-
Stevas and Albert Schweitzer). These principles require that the life
of all animate, organic things be protected and even revered; that it
never be intentionally or perhaps even knowingly destroyed if it is at
all possible to avoid doing so. Given that from conception, certainly
from implantation, the (embryo-cum-) fetus is undoubtedly animate, it follows that abortion, which is the knowing, in most if not
all cases the intentional, destruction of the life of the fetus can be
justified, if at all, only in cases in which it is the only alternative to
the knowing, perhaps the intentional, destruction of some other
living thing. Traditionally, this has been taken to mean that abortion is justified only if refusing it will cause the death of the mother,
perhaps even constitute the intentional killing of the mother.[8] And
because advances in medical science have all but eliminated the
possibility that such dilemmas will in fact present themselves, abortion is virtually always wrong.

There is very little that can be said for this argument. As noble as
the sanctity of life principle may at first sight appear, accepting and
acting consistently on it would, of certainty, lead to horrendous and
utterly indefensible results. I will give but one of the many examples
that not only support but require this judgment. In preparing for
most medical procedures, doctors and nurses use antiseptics that
are known and intended to destroy the lives of countless animate
things. It could not be said that doing so is indispensable to preserving other lives, particularly not the life of the patient. Countless
patients survived medical procedures very nicely before antiseptics
and indeed germs were discovered. More to the point here, given the
availability of antiseptics, antibiotics, and other such medications,

---

[8]The distinction between knowing and intentional destruction of the fetus is at
the basis of what is commonly called the doctrine of the double effect. I do not find
the distinction or the doctrine helpful in respect to questions about abortion, but I
cannot deal with the matter here. For a sensitive and helpful discussion, see esp.
Philippa Foot, "The Problem of Abortion and the Doctrine of Double Effect,"
Oxford Review, no. 5 (1967), pp. 5ff.

we could now postpone their use until such time as definite evidence of infection presented itself. Since infection would very often not develop, such a practice would save the lives of untold numbers of living things at minimal if any risk to patients.

But such a procedure would be unthinkable. Let one human person die or even suffer from it and its outrageous character would be condemned by everyone who heard of it. We do not treat all animate things as of equal value. Avoiding the slightest risk to some creatures—say, sentient creatures—justifies the destruction of millions of animate but insentient ones. The most generous thing that could be said for the proposal to do otherwise is that it would reflect a truly wild and irrational form of sentimentality. To pretend that we do in fact or would ever take such a proposal seriously would be the sheerest hypocrisy.[9]

The Fetus as Sentient

The argument from the merely animate character of the fetus, then, is no argument at all. But the fetus as such is not merely animate; from a short time after implantation it begins to show clear signs of sentience or what is sometimes called simple (as opposed to reflexive or self-) consciousness. These signs multiply rapidly in the early stages of its development and are undeniable through much of its existence. Thus with the possible exception of its very earliest stages the fetus as such falls under the protections, whatever they are, of any principles that hold for sentient life, not just those that protect life itself.

There is at least one principle that applies to all sentient but no

[9]On this point, see Werner J. Pluhar, "Abortion and Simple Consciousness," *Journal of Philosophy* 71 (1974):165. "As sentience . . . grows dimmer and dimmer as we descend toward ever simpler organisms, the *prima facie* wrongness of destroying an organism inevitably decreases in proportion, ultimately to a degree of negligibility where it becomes in practice more misleading to affirm than to deny that there remains a residual *prima facie* wrongness at all, since it is standardly overridden by just about any countervailing consideration, moral or other."
It does not follow that no consideration whatever is owed to life as such. The wanton, pointless destruction of any living thing, aside from being terribly stupid from a self-interested point of view, is indefensible. As Pluhar suggests, the point is rather that terms such as *wanton* are not and should not be employed if the killing finds justification from the resultant improvements in the well-being of higher creatures.

nonsentient life, and that is the principle that forbids cruelty.[10] Thus if there were grounds for saying that abortion as such is cruel it would be categorically impermissible. Equally, if a particular person's desire for an abortion proceeded exclusively from cruel motives or dispositions—say, to torture a fetus at an advanced stage of development after it had been removed from the womb but before it died, or simply because that person took pleasure in the thought of any suffering the fetus might undergo during abortion—that abortion would be wrong.

There are, however, no grounds for treating abortion as such as a cruel act. "Cruelty" requires that the act be done for the sake of producing pain or other suffering. There may be individuals who seek abortions out of such motives, but there is surely no evidence to support the generalization that all or any significant number of persons do so. Anyone who did so, moreover, would have to have the abortion performed in a medically improper manner since all accepted procedures employ techniques, such as the use of anesthetics, designed to eliminate pain on the part of the fetus and pain and suffering on the part of the mother. It may be true, however, that the possibility of pain increases as the fetus develops. If so, this would be one of a number of considerations in favor of having abortions performed at the earliest possible date in the pregnancy. It is also true, to reiterate, that we have identified a condition under which abortion cannot be justified.

A further albeit less demanding principle that holds for sentient creatures concerns what we might call insensitivity or indifference. In extreme forms insensitivity is difficult to distinguish from cruelty. But one can be insensitive to another creature without positively seeking to harm it or to cause it to suffer. This is a more plausible charge against those seeking abortions. They do not cruelly or maliciously seek to cause the fetus to suffer, but they are insensitive to the fact that it is impossible to achieve their objective without causing severely adverse effects for the fetus. They and those who defend them simply do not concern themselves with, do not care about, the consequences of their actions for the fetus.

This charge has a more plausible ring than that of cruelty. It takes

[10]It is, I think, conceptually impossible to be cruel to a creature or thing—a microbe, a plant, and so on—incapable of any kind of pain or undergoing any kind of suffering or anguish.

a good part of its plausibility from the fact that a considerable number of persons view the fetus as nothing more than a bit of tissue or a blob of coagulated protoplasm and accordingly believe that no consideration whatever is owed to it. Thus we have stories, retailed by anti-abortionists, such as the tale of the couple who, despite wanting a child and fully intending to try to conceive again in a few months, sought an abortion so that a mistimed pregnancy would not interfere with a planned vacation. More generally, since abortion is the destruction of the fetus, the charge that those who seek or support the procedure are insensitive, even indifferent, to a sentient organism has an air of plausibility about it.

If more credible than the charge of cruelty, however, the allegation that abortion involves indifference or insensitivity is also wide of the mark. Those who deny that the fetus is sentient are mistaken. But if they are genuinely mistaken in their views in this regard, they cannot also be indifferent to the pain that the fetus undergoes. And for those who recognize its sentience, seeking or defending abortion may be a question not of insensitivity to the fetus but of placing higher value on the interests and desires, objectives and purposes, of the mother than on the survival of the fetus. To choose a greater good over a lesser one is not in itself to deny or to be indifferent to the lesser good. In other circumstances, not faced with such a choice, the very persons who favor abortion may well show the most exquisite sensitivity to the well-being of the fetus. Certainly it is common for women who support abortion on demand and indeed who have had abortions to take every possible care for the fetus during a desired or merely accepted pregnancy and to go out of their way in assisting others who are pregnant.

The point of these last remarks can be generalized. Criticisms that focus on alleged defects of character, motive, or disposition on the part of proponents of abortion beg the issue in question. If abortion is right or justified, it is not wrong or a defect of character to seek it or to defend it. No doubt individuals have sought and defended abortions out of bad motives and owing to serious defects of character. But one suspects that their numbers are at least matched by those who oppose abortion out of a belief that pregnant women ought to be made to carry and to rear the child as due punishment for carelessness, promiscuity, or even Eve's primeval sin against God. (A view that the fetus, if it had views, or the child that the fetus becomes, might find something less than flattering!) No amount of railing against either sort of person will help us to decide the merits of the issues about abortion.

Cruelty and insensitivity to the fetus, then, are as wrong as cruelty and insensitivity to any sentient creature. But the question remains whether abortion is wrong *because* the fetus is a sentient creature. Here again, if the value to the mother of a right to abortion is even remotely as great as I have suggested, the answer is clearly in the negative.[11] Even if we put the matter in the crudest of quantitative terms, since the fetus is merely sentient, the instant of pain that it may undergo in abortion simply cannot begin to compare with the fear, the mental anguish, the frustration and derangement of life plans, that unwanted pregnancies impose on women. But *of course* it is *wrong* to put the matter this way; it is wrong to act as if human persons are as it were to be weighed on the same moral scales as merely sentient creatures.

The Fetus as Possessed of Reflexive Consciousness

Animate and *sentient:* those two terms exhaust the list of un-doubted and undoubtedly morally relevant properties of the fetus as such.[12] Because the fetus has these properties it falls under the protection of moral principles of undoubted gravity and impor-tance. But there is simply no case at all for thinking that those protections do or should extend to the refusal of a right to abortion on demand. Any conflict between those principles and the principles

[11]I leave aside the fact that humans routinely destroy and cause pain to sentient creatures for reasons vastly weaker than those that support a right to abortion on demand. Many of these practices are clearly indefensible. It should nevertheless be said that if one were to start a campaign against mistreatment of sentient creatures, on any view of the matter abortion would have to take a much lower priority than those many practices that are virtually without justification.

[12]Of course the fetus as such has a veritable host of other properties. Among those that figure with disturbing prominence in the anti-abortion literature are its undeniable aesthetic properties. The fetus is commonly said to be very beautiful: delicate in features, extraordinarily intricate in its complexities, and so forth. Insofar as I can judge from photographs I have seen, I concur with these judgments. The judgments are also true of, for example, snowflakes and rock crystals. And these are reasons, albeit certainly not moral reasons, for preserving snowflakes and rock crystals under some circumstances. They are not reasons for countenancing adverse effects on human beings. Nor, incidentally, are they reasons that pro-abortionists should adopt for protecting the fetus. If it turned out that some or most fetuses were ugly, would we therefore be justified in destroying them?

that celebrate and defend significant life values of human persons must be decided in favor of the latter.

It is sometimes suggested, however, that the fetus as such, at least at some stages of its development, displays some degree of complex or reflexive consciousness, not merely sentient or simple consciousness. It not only feels pain in a purely phenomenal sense that we can detect with (and indeed define in terms of readings on) scientific instruments, but it is aware of pain, may seek to avoid it, may fear it, may suffer anguish in respect to it, and so forth. If this is true, the case for thinking of the fetus as human in a moral as well as a purely genetic or biological sense would be stronger, and hence the argument that the mother should have a right to prefer her interests and desires to the survival of the fetus would be vastly more difficult to make.

The evidence proffered in support of this characterization of the fetus concerns its alleged ability to adapt to changes in its environment in ways at least analogous to the deliberate, intentional adaptations made by human persons and higher animals. Some of this evidence is purely biological or neurological. Heartbeat, brain waves, the chemical composition of blood and other bodily fluids and substances alter in response to various changes in the environment. But changes of this sort are common to all animate creatures and do not support the contention in question.[13] Other evidence has at least something of a behavioral dimension and can be interpreted to indicate primitive kinds of intentionality, purposiveness, and consciousness of self. For example, the position of the fetus in the womb is known to change in response not only to chemical changes that as it were produce their own effects in it but to such influences as pressures on the womb resulting from changes in the mother's posture and related events—changes the response to which would not appear to be dictated by the changes themselves. If we can say that the *fetus changes* its position in the womb in something like a knowing, intentional, chosen response to such pressures, we would have at least a primitive kind of reflexive consciousness.

[13]Of course some of this "biological" evidence, particularly evidence concerning the central nervous system, distinguishes human fetuses from other creatures and establishes that they have the neurological potential for (the neurologically necessary conditions of) reflexive consciousness. But this evidence bears on the question of the potential immanent in the fetus, not the actuality that the fetus as such presents. I take up the question of potentiality in the following section.

This evidence is difficult to interpret and evaluate. Part of the difficulty is due to lack of clarity in the concepts we use (and, as matters stand, must use) in interpreting it. The notion of reflexive or complex consciousness (and the idea of human personhood in the moral sense that is intimately connected with it) has a relatively straightforward and unproblematic application to the ordinary human person of, say, more than a couple years of age. In the absence of evidence of the influence of drugs, serious disease, blows on the head, and so forth, such persons present what can properly be called the paradigm of reflexive consciousness; the pattern or family of characteristics that they so abundantly and continuously display are what we *mean* by reflexive consciousness. But as we move away from the paradigm case, the clarity of the concept and the certainty with which we apply it slips away from us. As we consider persons who are very drowsy but not asleep, under the influence of hypnosis, drunk or otherwise drugged, temporarily amnesiac owing to an injury or severe emotional stress, suffering severe depression in the psychiatric sense, mentally defective owing to birth trauma, we are increasingly doubtful as to what to say. The same is true of movement down the ranks of the animal kingdom and, for some, of movement up the ranks of increasingly complex and adaptive machines. Because the fetus is, on any reading of the evidence, very far indeed from the paradigm case of reflexive consciousness, it is not surprising that there is controversy over how to characterize it.

There is also a special problem involved in judgments about the fetus in this regard. The problem arises from one of the elementary but also elemental facts concerning it, namely, that it is in the womb and hence can interact with those (namely, us) who must make the judgments[14] only in the most narrowly circumscribed ways and for the most part only through the medium of elaborate scientific instruments (instruments that play no role in our ordinary uses of the concept of reflexive consciousness). There is a family of concepts the applicability of which makes up our notion of reflexive consciousness. "Intention," "deliberation," "choice," "reasoning," "understanding," "judgment," "having an interest" (and of course a num-

---

[14]It is hardly irrelevant to this matter that the fetus does not itself have the concept of reflexive consciousness—or any other concept—and for this among other reasons cannot tell us that it deserves this characterization. On this point, see Tooley, "Abortion and Infanticide," in *Rights and Wrongs of Abortion*, ed. Cohen et al.

ber of more specifically moral and jural concepts to which I return below) are among the more important of these. When we can apply these concepts to a person or other creature in a positive way, we have no difficulty about characterizing that person or creature as possessed of some degree of reflexive consciousness. If, as I believe, Wittgenstein and others are correct that these concepts are built up in the course of, that their uses and their meanings take their characteristic shapes from, the interactions in which they figure and which they partly constitute, then the fact that our interactions with the fetus are so severely limited goes far to explain the difficulties we experience in trying to apply these concepts to the fetus. As Roger Wertheimer has said: "There isn't much we can do with a fetus; either we let it out or we do it in. . . . As things stand, the range of interactions is so minimal that we are not compelled to regard the fetus in any particular way."[15]

Because the interaction is minimal rather than nonexistent, it may be that something at least analogous to reflexive consciousness can cogently be attributed to the fetus. If so, the case against cruelty and indifference would certainly take on additional dimensions, as would the argument against utterly casual, thoughtless uses of any rights to abortion that might be established. Given that there is no evidence supporting such attributions prior to what has traditionally been called quickening, it may be that these considerations support a strong moral preference for abortions prior to that development and in any case as early as possible.

In addition to these speculations, however, there are a number of certainties concerning the alleged reflexive consciousness of the fetus as such. Prominent among these certainties are the following: *none* of those moral and jural attributes that we alluded to above has any application whatsoever to the fetus. A fetus cannot be generous or selfish, kind or malevolent, honest or dishonest, courageous or cowardly, just or unjust. Accordingly, a fetus cannot

[15]Roger Wertheimer, "Understanding the Abortion Argument," in *Rights and Wrongs of Abortion*, ed. Cohen et al., p. 44. A really uncompromising interpretation of Wittgenstein's discussion of logical privacy might support the conclusion that the very idea of applying the above concepts to the fetus is and must be incoherent. The conditions necessary for such an attempt to so much as get a foothold, the argument would run, are simply not satisfied. I will not try to develop such an argument here, but the possibility, which is suggested by Wertheimer's remarks as well as my own, is worth exploring.

deserve praise or blame, cannot be found guilty or innocent.[16] Again, the fetus can be said to have needs and sensitivities and to undergo damage and pain. It is for this reason that notions such as good and bad treatment apply to it (just as they apply to all animate organisms). But not even the most expansive interpretations of the available evidence suggest that it is capable of anxiety, fear or anguish, repose, equanimity or happiness (except, of course, in the sense of "happy as a clam"). The fetus does not have hopes that can be dashed, expectations that can be disappointed, desires that can be frustrated, objectives that it can fail to attain.

These last remarks are of course no more than an elaboration on the contention that our interactions with the fetus are extremely limited. One further such elaboration may be forgiven. The fetus can be said to be a subject of our moral actions; it cannot be an agent in our moral interactions. Together with certain propositions about the logic of the concept of rights which were touched on above, it follows from these facts about it that the fetus should not be thought of as a bearer or possessor of rights. To have a right is to be in a position to choose to exercise that right or not, to waive it if one wishes, to hold others to their obligations respecting it, or to release them from those obligations. And to be a participant in the practice of rights is to be subject to the duties and obligations that correlate with the rights of others. The fetus is capable of none of these (if it is capable of any) actions. Accordingly, while the fetus is properly regarded as the subject of good and bad (including morally good and bad) treatment by human agents, it is not properly regarded as bearing, possessing, or exercising rights or of having its rights respected or violated.

It follows from the last of this set of certainties that one of the strongest possible arguments against a legal right to abortion on demand—namely, that such a right would conflict with the established and justified rights of the fetus—is without foundation. It follows from the entire set of certainties, and from our entire discussion of reflexive consciousness, that the evidence on this subject

[16]The constant references to the innocence of the fetus, to abortion as the taking of innocent life, are of course misplaced. Aside, perhaps, from contexts involving religious doctrines concerning original sin, the concept of innocence has no more application to the fetus than the concept of guilt. (And of course in the Christian religious doctrine, if the fetus is a human being it is guilty, not innocent.)

adds very little to the arguments against abortion which are based on the undeniable fact that the fetus is animate and sentient. In particular, there is virtually no basis for the claim that the fetus as such is a human person in a moral as well as a biological sense or that it should be protected by those moral principles that apply distinctively to creatures who are human in the moral sense.

Arguments Grounded in the Potential Carried by (Immanent in) the Fetus as Such

Abortions do not destroy human persons. Abortions destroy fetuses. Of course we know that the fetus will, with due care on the part of human persons (and a little luck), almost certainly become a human person. This fact does not warrant us in saying that a fetus *is* a human person. The fact that a bowl of batter will, with due care (and a great deal of luck) become a gorgeous and delectable soufflé does not transmute the bowl of batter into a soufflé. A soufflé is one thing, a bowl of soufflé batter is another. A fetus is one thing, a human person is another. No amount of emphasis on the indeed wonderful genetic and other biological properties of the fetus can change this.

Still, we treat the bowl of soufflé batter differently from, say, a dustpan of dirt swept up from the kitchen floor. Since the bowl of batter is not notably admirable or useful as such, our doing so makes no sense apart from what the bowl of batter can become. If we admire and enjoy soufflés, we can hardly be altogether contemptuous of or indifferent to the batches of batter from which they rise so majestically. If we assign great value to human persons, we can hardly altogether withhold value from the fetuses from which human persons develop. Thus the question is not whether to assign value to the fetus but what sort of value to assign to it and how to assess that value when serving and respecting it conflicts with the value we accord to human persons and the quality of lives they are able to lead.

Before taking up the latter question—which is of course the crucial one under this heading and perhaps in the whole issue about abortion—there are two associated questions that require discussion. The questions concern the "slide" down one or another of the "slippery slopes" that are said to descend precipitously from the plateau of safe argumentative ground that both pro- and anti-abortionists seek to attain and hold.

Many contemporary anti-abortionists want to defend the fetus but to allow the use of contraceptives (and perhaps masturbation, so-called unnatural sexual acts, and so forth). Most pro-abortionists want to allow destruction of the fetus but to disallow infanticide (and the killing of other creatures who are human in the biological sense but who are said not to be human persons in the full moral sense of the term). Pro-abortionists regularly contend that anti-abortionists cannot rationally or nonarbitrarily stop the "slide" or "regress" to positions that they themselves reject. If it is the fetus's potential to become a human person that requires a prohibition against abortion, and if that same potential is immanent in any spermatozoon or ovum, then should there not also be a prohibition against the use of contraceptives, against masturbation to climax, against "wasting" the fluids by ejaculating them into various "inappropriate" orifices? Indeed if human beings have the capacity to produce ova and spermatozoa, should they not be prohibited from any actions or practices that may damage, destroy, or fail to utilize that capacity? If poor dietary habits, the use of alcohol, tobacco, marijuana or other drugs, excessive work, too little sleep, and so forth produce sterility, impotence, or frigidity, should they not be banned? Should vows of chastity and the beliefs and teachings that promote them not be forbidden? With comparable gusto anti-abortionists contend that there is no rational barrier to the "slide" or "progress" of the pro-abortion position to defense of a right to destroy any and all creatures who are like the fetus in lacking those attributes that define a human person in the full moral sense. If it is true that the cortical development necessary to full reflexive consciousness is not complete until approximately the infant's first birthday, is infanticide not every bit as defensible as feticide? If the development of full personality is prevented or arrested due to disease, accident, or other untoward events, should not those who are burdened by the life of the unfortunate victim of such events have a right to take that life?

It is not surprising that both sides have had difficulty in dealing with these questions and meeting these objections. The anti-abortionist can hardly resist the move from arguments grounded exclusively in the characteristics of the fetus as such to arguments relying on what it will become. But from the moment that move has been made the argument has to contend with the fact that the fetus represents (among other things) one moment or stage in a continuous biological process that can be, in the wider sense of the word, aborted at any moment or stage. If it is the culmination of that process that matters, one interruption in it can be made to appear as indefensible as any other. The pro-abortionist is faced with a comparable difficulty. As we have seen, concepts such as "human person," "moral personality," "reflexive consciousness," "capacity for distinctively human interaction" apply over a range or continuum of cases that is by no means precisely delineated. They are, in Wittgenstein's fashionable phrase, family resemblance concepts for the proper use of which it is impossible to state necessary and sufficient conditions. Moreover, many if not all of the characteristics over which their applications range are themselves fluid and developmental, not static or fixed. The moral personality of a two-year-old child is a vastly different thing than that of an adult.

Recognizing that, and why, both positions face such closely analogous difficulties ought to persuade us to a certain humility in discussing these matters. The game of trading charges in this regard is an amusement in which it is easy enough to score points; but the high scores that result aren't likely to signal progress in resolving issues about abortion.

For what it is worth, I am inclined to allow that there is a valid and morally significant distinction between conception (or perhaps implantation) and everything that precedes it. The union of a spermatozoon and an ovum (or that union plus segmentation and implantation) produces a new entity with characteristics not possessed by its causal antecedents in the biological process, characteristics deserving of at least the kinds of moral consideration discussed above. Abortion *is* a more serious matter than the use of contraceptives. But the distinction between a fetus and an infant is at least as clear and at least as morally significant. This is true from the outset (that is, from parturition), and the clarity and moral significance of the distinction are heightened and enhanced very rapidly from the instant of birth forward. From that instant the infant displays a repertoire of behaviors (crying, gurgling, sucking, eye and other facial and bodily movements) which are either impossible in the womb or impossible for us to perceive and interact with when occurring in the womb. Items in that repertoire, as well as the remarkable responses they commonly evoke in the human persons about the infant, multiply in number and increase in complexity in ways that are not only extraordinary (except that they are entirely ordinary!) but that could not occur if the creature remained a fetus. Given these facts, and given that our moral conceptions and relationships concern the experiences we in fact have and the interactions in which we in fact engage (if only vicariously), it would be astonishing if the fetus-infant distinction ceased to be accorded substantial moral significance. The infant is not a human person in the full sense; there are significant distinctions between the infant and the child, the child and the adolescent, and so forth. (One of these is that, in my view, the infant and the youngish child should not be thought of as bearers of rights.) But this does not alter the fact that there is a clear and morally significant distinction between the fetus and the infant.

But should that distinction be accorded the degree of significance necessary to justify a legal right to abortion on demand? If there were no substantial, no weighty considerations in favor of such a right, the answer to this question would be no. If sexual relations, pregnancy, childbirth, and child rearing were biologically, economically, socially, emotionally, and above all morally trivial, inconsequential, and easily accommodated, the fact that the fetus is biologically human and is very likely to become a human person if not aborted would be enough to justify narrow limitations on abortion. But of course the conditional just mentioned is wildly counterfactual. Sexual relations, childbearing and rearing, especially for women, are manifestly among the weightiest, the most consequential and demanding, of life's experiences. Because this is so, it is difficult to think of any very large number of actions that are prima facie more eligible for the protection of a legal right (liberty) than the act of having an abortion.

Against the argument for such a right stands the potential for human interaction, human personhood and personality, that is immanent in the fetus. A particular instantiation of that potential is destroyed every time an abortion is performed. This is no insignificant consideration. But there is a material difference between potentiality and actuality. The millions of women whose day-to-day lives are so heavily affected by the availability (or not) of a legal right to abortion are not to be thought of in the subjunctive or the future tense. Their interests and desires, their objectives and purposes, and the joy and delight, the pain and the anguish that they experience in pursuing their objectives are real and material, vivid and intense. It is in no small part because the human person that the fetus becomes will have such experiences that we ought to value its potential. It is dubious in the extreme to claim that we place immense, even absolute value on what the fetus will become at the same time that we go on sacrificing vital aspects of the well-being of those who now are what the fetus may someday be. If sensitivities even comparable to those sometimes lavished on the potential carried by the fetus are allowed in respect to the actuality presented by women, the case for a right to abortion on demand would be very strong. But such "evenhandedness" would be altogether misplaced. Beyond those characteristics of the fetus as such that were discussed above, the fetus is a bundle of human potential. But the woman who may want (now or sometime) but cannot have an abortion is a thinking, judging, feeling, hoping, believing human person who suffers in a here and now that may last much of her life.[17]

To deny a legal right (liberty) to abortion is knowingly to condemn very large numbers of actual human persons to pain and anguish and severely to restrict the freedom and quality of life of many more. We must accord this preeminently moral feature of the situation the serious consideration it obviously deserves. If we do so, the uncertain protection[18] that prohibiting abortions provides

[17]For an extreme case of this sort of "impartiality," see Baruch A. Brody, "Abortion and the Sanctity of Human Life," *American Philosophical Quarterly* 10 (April 1973):133ff. Brody argues that a fetus may be aborted to save the life of the mother only if the following conditions are satisfied: (1) in the absence of an abortion both the mother and the fetus will die "relatively soon"; (2) the decision to abort the fetus (rather than let the mother die and save the fetus) is made by a fair—that is, presumably a random—procedure. In short, in Brody's view there is no morally relevant difference between the mother and the fetus. For the full range of Brody's views on this subject, see his book *Abortion and the Sanctity of Human Life* (Cambridge: MIT Press, 1975).

[18]Although I have chosen not to emphasize the kind of consideration alluded to in the text, it is worth noting that at least some of the adverse effects of prohibiting abortion fall with virtual certainty on women, while the benefits, to the fetus, of the prohibition are uncertain at best.

Having allowed questions of a probabilistic sort into the discussion to this extent, it should also be mentioned that questions about abortion would be substantially complicated if in fact so few women wanted to bear children that a right to abortion actually threatened the continued existence of the human race. Because this is not the case, I will take up these complexities only to the extent of saying that it is less than obvious that denial of the right would be the morally appropriate response to

the fetus will not stand against the argument for a right to abortion on demand.[19]

The major (secular) arguments against a legal right (liberty) to abortion on demand have now been considered. Before concluding this part of the discussion, however, two related but in some respects distinct objections must be considered.

First, there is the objection that according a right to abortion will have psychological or cultural (that is, causal) consequences going beyond the effects of abortion itself. Specifically, it will produce a generalized weakening in respect for and the resolve to protect life and it will lead to the acceptance of infanticide, euthanasia, and other forms of killing. To my knowledge this objection, as commonly encountered as it now is, has not been formulated with the precision necessary to a determination of whether the empirical evidence that its cogency presupposes is in fact available. Nor has that evidence been produced.

For present purposes the more important consideration is that establishing the truth of the empirical propositions on which the objection depends would not itself constitute a conclusive argument against a legal right to abortion on demand. If a right to abortion is

---

such a development. It is not self-evident that the fact that women have the biological capacity to conceive and bear children justifies treating them and their lives as resources implicitly available for this or any other project.

[19]The important reflections of Judith Jarvis Thomson and Mary Anne Warren should be mentioned at this point. Thomson calls our attention to how seldom any of us are legally or morally *required* to make sacrifices even remotely comparable to those involved in unwanted pregnancy, child rearing, and the fear thereof. See her "A Defense of Abortion," in *Rights and Wrongs of Abortion*, ed. Cohen et al. Warren presents an analogy that helps to focus thought on the sacrifices we would be willing to make or impose on behalf of potential such as the fetus carries. She asks us to imagine (I have entered some minor modifications in her analogy) that our bodies could be split up into parts with each part (like so many plant cuttings) capable of becoming or generating a human person. If so, we would be presented with a choice between keeping our bodies whole and thereby wasting the immense human potential they carry or splitting them up so as to let that potential be realized. Perhaps some truly heroic persons would be willing to sacrifice their lives so as to utilize their capacity in this regard to the full; perhaps some number of others would be willing to give up an arm, a leg, some flesh from an inconspicuous part of their body, and so forth. Would there be any justification of requiring anyone to do any of these things; for punishing them or holding them morally blameworthy if they refused? See Mary Anne Warren, "The Moral and Legal Status of Abortion," *Monist* 52 (1973):42ff. For a related analogy, see Tooley, "Abortion and Infanticide," in *Rights and Wrongs of Abortion*, ed. Cohen et al.

justified, and if the alleged causal consequences of according that right are objectionable, it would be open to us to accord the right and to take independent steps to prevent the objectionable consequences from ensuing. The most important of such steps would be to show that, and why, infanticide, euthanasia, or whatever kind of killing we wish to oppose is distinct from abortion such that the latter is justified and the former is not and to try to get others to accept that judgment. Doing this much would presumably help to block the objectionable consequences. It would also put us in a position to defend whatever legal prohibitions against other forms of killing prove to be necessary to our objective.[20]

The second objection (or group of connected objections) relates to concessions that I have made to anti-abortion arguments. I have

[20]Owing to the reliance my argument for abortion makes on reflexive consciousness and moral interaction, a word must be said about kinds of killing, in addition to abortion, that would appear to be justified by that argument. I refer in particular to cases in which a human person ceases to display reflexive consciousness and ceases to be an agent in (as opposed to a subject of) moral interactions. If the loss is known (that is, known with the greatest certainty medical science allows) to be permanent, the case for a right to take the life of the erstwhile person seems to me to be at least as strong as the case for a right to abortion. It is, in fact, clearly stronger in one obvious respect; namely, that the organism in question does not possess the potential carried by the fetus. Such cases, however, are seriously complicated (as against the case of abortion) by two factors, the first of sometimes wrenching practical difficulty but of no great theoretical significance, the second of both practical and theoretical significance. The first is that it is often difficult to determine who should have the right to terminate the life of the organism. In the case of the fetus the mother's interests are sufficiently clear and paramount to make this decision unproblematic in most cases. But when tragedy befalls mature persons the matter is often anything but clear. The second complication arises from the fact that, unlike the fetus, such organisms have histories as persons in the full moral sense. These are largely histories of interactions with others who continue to be persons, interactions that will of course have produced attitudes, beliefs, emotional ties, and so forth that do not simply cease at the moment the interactions cease.

This second consideration is not a reason against a right to terminate the life of an organism that was once a person. It is a reason to expect that exercising such a right will be an agonizing, wrenching experience for those who must decide whether to do so and to expect that the latter will in fact often make great sacrifices rather than take the life. (Just as the fact that mothers, at least those not taught to look on the fetus as some kind of punishment inflicted upon them, can easily imagine a personal history for the fetus explains that they so often make the extraordinary sacrifices that the bearing and rearing of children entail.)

For present purposes, however, the importance of the second consideration is that it provides the necessary distinction between the fetus and persons who have temporarily lost reflexive consciousness and the capacity for moral agency and agreed that the fetus has moral value and standing and found that certain ways of treating it are morally wrong. If so, the objection runs, will not a legal right (liberty) to abortion on demand encourage, indeed license, wrongful treatment of the fetus?

There are actually several objections lurking here. The first is essentially the same as the objection just rejected. And the answer to it is the same. If certain ways of treating the fetus are known to be wrong, indeed if the argument for abortion itself includes a demonstration that they are wrong, then a right to abortion could be shown to "encourage" the wrongful treatments only by establishing contingent causal connections that have not in fact been established and that in any case would not be decisive against a right to abortion. Nor could such a right be said to "license" the wrongful treatments in the sense of explicitly and positively providing a warrant for them.

It might be argued, however, and this is the second of this second set of objections, that a legal liberty does license wrongful treatments of the fetus in the sense that it withdraws legal protection from it and leaves the question of how it will be treated to the discretion of private persons. But the assumption on which this objection rests is false. To accord a legal right to abortion on demand no more withdraws all legal protection from the fetus than does according a right to kill animals for human consumption withdraw such protections for animals as, for example, are provided by laws against cruelty to them. If cruelty or insensitivity were features of abortion itself, this argument would be cogent. Because they are not, the argument fails.

The third and last of this set of objections is that the right itself will be abused and that abuses will be difficult or impossible to prevent. People will seek and will obtain abortions for reasons as bad as or worse than those of the avid vacation seekers mentioned earlier. I don't suppose anyone knows, or knows how to find out or predict, exactly how often this sort of thing has occurred or will occur. Most rights are sometimes abused in the sense that people

---

interaction. Unlike the fetus, they do not merely have the potential to develop these characteristics, they have a history of such characteristics. And because they have such a history, they have a relationship to other moral agents that no fetus as such can ever have. For an opposing position, see Eike-Henner Kluge, *The Practice of Death* (New Haven: Yale University Press, 1975), chap. 1.

put them to uses distant from and even antithetical to the interests and objectives in terms of which the rights are usually justified. Think of the abuses of the right to private property—for example, the ways in which wealthy property owners hold the disadvantaged to the strict letter of their obligations in respect to those rights. Think of the abuses that have been made of rights such as freedom of speech, press, and association by individuals seeking to destroy such rights altogether. Where the argument for the value of these rights has continued to command widespread allegiance, the recurrence of such abuses has not been viewed as a sufficient reason for disestablishing the rights themselves.

There are, however, conceptual issues of some importance here, one of which points ahead to questions about moral rights in the sense of liberties and both legal and moral rights in the strict sense. The first point takes us back to the logic distinctive of a right. Rights are conclusive against some range of known or anticipated objections. In the case of a legal right (liberty), the right is conclusive against all legal objections to the action protected by the right. Now, one could attempt to define the legal right to having an abortion in such a way as to exclude from the actions protected by it abortions sought for indefensible reasons. In the same way, one could define the rights of contract so as to exclude from them, say, the right of a wealthy person or a bank to foreclose on a mortgage held against a poor person unable to meet the mortgage payments. This would be to preserve the stringency or conclusiveness of the warrant the right provides but to restrict the range of objections against which it is in fact conclusive.

But there is another kind of move available, one that is preferable in this kind of case. It is well established that it can be morally wrong to do something that one has a legal right to do. No legal action can be taken or brought against the person who exercises the right in a morally wrongful manner, but that person is nevertheless subject to certain kinds of criticism and disapproval. For reasons that I will take up in the next section, this seems to me to be the best way of handling the kind of abuse of the legal right (liberty) to abortion on demand that I am now discussing.

The case for a legal right (liberty) to abortion on demand deserves acceptance. The considerations in favor of this right are firmly grounded in deep and vital human interests and purposes, interests and purposes that themselves arise out of some of the most continuing and morally salient dimensions of the lives of human persons. The arguments against the right are sufficient to establish that the fetus should be accorded moral value and standing of a kind that any moral person will respect and seek to protect. They are not sufficient to disjustify the right. The fetus is an animate and barely more than sentient creature with the potential to become a human person. It would be wrong to prefer preservation of instances of it to the service of profound and pervasive concerns of actual human persons.

Can a Moral Right (Liberty) to Abortion on Demand Be Justified?

Some arguments for a legal right (liberty) to abortion on demand rely heavily on distinctive characteristics of legal prohibitions or requirements such as that they are enforced by the coercive power of the state. Given the widespread and cogently argued disagreement over abortion, for both normative and prudential reasons the state ought to withdraw and let the issue be resolved by the moral rather than the legal community.[21]

Although not without their merits, I have not relied on such arguments here. Rather, I have contended that the moral case for abortion on demand is very strong and that it deserves the positive support that is accorded by giving it the standing of a right. (If this argument were widely rejected, I might fall back to the "weaker" position that abortion ought to be "decriminalized." But that would be a tactical retreat.) For this reason, my argument for a legal right (liberty) is also an argument for a moral right (liberty) to that action. There ought to be such a moral right.

Accordingly, the only distinct issue to be taken up under the present heading concerns the implications, for the *B*'s, of *A* having a moral right (liberty) as well as a legal right (liberty) to abortion on demand. In the latter case the implication is that *B* cannot properly act to make abortion legally wrong, and cannot attempt to punish *A* for having an abortion or punish any other person for giving *A* an abortion that *A* desires. In the former case, *B* cannot properly

[21]See, for example, Wertheimer, "Understanding the Abortion Argument," in *Rights and Wrongs of Abortion*, ed. Cohen et al., the final paragraphs.

contend that it is morally wrong for *A* to have an abortion and cannot bring moral criticism to bear on *A* for doing so. Thus far the implications are entirely parallel. But there is at least one important difference between the two cases. In the law, any given abortion either is or is not legally wrong. That is the only judgment that the law as such can make. But morality and moral judgment commonly allow of differentiations that are more subtle and refined than are ordinarily possible in the law. The *B*'s might accept the position that there is a right to abortion and accept the implication that they should therefore ordinarily refrain from criticizing *A*'s for seeking or having one. Consistent with this position, however, they might hold out the possibility of making and expressing a number of kinds of judgments about conditions ancillary to or associated with the seeking and having of abortions. To our vacationists, for example, they might say: "We recognize and respect your right to abortion on demand and we will interfere in this case only to the extent of saying that we think your reasons for wanting this abortion are vile and repugnant." Persons who said this kind of thing about any very wide array of reasons for having an abortion would probably demonstrate by doing so that they did not in fact accept that right. It is nevertheless a valuable feature of moral as opposed to legal rights that genuine acceptance of and respect for them is compatible with recognizing and forcefully recording one's objections to their abuse. Thus a moral right (liberty) to abortion on demand is valuable both for the protections it accords the *A*'s and for the flexibility of response that it makes available to *B*'s who respect *A*'s right.

Can a Legal or Moral Right in the Strict Sense to Abortion on Demand Be Justified?

As noted earlier, it is a feature of the concept of a right in the strict sense that such rights impose some definite and affirmative obligation or obligations on some identifiable *B*'s. The concept itself, however, tells us no more than this. Specifically, it tells us nothing about the incidence or the content of those obligations in respect to any particular right.[22] Thus there could be a legal or a moral right in

---

[22]In fact, the obligations are sometimes specified in the rules that establish the right; sometimes they must be inferred from the characteristics of the right itself and what would be destructive of or perhaps necessary to its successful exercise.

the strict sense that imposed obligations on doctors or other quali-fied medical personnel, on hospitals and clinics, on the state, on insurance companies, and the like. And the obligations could be to perform or to see to or to pay for the performance of abortions; to do so unqualifiedly on demand, only in the first trimester or under other conditions; to provide postabortion care and counseling; and so forth through a considerable list of possibilities.

Because I cannot begin to deal with this array of possibilities, I restrict myself, by way of concluding this chapter, primarily to comments on the possible obligations of medical or paramedical personnel qualified to perform abortions. Given that some persons in this category hold strongly felt moral objections against abortion, can we say that the right to abortion on demand includes the right to demand that persons competent to perform an abortion actually do so? Specifically, does a woman have a right to demand an abortion from a medically competent (and otherwise available) individual who personally believes that abortion is morally wrong? Is the argument for a right to abortion on demand strong enough to justify the imposition of such an obligation on persons who do not find that argument convincing? (Note that the question also arises in somewhat less dramatic ways in respect to persons other than those who actually perform the operation. It arises in regard to nurses and many others who must assist more or less directly with the procedure. And in jurisdictions in which the government has undertaken to provide or to assist with the costs of abortion it arises in some degree in respect to all citizens or subjects.)

The answer to these questions is a qualified yes. It is yes because (1) the argument for abortion on demand is very strong and (2) because, as things stand, a woman cannot safely (or even surely) abort herself. Owing to (1), we can say that the views of those who contend that abortion is morally indefensible are not well grounded. Having considered the arguments for this position and found them wanting, we cannot turn about and say that they nevertheless pro-vide adequate support for the position they defend. Owing to (2) we can say that the right to abortion on demand could be, as a practical matter, a nullity if abortions could not in fact be obtained from those competent to perform them. Thus if it were the case that the demand for abortions were too great to be met by those both competent and willing to perform them, there would be adequate justification for establishing either a legal or a moral right (or both) in the strict sense that imposed (on those medically competent to do so) an obligation to provide abortions. (There is also adequate justification for using public funds to pay for abortions for persons—in jurisdictions with free enterprise medical practice—who cannot afford them.)

The yes is qualified for the same kinds of reasons that have convinced a number of societies to qualify the obligations imposed on pacifists and other conscientious objectors to do military service in what are believed to be justified wars. It is not that their arguments are judged to be convincing. If that were the case, others would have to give up their position in favor of the position of the pacifists. But where the position of the pacifist or other objecting position is believed by others to be cogent and sincerely held, and where it is believed that the justified objectives can be achieved while conceding something to the views of the objectors, an effort is made to find ways of making such concessions. Conditions of this kind have not always been satisfied in respect to abortion. But because they do seem to be satisfied at the present time, it would be morally insensitive (it would be a violation of LP) not to accommodate to the views of those who object to abortion insofar as we can. Thus we should establish both a legal and a moral right in the strict sense to abortion on demand. And so far as we can do so without nullifying the right, we should excuse from the correlative obligations those persons for whom abortion remains morally unacceptable.

Conclusion

The concept of a right is one of the most widely used, and most commonly abused, items in our moral and political lexicon. We hear claims to an extraordinary variety of rights and we find rights attributed to an astonishing diversity of creatures and things. Although this proliferation represents a kind of tribute to the not inconsiderable success of a comparatively recent legal and moral innovation of genuine value, there is reason to view the proliferation with skepticism. We may be experiencing a kind of inflationary spiral that will end by unnecessarily diminishing the real and distinctive goods that can be obtained with this part of our conceptual currency.

This concern, however, does not properly extend to the campaign for a right to abortion on demand. In adopting the language of rights, pro-abortionists have made precisely the correct conceptual choice. As I have tried to show, "a right" provides the conceptualization, and hence the moral and jural attribute, exactly appropriate to the case that the pro-abortionist wants to make. For this reason, because that case is very strong, and because its strength derives in no small part from the support it receives from the principle (LP) which provides the optimum basis for defending individual rights, a right to abortion on demand is exactly what women ought to have.

7

Egalitarian Blood and
Skeptical Turnips

Ackerman is surely correct that his conception of the basic problems of politics and political philosophy is grounded in assumptions familiar from most recognizably liberal thought. (1) Human beings are end-oriented, goal-seeking creatures whose actions and patterns of action cannot be understood or assessed apart from their conceptions of the good; (2a) conceptions of the good, and hence the goals of action, are irreducibly plural; (2b) there is a scarcity of the goods that human beings seek and of the resources necessary to effective pursuit of those goods; (3) hence there is certain to be disagreement and competition and very likely to be conflict among human beings; (4) disagreement, competition, and conflict neither can nor should be entirely eliminated, but conflict must be contained within nondestructive limits; (5) the primary if not the exclusive objective of politics is to arrange and order human interaction so that each individual has the greatest possible freedom to pursue goals compatible with effective constraints on destructive conflict; (6) the task of political philosophy is to achieve an understanding of human beings and their interactions which will contribute to this objective.

In its generic form (or rather its apparent generic form), moreover, the (putatively) master notion in Ackerman's political philosophy, the notion of "Neutral dialogue" or "constrained conversation," is also tolerably familiar. Recognizing, on any one of several grounds, the truth of 2a, and realizing that disagreement over conceptions of good is the source of the most destructive conflict (and/or the modes of stilling conflict most destructive of the freedom of some), in politics each of us must cease to claim the superiority of our conception of good and order our interactions by principles neutral among such conceptions. This self-denying ordinance (historically first or at least most emphatically adopted in respect to religious beliefs) will itself prevent the most violent and freedom-destroying conflicts, thereby permitting individuals and groups of like-minded individuals a great increase in freedom to pursue their goals as they see them.

Given its first systematic expression by a thinker, Thomas Hobbes, to whom Ackerman is much indebted, this understanding assigns to politics and the state the primary task of maintaining and enforcing the conversational constraints. In the most uncompromising versions of the understanding, perhaps best represented in our time by Michael Oakeshott's notion of a civil society or *societas*, the conversational constraint is extended so as entirely to exclude considerations of ends and purposes from politics and political interactions. A proper political association is an association exclusively in terms of subscription to what Oakeshott calls "adverbial rules," rules that speak not at all to the substance and purpose of proposals presented or actions attempted or taken. Driving to its limit the understanding that questions about ends and purposes are largely unresolvable and inveterately conflictogenic, Oakeshott insists that admitting any such questions into the life of a political association will, of certainty, either explode the association in civil war or transform it into that terrible mode of tyranny, a teleocracy.[1]

In most of its numerous versions, this understanding rests on a deep skepticism concerning the capacity of associations of human beings to resolve, to the mutual satisfaction of their several members, questions of undoubted importance to those members. This characteristic is in evidence in the opening and closing chapters of Ackerman's work, and he explicitly endorses what he calls the "principled uncertainty that is the hallmark of liberal policy" (p. 103).[2] At various points in his central chapters, moreover, he shows himself willing to accept what many have found to be decidedly bleak and dispiriting implications of these skeptical foundations. Pursuit of many interests and desires, objectives and purposes,

---

[1] See Michael Oakeshott, *On Human Conduct* (London: Oxford University Press, 1975), esp. the second essay.

[2] All page references in the text are to Bruce Ackerman, *Social Justice and the Liberal State* (New Haven: Yale University Press, 1980).

including some that could be regarded as worthy by most criteria, is found to be illegitimate because involving violations of the constraints generated by the skeptical assumptions.[3]

The extraordinary feature of Ackerman's book, however, is that its skeptical assumptions are not only conjoined with but asserted to be the unimpeachable ratiocinative foundations of a justification for an intensely activist and radically egalitarian welfare state—a justification that is as encompassing in scope and content as it is evangelical in tone. Ackerman claims that there is a direct line of argumentation from Neutrality concerning conceptions of good to largely incontrovertible conclusions concerning the basic issues of distributive justice within and among generations, freedom of expression and association, eugenics and other questions of population policy, of education, of abortion and infanticide, affirmative action, environmental conservation and use, treatment of animals, the qualifications for and responsibilities of citizenship, the optimal patterns of political institutions, and no doubt some others that I have neglected to record. Over a very considerable range the answers to these questions are to be sought within, not outside, of the political and governmental realm and process. Answering them, moreover, is not left to the private judgment of individuals and groups. There are authoritative answers that are allegedly dictated by Neutral conversation. Anyone who rejects those answers has made a specifiable error. Anyone who seeks to act on alternative answers has violated Neutrality and is therefore guilty of seeking illegitimate power over others.[4]

I

It happens that I agree with Ackerman's conclusions concerning many of the issues of morality and public policy which he addresses. It also happens that I find a number of the more proximate of his arguments for those conclusions cogent and convincing. For these and numerous other reasons, this is an important work. But the contention that the substantive conclusions are in fact derived, or are in principle derivable, from the elements constituting Neutral

[3]See ibid., esp. 15.2, "Satisfaction Guaranteed?" pp. 61–64.
[4]Ackerman does leave open the possibility that there are alternative ratiocinative paths to the conclusions he reaches; see ibid., pp. 13–15.

conversation is initially implausible, and I at least find it much less than convincing.

Crucial to Ackerman's policy conclusions is a principle of equality initially presented in the formal or *ceteribus paribus* form that has been salient in moral and political thought at least since the seventeenth century. Ackerman claims, however, that the method of dialogue constrained by Neutrality reveals this principle to carry a range of substantive egalitarian implications recognized by few if any of its previous proponents.

Rationality itself commits us to equality in the weak *ceteribus paribus* sense of treating admittedly like cases alike. This requirement, however, can be satisfied, consistent with great differences in treatment, by giving pertinent reasons for the distinctions and discriminations we are disposed to make. Notoriously, the weak principle of equality gives little guidance in choosing and assessing the pertinence of such reasons. Therefore the principle places minimal constraints on our thought and action.

Ackerman argues that Neutrality transforms this situation. It does so by excluding as illegitimate entire encompassing categories of what might otherwise pass muster as sufficient reasons for treating one person or class of persons differently from others. Debarred from arguing that I, my class, caste, or nation, is superior to you or your class; forbidden from claiming that my goals or objectives are superior to yours, I am deprived of many if not most of the considerations that are commonly advanced to justify preferment and discrimination. Thus the presumptive or prima facie case for equality is strongly protected against defeat or qualification; most other things are guaranteed to be "equal" and hence the usual justifications for departures from equality cannot so much as obtain a hearing. (Strictly, the force of the argument, at least over much of its sweep, depends on 2*b* as well as 2*a*. As we see below, for Ackerman equality is an instrumental good. Thus if there were an unlimited supply of the goods and resources necessary or contributive to the achievement of goals and purposes, then the question of equality and departures from it, or more generally the question of advancing and justifying claims, would arise over a much narrower range of activities and interactions.) Thus in a world unblemished by accumulated differences that put some persons in a disadvantaged position, all resources that (*a*) might contribute to achieving goals and purposes and (*b*) that are subject to deliberate, choiceful distribution and redistribution, must be distributed in a strictly, that is, an arithmetically, equal fashion. In the world we know, a world disfigured by gross, deeply disadvantaging and totally unjustified differences and distinctions, we must move to redistribute goods and resources so as to eliminate those disadvantages.[5]

II

There is a complex and often inventive apparatus of elaboration and application in and through which Ackerman brings this basic argument to bear on the issues listed above. Often fascinating and occasionally annoying in the science fiction character of its detail, this apparatus will doubtless attract a good deal of attention. Much of the apparatus, however, is introduced to free our minds of the sorts of philosophically distracting complications that present themselves in applying, even in thought, a general theory to times and places specific. Ackerman believes that his theory carries definite implications for contemporary societies. In later chapters he attends to the casuistic issues of "second" and "third" best—as distinct from "ideal"—theory.[6] These discussions moderate somewhat the frequently dogmatic character of the argumentation at the level of ideal theory, a fact that the reader should bear in mind in considering the following objections. It is clear, however, that in Ackerman's view the philosophically crucial contentions of the book reside in the ideal theory, not the casuistry. Accordingly, I concentrate on the first of these.

Will Neutrality solve the classic problem of transmuting weak, formal equality into a strong, substantive egalitarianism? It will be useful to begin by looking behind Neutrality to the skepticism that is supposed to convince us to accept it. In dialogue, Neutrality gets

[5]Or rather, the citizens of each of the nations into which our world is in fact divided must work such a redistribution among themselves. They have much more modest obligations to the citizens of other nations—no matter how severely disadvantaged; see, esp., ibid., pp. 256–57.

[6]"Second-best" theory attends to the transaction costs of implementing the conclusions of ideal theory, costs assumed away in ideal theory by positing a "perfect technology of justice." "Third-best" theory concerns itself with the vast array of additional complications created by the fact that the human beings we know often willfully refuse to act on (what they may concede to be) the correct conclusions of ideal theory. See ibid., esp. pp. 31–32, 232–33, for these distinctions.

expressed by the phrase "I am (my goals are, my conception of good is) at least as good as you are (as yours are)." This endlessly repeated phrase does not reflect a very deep or robust skepticism. To take the obvious as a benchmark, it allows what the much deeper skepticism of the emotivist denied, namely, that we share a concept (as opposed to a conception) of good;[7] it allows that we can use that concept in a mutually intelligible manner.[8] A deep skepticism would not yield "I am at least as good as you are" but the conclusion that we do not know what we are talking about in respect to good. This conclusion would presumably lead us to abandon such discourse altogether. Or it might lead to a nihilism scornful of Ackerman's entire enterprise of legitimating power.

But Ackerman assumes a shared conception as well as a shared concept of good. I suggest that it is this assumption that does the work of supporting his egalitarian conclusions. For starters, if the members of a society did not agree that destructive conflict is bad, if they rejected the idea that power ought to be legitimated, they would be untouched by Ackerman's arguments. Again, if there were no consensus as to what counts as a resource, as to the wherewithal necessary or contributive to achieving their goals and purposes, they could not agree on what should be included in and excluded from the scheme of distribution and redistribution. In its turn, agreement on wherewithal presupposes a shared understanding of the range over which the notions "good" and "goods" can move. Through much of his discussion Ackerman masks these (and, as I argue just below, some rather more controversial) assumptions with his notion of "Manna," an infinitely fungible something or other that can be put to the service of any good whatever. But whether masked or standing out in bold relief the assumptions are indispensable to his arguments.

Nor do these considerable items exhaust the axiological consensus presupposed by Ackerman's arguments. Why should I accept that resources be distributed equally? As we have seen, Ackerman's general answer is that all of the arguments for unequal distributions

[7] I follow Rawls's distinction between a concept and a conception. See John Rawls, *A Theory of Justice* (Cambridge: Harvard University Press, 1971), pp. 5ff.

[8] If we took "I am at least as good as you are" at all literally, simple grammar might prompt us to query whether persons able to discern and agree about instances of good could not (thereby?) discern and agree about at least some instances of better and best.

depend on illegitimate claims to superiority. Thus equal distribution falls out as the only policy that does not breach the conversational constraints.

I leave aside the question of whether this argument would go through in a world blessed with Manna; Ackerman does not have any Manna to distribute. The resources he is concerned to divide as equally as the nature of the resources allow are such goods as genetic endowments; stable families; liberal educations; freedoms to speak, assemble, associate, and reproduce; the liberty to accumulate money and other forms of property; clean, healthful environments; and so forth. In a world of finite resources, these goods compete with one another and with other goods; allocating resources to achieve, acquire, or maintain one among them reduces our capacity (both individually and collectively) to achieve the others. This being the case, Ackerman's proposed allocations necessarily involve rankings of and choices among goods and hence among conceptions of good. The policies are grounded not in Neutrality among conceptions of good but in a preference for one conception of good over others.

If there were unanimity concerning the rankings and the consequent allocations, it would perhaps *appear* that respect for Neutrality had been maintained. As with all of the attempts known to me to solve this problem, Ackerman's attempt ultimately depends on achieving such an agreement.[9] That is, the argument "succeeds" only by denying the chief assumption, the unresolvability of disagreements over conceptions of good, which sets it into motion.

Ackerman's skepticism, while not very deep-going, is nevertheless strong enough to prevent him from openly positing actual, express agreement concerning his proposed policies and the goods they serve. Accordingly, he takes the familiar tack of contending that in reason everyone should or ought to agree to those policies and that those who do agree are justified in imposing the policies on those who fail to see the light. The distinctive feature of his version of this maneuver is his contention (at the level of ideal theory) that anyone who dissents from the proposals has violated Neutrality.

---

[9]The best known of other recent attempts is of course Rawls's, where the assumption that agreement can be reached on the primary goods and on the maximin principle is intended to do the same job.

Any and all cases of dissent from these proposals are characterized as cases of someone illegitimately claiming that her conceptions of good are superior to rival conceptions.

III

As I said at the outset, this is implausible. On Ackerman's own beginning assumptions it is deeply implausible. Ackerman labors mightily to make it convincing.[10] He does so by trying to show that his proposed policies are required by Neutrality itself. In the course of this effort Neutrality takes on a rather more variegated coloration; it sheds its appearance as nothing more than an inference from skepticism about the possibilities of resolving disagreement over normative questions and presents itself as a social ideal, as a doctrine about what at bottom is "good" for humankind.

The argument is that egalitarian genetic, population, family, educational, and perhaps other policies are required in order that all citizens be sustained[11] in their "dialogic competence"; that none of them be so "dominated" as to be unable effectively to argue against (and otherwise to resist?) attempts by others to impose conceptions of good on them. The ideal life is one in which the capacity for free activity through dialogic interaction is supported by a position of "undominated equality."

Neutrality as a social ideal (call it Neutrality$_1$) does have important connections with Neutrality understood as a conversational constraint grounded in skepticism (Neutrality$_2$). Society adopts egalitarian policies on certain fundamental questions. It does so in order to put all those eligible for citizenship in a position to conduct

[10]The deep implausibility of the contention, it seems to me, is what leads Oakeshott to adopt, and to accept the consequences of adopting, the conclusion that a civil political association must keep its hands off of questions about ends.

[11]I say "sustained" because Ackerman makes capacity for dialogic competence the chief condition of eligibility for the status of citizenship; see *Social Justice,* chap. 3. Lacking the capacity for such competence, the mental defective ("idiots"), the fetus, subhuman animals, etc. are not eligible for citizenship. In Ackerman's view it follows that the egalitarian distribution rules do not hold in respect to these creatures. Indeed, it follows that citizens should regard these creatures as bits of Manna to be put to use. There are a host of difficulties here, but I cannot take them up in this essay.

their further activities within, and to order their further relationships by, the conversational constraints of Neutrality$_2$. In those further activities and relationships citizens are at liberty to adopt whatever goals and purposes they find attractive. But if their efforts to achieve those goals bring them into conflict with other citizens, they cannot seek to resolve the conflict by claiming that their goals are superior to the goals of others. If they cannot obtain the resources they need to attain their goals without resort to such arguments, they must give up those goals.

Thus Neutrality$_2$ does reflect a certain skepticism about the resolvability of disagreements over ends and goals. And it is intended to prevent those disagreements from leading to conflicts that are destructive of freedom. Moreover, Neutrality$_2$, or rather the capacity of citizens to conduct themselves within and otherwise to maintain the constraints of Neutrality$_2$, is integral to Neutrality$_1$. Sustaining the capacity for such conduct is the primary reason for adopting the egalitarian policies characteristic of Neutrality$_1$. *In this sense* Ackerman is entitled to claim that Neutrality$_2$ is a basis for or ground of his argument for egalitarian policies. But this is a very different sense than the one with which he began. Justifying policies by arguing that they contribute to this (or any other) agreed-upon end is a far cry from claiming that they are required because we cannot agree upon ends.

IV

To sum up, we have another attempt to delineate and defend a political and moral ideal that integrates and reconciles equality and freedom. The ideal seeks to maximize freedom to pursue self-chosen goals and purposes within the limits set by egalitarian constraints. The constraints operate at three levels. First, everyone must accept the objective of maintaining the greatest possible scope for freedom for each citizen consistent with the avoidance of destructive conflict. Second, everyone must accept that this ideal can be attained only if each citizen is in a position of undominated equality (p. 18) and must accept the policies implied by that proposition. Third, all citizens must forego arguments alleging their personal superiority or the superiority of their goals or purposes. Perfectionist arguments are permitted only as the basis for the constraints that form the first and second levels of the ideal.[12]

Whether this is the liberal ideal, it is undeniable that something akin to it has been attractive to many self-denominated liberals. The three "levels" or dimensions into which Ackerman's vision (I suggest) resolves itself are neither an unfamiliar nor an implausible rendering of the implications of the six assumptions I noted at the outset of this essay. In particular, it is difficult to see how the ideal could now be made plausible without including in it some version of the substantive (level 2) and procedural (level 3) limitations on freedom to pursue individual and group goals and objectives (level 1).

The all but standard difficulty, of course, is to find an understanding of the egalitarian constraints of level 2 that renders them compatible with the freedom and diversity of level 1. Ackerman recognizes this and is at pains to deny that his level 2 proposals will have narrowly restricting or notably flattening and homogenizing effects. His egalitarian policies are instrumental to freedom rather than ends in themselves, and they forbid only those inequalities that leave some citizens in a dominated position. For these reasons he believes that the policies are consistent with a wide scope for individual initiative and experimentation and a rich, variegated pluralism.

My own suspicion is that his level 2 policies would prove to be voracious of resources and that the resulting limitations, in company with the ban on perfectionist arguments, would be more constraining of diversity than Ackerman recognizes. For our purposes, however, the important question is not the outcome, which might be as I suggest and yet highly desirable, but the justification that Ackerman is able to give for it. This question takes us back to Ackerman's attempt to rely, or at least his avowed reliance, on the essentially procedural consideration of Neutrality$_2$.

Ackerman is not the first to try to derive substantive egalitarian conclusions from premises that are formal or procedural in the sense that they impose constraints on reasoning. The best known recent attempt along the same lines is Rawls's use of the Veil of Ignorance to exclude large classes of information and hence any

[12]Of course Ackerman claims to have excluded perfectionist arguments altogether. In saying that they are permitted as the basis for first- and second-level constraints I am assuming the correctness of my own argument against Ackerman.

reasons that might be partly based on that information. Ackerman claims that his approach is preferable to Rawls's just because he suppresses less of what actually influences thought and action, an objective for which I have a good deal of sympathy. Perhaps Ackerman qua theorist excludes less information than Rawls. Neutrality$_2$ nevertheless requires citizens disposed to challenge egalitarian distributions to set aside no less than their convictions about what is best and worst. They are to do so on the skeptical grounds that they cannot hope to win agreement concerning those conceptions and cannot justify imposing them if they cannot win agreement to them. But this argument posits an impossibility. As the old saying has it, you cannot get blood out of a turnip. From the premise that we cannot reason our way to agreement about conceptions of good you cannot get reasoned agreement that undominated equality is the good that should take precedence over all others with which it conflicts. If all that Ackerman gave us in support of the egalitarian policies of Neutrality$_1$ was the skeptical foundations of Neutrality$_2$, he would have given us precisely nothing in support of those policies. The substantive egalitarian policies of level 2 would present themselves as arbitrary restrictions on the freedom of level 1. If we take seriously the announced program of the book, we have to say that it is another failed attempt to provide a reasoned, a principled, reconciliation of freedom and equality.

V

For reasons already mentioned in passing, it would be foolish to dismiss the book in this way. Despite his program, Ackerman presents a rich array of arguments for his several egalitarian proposals. I cannot assess the particulars of these arguments here, but I hesitate not at all in saying that everyone interested in the issues they address will profit from thinking them through. Having delivered up this pronouncement of my own, I end with a general comment concerning the disjunction between the program Ackerman sets out and his performance over substantial stretches of his book.

A preponderance of Ackerman's chapters conclude with comparisons between his "liberal" position and the conclusions yielded by contractarian and utilitarian thought. To oversimplify somewhat, the recurrent themes in these comparisons are as follows. Contractarians place themselves under constraints so narrow as to do themselves out of the wherewithal necessary to so much as make contact with the important issues. Huge classes of considerations that do and must play an important part in moral and political discourse are excluded; and those admitted must be marshaled and processed according to fixed, inflexible rules and procedures. In respect to vital issues of moral and political philosophy, contractarian thought is either dogmatic or barren. By contrast, utilitarianism engages the issues and consistently advances pertinent proposals for resolving them. Indeed Ackerman not infrequently finds himself in agreement with the resolutions that utilitarians have proffered. But utilitarianism commits mistakes that are the converse of its contractarian opponents. Owing to its consequentialism, there are virtually no classes of considerations that utilitarianism can exclude from moral and political discourse. For the same reason plus its commitment to maximizing aggregate satisfaction, prohibitions and requirements salient in nonphilosophical thought are downgraded to the standing of rules of thumb or reduced to the weak requirements of the formal principle of equality together with a latitudinarian if not vacuous teleology. In particular, individual dignity and freedom are left hostage to the ebbs and flows of power.

Ackerman's "liberalism" is intended to let in a wider array of considerations than contractarianism, thereby avoiding dogmatism and gaining purchase on the real issues of moral and political life, while at the same time avoiding the dangerously indiscriminate character of utilitarianism. In this perspective the burden of my argument has been that Ackerman fails to delineate a stable and defensible alternative position. The programmatic restrictions imposed by Neutrality$_2$ exclude considerations essential to moral and political thought and action and leave his liberalism in the very difficulty he ascribes to contractarian thought; that is, his liberalism is either incapable of joining major issues or forced to make (as I have argued he in fact does make) ad hoc appeals to considerations that are illicit by his own canons.

If assumption 1 in our original list is correct, it would seem that attempts to banish or restrict the use of conceptions of good must yield this result. If moral and political life takes its distinctive character from, if moral and political issues and disputes are about, ends and purposes, how can moral and political philosophy do other than address and attempt to resolve questions about ends and purposes?

As teleologists from Aristotle to the utilitarians have argued, moral and political philosophy can do no other. Does it follow that there is no alternative to the sort of unrestricted and undiscriminating utilitarianism that Ackerman and a small legion of deontologists deride? We do not have a satisfactory answer to this question. Despite a number of thoughtful attempts to revise and refine classical utilitarian theory, no fully satisfactory version of the doctrine has been achieved. I suggest, however, that (at the level of systematic theory) Ackerman's book is important because it contributes to this objective.

Neutrality$_2$ is one species of a genus familiar in those strands of liberal thought that accept assumptions 1 and 2a. Nor is Ackerman the first to reason from these assumptions to the notion of formal or procedural restrictions on the ways in which political actors may pursue their goals and purposes. Law and the rule of law, constitutionalism, rules of order and debate, bills of rights and indeed the notion of rights in all its forms—all of these are ways of putting constraints on such activity. Constraints of these kinds have an honored place in most liberal thinking—albeit a theoretically insecure place in utilitarian versions of liberalism. If Ackerman's argument for such constraints is in fact distinctive, it takes its special character from two of its alleged features. The first is that the constraints of Neutrality$_2$ are said to be absolute within their realm of application. No one can ever, under any condition or circumstance, seek to win a political argument or to settle a political dispute by appeal to the superiority of a conception of good. (In this respect Ackerman's argument has the form of some natural rights theories.) The second and intimately related feature is the claim that the constraints established by Neutrality$_2$ are justified not on the ground that they contribute to some good (or on natural rights grounds) but on the skeptic's assumption that we cannot resolve, to our mutual satisfaction, questions about good. By contrast, numerous proponents of the rule of law, constitutionalism, parliamentary procedures, individual rights, and the like, including non- or anti-utilitarian proponents, recognize the possibility of justified departures from and even violations of the constraints that these arrangements and institutions establish. They argue for the constraints, and for and against proposed exceptions to and departures from them, on the ground that the constraints contribute to especially important ends, serve particularly important goals and purposes. Their skepticism concerning the possibilities of resolving questions about good and bad does not lead to a bootless effort to banish views about such questions from political debate and interaction.[13] Rather, they attempt to achieve, through argumentation, the widest possible consensus about certain of those questions that they regard as fundamentally important. If, or to the extent that, such a consensus can be achieved and maintained, perhaps in part by giving it various institutionalized expressions and embodiments, it may be possible to contain the all but inevitable, and the all but inevitably expressed, disagreements about other questions of value within nondestructive bounds. And just as there can be no guarantee of success in this endeavor—indeed not more than a dim prospect of partial and in all likelihood short-lived successes—so there is no alternative to it.

Ackerman's programmatic statements to the contrary notwithstanding, much of his performance in this book in fact fits this latter pattern and contributes importantly to this latter tradition. Although his claims for Neutrality$_2$ are excessive, his argument concerning it might be read as reiterating, in the name of such values as individual freedom and dignity, the case for understanding and respecting the diversity of conceptions of good with which we are in fact presented. More important, if we set aside the distracting claim that the moral and political ideal that is Neutrality$_1$ is or could be an incorrigible inference from Neutrality$_2$ or an inescapable outcome of the dialogic method, we will see that he often provides excellent reasons of an axiological and teleological (and hence a broadly utilitarian) kind, for the further and deeply normative choices and commitments he urges on us. These reasons will not exclude the possibility of cogent disagreement. But as with the arguments that have thus far convinced some societies to establish and maintain various civil and political rights and liberties, to extend the suffrage widely, to cushion their citizens against the worst effects of at least some of the grosser forms of disadvantage, these arguments might

[13]I have attempted to defend the claim that such efforts are bootless in a discussion of Oakeshott's more consistent effort to follow this course. See my *Practice of Political Authority* (Chicago: University of Chicago Press, 1980), esp. chaps. 2 and 3.

extend and deepen acceptance of the beliefs that Ackerman promotes. This process will not itself yield a utilitarianism satisfactory by the criteria of systematic moral and political philosophy. But it might contribute to that objective. It might do so by providing the best kinds of reasons we can hope to have for commitments to which, as Ackerman recognizes, many flesh and blood utilitarians have been strongly attracted.

Index

Index

Library of Congress Cataloging-in-Publication Data

Flathman, Richard E.
  Toward a liberalism.

  Includes bibliographical references and index.
  1. Liberalism. 2. Authority. 3. Individualism. 4. Pluralism (Social sciences)
I. Title.
HM276.F62   1989   320.5'1   88-47922
ISBN 0-8014-2243-4 (alk. paper)
ISBN 0-8014-9536-9 (pbk. : alk. paper)